Sermons to the Natural Man

Lessons on the Will and Love of God, the Spiritual Slavery of Sin, and the Goodness of a Christian Life

By William G. T. Shedd

Published by Pantianos Classics

ISBN-13: 978-1-78987-047-3

First published in 1871

Contents

Preface .... *iv*

I - The Future State A Self-Conscious State. 9

II - The Future State A Self-Conscious State. 17

III - God's Exhaustive Knowledge of Man. 24

IV - God's Exhaustive Knowledge of Man. (continued) 32

V - All Mankind Guilty; Or, Every Man Knows More Than He
Practises 40

VI - Sin in The Heart the Source of Error in The Head 49

VII - The Necessity of Divine Influences 58

VIII - The Necessity of Divine Influences. (continued) 65

IX - The Impotence of The Law 73

X - Self-Scrutiny in God's Presence 81

XI - Sin Is Spiritual Slavery 89

XII - The Original and The Actual Relation of Man to Law 101

XIII - The Sin of Omission 108

XIV - The Sinfulness of Original Sin 115

XV - The Approbation of Goodness is Not the Love of It 123

XVI - The Use of Fear in Religion 132

XVII - The Present Life as Related to The Future 143

XVIII - The Exercise of Mercy Optional with God 152

XIX - Christianity Requires the Temper of Childhood 161

XX - Faith the Sole Saving Act 169

Preface

It is with a solemn feeling of responsibility that I send forth this volume of Sermons. The ordinary emotions of authorship have little place in the experience, when one remembers that what he says will be either a means of spiritual life, or an occasion of spiritual death.

I believe that the substance of these Discourses will prove to accord with God's revealed truth, in the day that will try all truth. The title indicates their general aim and tendency. The purpose is psychological. I would, if possible, anatomize the natural heart. It is in vain to offer the gospel unless the law has been applied with clearness and cogency. At the present day, certainly, there is far less danger of erring in the direction of religious severity, than in the direction of religious indulgence. If I have not preached redemption in these sermons so fully as I have analyzed sin, it is because it is my deliberate conviction that just now the first and hardest work to be done by the preacher, for the natural man, is to produce in him some sensibility upon the subject of sin. Conscience needs to become consciousness. There is considerable theoretical unbelief respecting the doctrines of the New Testament; but this is not the principal difficulty. Theoretical skepticism is in a small minority of Christendom, and always has been. The chief obstacle to the spread of the Christian religion is the practical unbelief of speculative believers. "Thou sayest,"—says John Bunyan,—"thou dost in deed and in truth believe the Scriptures. I ask, therefore, Wast thou ever killed stark dead by the law of works contained in the Scriptures? Killed by the law or letter, and made to see thy sins against it, and left in an helpless condition by the law? For, the proper work of the law is to slay the soul, and to leave it dead in an helpless state. For, it doth neither give the soul any comfort itself, when it comes, nor doth it show the soul where comfort is to be had; and therefore it is called the 'ministration of condemnation,' the 'ministration of death.' For, though men may have a notion of the blessed Word of God, yet before they be converted, it may be truly said of them, Ye err, not knowing the Scriptures, nor the power of God."

If it be thought that such preaching of the law can be dispensed with, by employing solely what is called in some quarters the preaching of the gospel, I do not agree with the opinion. The benefits of Christ's redemption are pearls which must not be cast before swine. The gospel is not for the stupid, or for the doubter,—still less for the scoffer. Christ's atonement is to be offered to conscious guilt, and in order to conscious guilt there must be the application of the decalogue. John Baptist must prepare the way for the merciful Redeemer, by legal and close preaching. And the merciful Redeemer Himself, in the opening of His ministry, and before He spake much concerning remission of sins, preached a sermon which in its searching and self-revelatory character is a more alarming address to the corrupt natural heart, than was the first edition of it delivered amidst the lightnings of Sinai. The Sermon on the Mount is called the Sermon of the Beatitudes, and many have the impression that it is a very lovely song to the sinful soul of man. They forget that the blessing upon obedience implies a curse upon disobedience, and that every mortal man has disobeyed the Sermon on the Mount. "God save me,"—said a thoughtful person who knew what is in the Sermon on the Mount, and what is in the human heart,—"God save me from the Sermon on the Mount when I am judged in the last day." When Christ preached this discourse, He preached the law, principally. "Think not,"—He says,—"that I am come to destroy the law or the prophets. I am not come to destroy, but to fulfil. For verily I say unto you, Till heaven and earth pass, one jot or one tittle shall in no wise pass from the law till all be fulfilled." John the Baptist describes his own preaching, which was confessedly severe and legal, as being far less searching than that of the Messiah whose near advent he announced. "I indeed baptize you with water unto repentance: but he that cometh after me is mightier than I, whose shoes I am not worthy to bear: he shall baptize you with the Holy Ghost and with fire; whose fan is in his hand, and he will thoroughly purge his floor, and gather his wheat into the garner; but he will burn up the chaff with unquenchable fire."

The general burden and strain of the Discourse with which the Redeemer opened His ministry is preceptive and mandatory. Its keynote is: "Thou shalt do this," and, "Thou shalt not do that;" "Thou shalt be thus, in thine heart," and, "Thou shalt not be thus, in thine heart." So little is said in it, comparatively, concerning what are called the doctrines of grace, that it has often been cited to prove that the creed of the Church has been expanded unduly, and made to contain more than the Founder of Christianity really intended it should. The absence, for example, of any direct and specific statement of the doctrine of Atonement, in this important section of Christ's teaching, has been instanced by the Socinian opponent as proof that this doctrine is not so vital as the Church has always claimed it to be. But, Christ was purposely silent respecting grace and its methods, until he had spiritualized Law, and made it penetrate the human consciousness like a sharp sword. Of what use would it have been to offer mercy, before the sense of its need had been elicited? and how was this to be elicited, but by the solemn and authoritative enunciation of law and justice? There are, indeed, cheering intimations, in the Sermon on the Mount, respecting the Divine mercy, and so there are in connection with the giving of the Ten Commandments. But law, rather than grace, is the main substance and burden of both. The great intention, in each instance, is to convince of sin, preparatory to the offer of clemency. The Decalogue is the legal basis of the Old Dispensation, and the Sermon on the Mount is the legal basis of the New. When the Redeemer, in the opening of His ministry, had provided the apparatus of conviction, then He provided the apparatus of expiation. The Great High-Priest, like the Levitical priest who typi-fied Him, did not sprinkle atoning blood indiscriminately. It was to bedew only him who felt and confessed guilt.

This legal and minatory element in the words of Jesus has also been no-ticed by the skeptic, and an argument has been founded upon it to prove that He was soured by ill-success, and, like other merely human reformers who have found the human heart too hard, for them, fell away from the gentleness with which He began His ministry, into the anger and denunciation of morti-fied ambition with which it closed. This is the picture of Jesus Christ which Rénan presents in his apocryphal Gospel. But the fact is, that the Redeemer began with law, and was rigorous with sin from the very first. The Sermon on the Mount was delivered not far from twelve months from the time of His inauguration, by baptism, to the office of Messiah. And all along through His ministry of three years and a half, He constantly employs the law in order to prepare his hearers for grace. He was as gentle and gracious to the penitent sinner, in the opening of His ministry, as he was at the close of it; and He was as unsparing and severe towards the hardened and self-righteous sinner, in His early Judaean, as He was in His later Galilean ministry.

It is sometimes said that the surest way to produce conviction of sin is to preach the Cross. There is a sense in which this is true, and there is a sense in which it is false. If the Cross is set forth as the cursed tree on which the Lord of Glory hung and suffered, to satisfy the demands of Eternal Justice, then indeed there is fitness in the preaching to produce the sense of guilt. But this is to preach the law, in its fullest extent, and the most tremendous energy of its claims. Such discourse as this must necessarily analyze law, define it, en-force it, and apply it in the most cogent manner. For, only as the atonement of Christ is shown to completely meet and satisfy all these legal demands which have been so thoroughly discussed and exhibited, is the real virtue and power of the Cross made manifest.

But if the Cross is merely held up as a decorative ornament, like that on the breast of Belinda, "which Jews might kiss and infidels adore;" if it be pro-claimed as the beautiful symbol of the Divine indifference and indulgence, and there be a studious avoiding of all judicial aspects and relations; if the natural man is not searched by law and alarmed by justice, but is only soothed and narcotized by the idea of an Epicurean deity destitute of moral anger and inflicting no righteous retribution,—then, there will be no convic-tion of sin. Whenever the preaching of the law is positively objected to, and the preaching of the gospel is proposed in its place, it will be found that the "gospel" means that good-nature and that easy virtue which some mortals dare to attribute to the Holy and Immaculate Godhead! He who really, and in good faith, preaches the Cross, never opposes the preaching of the law.

Still another reason for the kind of religious discourse which we are de-fending is found in the fact that multitudes are expecting a happy issue of this life, upon ethical as distinguished from evangelical grounds. They deny that they deserve damnation, or that they need Christ's atonement. They say that they are living virtuous lives, and are ready to adopt language similar to that of Mr. Mill spoken in another connection: "If from this position of integrity and morality we are to be sent to hell, to hell we will go." This tendency is strengthened by the current light letters, in distinction from standard literature. A certain class, through ephemeral essays, poems, and novels, has been plied with the doctrine of a natural virtue and an innate goodness, until it has become proud and self-reliant. The "manhood" of paganism is glorified, and the "childhood" of the gospel is vilified. The graces of humility, self-abasement before God, and especially of penitence for sin, are distasteful and loathed. Persons of this order prefer to have their religious teacher silent upon these themes, and urge them to courage, honor, magnanimity, and all that class of qualities which imply self-consciousness and self-reliance. To them apply the solemn words of the Son of God to the Pharisees: "If ye were blind, ye should have no sin: but now ye say, We see, therefore your sin remaineth."

It is, therefore, specially incumbent upon the Christian ministry, to employ a searching and psychological style of preaching, and to apply the tests of ethics and virtue so powerfully to men who are trusting to ethics and virtue, as to bring them upon their knees. Since these men are desiring, like the "foolish Galatiana," to be saved by the law, then let the law be laid down to them, in all its breadth and reach, that they may understand the real nature and consequences of the position they have taken. "Tell me," says a preacher of this stamp,—"tell me, ye that desire to be under the law, do ye not hear the law,"—do ye not hear its thundering,—"cursed is every one that continueth not in ALL things that are written in the law, to do them!" Virtue must be absolutely perfect and spotless, if a happy immortality is to be made to depend upon virtue. If the human heart, in its self-deception and self-reliance, turns away from the Cross and the righteousness of God, to morals and the righteousness of works, then let the Christian thinker follow after it like the avenger of blood. Let him set the heights and depths of ethical perfection before the deluded mortal; let him point to the inaccessible cliffs that tower high above, and bid him scale them if he can; let him point to the fathomless abysses beneath, and tell him to descend and bring up perfect virtue therefrom; let him employ the very instrument which this virtuoso has chosen, until it becomes an instrument of torture and self-despair. In this way, he is breaking down the "manhood" that confronts and opposes, and is bringing in the "childhood" that is docile, and recipient of the kingdom.

These Sermons run the hazard of being pronounced monotonous, because of the pertinacity with which the attempt is made to force self-reflection. But this criticism can easily be endured, provided the attempt succeeds. Religious truth becomes almighty the instant it can get within the soul; and it gets within the soul, the instant real thinking begins. "As you value your peace of mind, stop all scrutiny into your personal character," is the advice of what Milton denominates "the sty of Epicurus." The discouraging religious condition of the present age is due to the great lack, not merely in the lower but the higher classes, of calm, clear self-intelligence. Men do not know themselves. The Delphic oracle was never less obeyed than now, in this vortex of mechanical arts and luxury. For this reason, it is desirable that the religious teacher dwell consecutively upon topics that are connected with that which is within man,—his settled motives of action, and all those spontaneous on-goings of his soul of which he takes no notice, unless he is persuaded or impelled to do so. Some of the old painters produced powerful effects by one solitary color. The subject of moral evil contemplated in the heart of the individual man,—not described to him from the outside, but wrought out of his own being into incandescent letters, by the fierce chemistry of anxious perhaps agonizing reflection,—sin, the one awful fact in the history of man, if caused to pervade discourse will always impart to it a hue which, though it be monochromatic, arrests and holds the eye like the lurid color of an approaching storm-cloud.

With this statement respecting the aim and purport of these Sermons, and deeply conscious of their imperfections, especially for spiritual purposes, I send them out into the world, with the prayer that God the Spirit will deign to employ them as the means of awakening some souls from the lethargy of sin.

Union Theological Seminary,
New York, February 17, 1871.

I - The Future State A Self-Conscious State.

1 Cor. xiii. 12.—*"Now I know in part; but then shall I know even as also I am known."*

The apostle Paul made this remark with reference to the blessedness of the Christian in eternity. Such assertions are frequent in the Scriptures. This same apostle, whose soul was so constantly dilated with the expectation of the beatific vision, assures the Corinthians, in another passage in this epistle, that "eye hath not seen, nor ear heard, neither have entered into the heart of man the things which God hath prepared for them that love Him." The beloved disciple John, also, though he seems to have lived in the spiritual world while he was upon the earth, and though the glories of eternity were made to pass before him in the visions of Patmos, is compelled to say of the sons of God, "It doth not yet appear what we shall be." And certainly the common Christian, as he looks forward with a mixture of hope and anxiety to his final state in eternity, will confess that he knows but "in part," and that a very small part, concerning it. He endures as seeing that which is invisible, and cherishes the hope that through Christ's redemption his eternity will be a condition of peace and purity, and that he shall know even as also he is known.

But it is not the Christian alone who is to enter eternity, and to whom the exchange of worlds will bring a luminous apprehension of many things that have hitherto been seen only through a glass darkly. Every human creature may say, when he thinks of the alteration that will come over his views of religious subjects upon entering another life, "Now I know in part; but then shall I know even as also I am known. I am now in the midst of the vapors and smoke of this dim spot which men call earth, but then shall I stand in the dazzling light of the face of God, and labor under no doubt or delusion respecting my own character or that of my Eternal Judge."

A moment's reflection will convince any one, that the article and fact of death must of itself make a vast accession to the amount of a man's knowledge, because death introduces him into an entirely new state of existence. Foreign travel adds much to our stock of ideas, because we go into regions of the earth of which we had previously known only by the hearing of the ear. But the great and last journey that man takes carries him over into a province of which no book, not even the Bible itself, gives him any distinct cognition, as to the style of its scenery or the texture of its objects. In respect to any earthly scene or experience, all men stand upon substantially the same level of information, because they all have substantially the same data for forming an estimate. Though I may never have been in Italy, I yet know that the soil of Italy is a part of the common crust of the globe, that the Apennines are like other mountains which I have seen, that the Italian sunlight pours through the pupil like any other sunlight, and that the Italian breezes fan the brow like those of the sunny south the world over. I understand that the general forms of human consciousness in Europe and Asia, are like those in America. The operations of the five senses are the same in the Old World that they are in the New. But what do I know of the surroundings and experience of a man who has travelled from time into eternity? Am I not completely baffled, the moment I attempt to construct the consciousness of the unearthly state? I have no materials out of which to build it, because it is not a world of sense and matter, like that which I now inhabit.

But death carries man over into the new and entirely different mode of existence, so that he knows by direct observation and immediate intuition. A flood of new information pours in upon the disembodied spirit, such as he cannot by any possibility acquire upon earth, and yet such as he cannot by any possibility escape from in his new residence. How strange it is, that the young child, the infant of days, in the heart of Africa, by merely dying, by merely passing from time into eternity, acquires a kind and grade of knowledge that is absolutely inaccessible to the wisest and subtlest philosopher while here on earth![1] The dead Hottentot knows more than the living Plato.

But not only does the exchange of worlds make a vast addition to our stores of information respecting the nature of the invisible realm, and the mode of existence there, it also makes a vast addition to the kind and degree of our knowledge respecting ourselves, and our personal relationships to God. This is by far the most important part of the new acquisition which we gain by the passage from time to eternity, and it is to this that the Apostle directs attention in the text. It is not so much the world that will be around us, when we are beyond the tomb, as it is the world that will be within us, that is of chief importance. Our circumstances in this mode of existence, and in any mode of existence, are arranged by a Power above us, and are, comparatively, matters of small concern; but the persons that we ourselves verily are, the characters which we bring into this environment, the little inner world of thought and feeling which is to be inclosed and overarched in the great outer world of forms and objects,—all this is matter of infinite moment and anxiety to a responsible creature.

For the text teaches, that inasmuch as the future life is the ultimate state of being for an immortal spirit, all that imperfection and deficiency in knowledge which appertains to this present life, this "ignorant present" time, must disappear. When we are in eternity, we shall not be in the dark and in doubt respecting certain great questions and truths that sometimes raise a query in our minds here. Voltaire now knows whether there is a sin-hating God, and David Hume now knows whether there is an endless hell. I may, in certain moods of my mind here upon earth, query whether I am accountable and liable to retribution, but the instant I shall pass from this realm of shadows, all this skepticism will be banished forever from my mind. For the future state is the final state, and hence all questions are settled, and all doubts are resolved. While upon earth, the arrangements are such that we cannot see every thing, and must walk by faith, because it is a state of probation; but when once in eternity, all the arrangements are such that we cannot but see every thing, and must walk by sight, because it is the state of adjudication. Hence it is, that the preacher is continually urging men to view things, so far as is possible, in the light of eternity, as the only light that shines clearly and without refractions. Hence it is, that he importunes his hearers to estimate their duties, and their relationships, and their personal character, as they will upon the death-bed, because in the solemn hour of death the light of the future state begins to dawn upon the human soul.

It is very plain that if a spiritual man like the apostle Paul, who in a very remarkable degree lived with reference to the future world, and contemplated subjects in the light of eternity, was compelled to say that he knew but "in part," much more must the thoughtless natural man confess his ignorance of that which will meet him when his spirit returns to God. The great mass of mankind are totally vacant of any just apprehension of what will be their state of mind, upon being introduced into God's presence. They have never seriously considered what must be the effect upon their views and feelings, of an entire withdrawment from the scenes and objects of earth, and an entrance into those of the future state. Most men are wholly engrossed in the present existence, and do not allow their thoughts to reach over into that invisible region which revelation discloses, and which the uncontrollable workings of conscience sometimes force upon their attention for a moment. How many men there are, whose sinful and thoughtless lives prove that they are not aware that the future world will, by its very characteristics, fill them with a species and a grade of information that will be misery unutterable. Is it not the duty and the wisdom of all such, to attempt to conjecture and anticipate the coming experience of the human soul in the day of judgment and the future life, in order that by repentance toward God and faith in the Lord Jesus Christ they may be able to stand in that day? Let us then endeavor to know, at least "in part," concerning the eternal state.

The latter clause of the text specifies the general characteristic of existence in the future world. It is a mode of existence in which the rational mind "knows even as it is known." It is a world of knowledge,—of conscious knowledge. In thus unequivocally asserting that our existence beyond the tomb is one of distinct consciousness, revelation has taught us what we most desire and need to know. The first question that would be raised by a creature who was just to be launched out upon an untried mode of existence would be the question: "Shall I be conscious?" However much he might desire to know the length and breadth of the ocean upon which his was to set sail, the scenery that was to be above him and around him in his coming history,—nay, however much he might wish to know of matters still closer to himself than these; however much he might crave to ask of his Maker, "With what body shall I come?" all would be set second to the simple single inquiry: "Shall I think, shall I feel, shall I know?" In answering this question in the affirmative, without any hesitation or ambiguity, the apostle Paul has in reality cleared up most of the darkness that overhangs the future state. The structure of the spiritual body, and the fabric of the immaterial world, are matters of secondary importance, and may be left without explanation, provided only the rational mind of man be distinctly informed that it shall not sleep in unconsciousness, and that the immortal spark shall not become such stuff as dreams are made of.

The future, then, is a mode of existence in which the soul "knows even as it is known." But this involves a perception in which there is no error, and no intermission. For, the human spirit in eternity "is known" by the omniscient God. If, then, it knows in the style and manner that God knows, there can be no misconception or cessation in its cognition. Here, then, we have a glimpse into the nature of our eternal existence. It is a state of distinct and unceasing knowledge of moral truth and moral objects. The human spirit, be it holy or sinful, a friend or an enemy of God, in eternity will always and forever be aware of it. There is no forgetting in the future state; there is no dissipation of the mind there; and there is no aversion of the mind from itself. The cognition is a fixed quantity. Given the soul, and the knowledge is given. If it be holy, it is always conscious of the fact. If it be sinful, it cannot for an instant lose the distressing consciousness of sin. In neither instance will it be necessary, as it generally is in this life, to make a special effort and a particular examination, in order to know the personal character. Knowledge of God and His law, in the future life, is spontaneous and inevitable; no creature can escape it; and therefore the bliss is unceasing in heaven, and the misery is unceasing in hell. There are no states of thoughtlessness and unconcern in the future life, because there is not an instant of forgetfulness or ignorance of the personal character and condition. In the world beyond this, every man will constantly and distinctly know what he is, and what he is not, because he will "be known" by the omniscient and unerring God, and will himself know in the same constant and distinct style and manner.

If the most thoughtless person that now walks the globe could only have a clear perception of that kind of knowledge which is awaiting him upon the other side of the tomb, he would become the most thoughtful and the most anxious of men. It would sober him like death itself. And if any unpardoned man should from this moment onward be haunted with the thought, "When I die I shall enter into the light of God's countenance, and obtain a knowledge of my own character and obligations that will be as accurate and unvarying as that of God himself upon this subject," he would find no rest until he had obtained an assurance of the Divine mercy, and such an inward change as would enable him to endure this deep and full consciousness of the purity of God and of the state of his heart. It is only because a man is unthinking, or because he imagines that the future world will be like the present one, only longer in duration, that he is so indifferent regarding it. Here is the difficulty of the case, and the fatal mistake which the natural man makes. He supposes that the views which he shall have upon religious subjects in the eternal state, will be very much as they are in this,—vague, indistinct, fluctuating, and therefore causing no very great anxiety. He can pass days and weeks here in time without thinking of the claims of God upon him, and he imagines that the same thing is possible in eternity. While here upon earth, he certainly does not "know even as also he is known," and he hastily concludes that so it will be beyond the grave. It is because men imagine that eternity is only a very long space of time, filled up, as time here is, with dim, indistinct apprehensions, with a constantly shifting experience, with shallow feelings and ever diversified emotions, in fine, with all the variety of pleasure and pain, of ignorance and knowledge, that pertains to this imperfect and probationary life,—it is because mankind thus conceive of the final state, that it exerts no more influence over them. But such is not its true idea. There is a marked difference between the present and the future life, in respect to uniformity and clearness of knowledge. "Now I know in part, but then shall I know even as also I am known." The text and the whole teaching of the New Testament prove that the invisible world is the unchangeable one; that there are no alterations of character, and consequently no alternations of experience, in the future life; that there are no transitions, as there are in this checkered scene of earth, from happiness to unhappiness and back again. There is but one uniform type of experience for an individual soul in eternity. That soul is either uninterruptedly happy, or uninterruptedly miserable, because it has either an uninterrupted sense of holiness, or an uninterrupted sense of sin. He that is righteous is righteous still, and knows it continually; and he that is filthy is filthy still, and knows it incessantly. If we enter eternity as the redeemed of the Lord, we take over the holy heart and spiritual affections of regeneration, and there is no change but that of progression,—a change, consequently, only in degree, but none of kind or type. The same knowledge and experience that we have here "in part" we shall have there in completeness and permanency. And the same will be true, if the heart be evil and the affections inordinate and earthly. And all this, simply because the mind's knowledge is clear, accurate, and constant. That which the transgressor knows here of God and his own heart, but imperfectly, and fitfully, and briefly, he shall know there perfectly, and constantly, and everlastingly. The law of constant evolution, and the characteristic of unvarying uniformity, will determine and fix the type of experience in the evil as it does in the good.

Such, then, is the general nature of knowledge in the future state. It is distinct, accurate, unintermittent, and unvarying. We shall know even as we are known, and we are known by the omniscient and unerring Searcher of hearts. Let us now apply this general characteristic of cognition in eternity to some particulars. Let us transfer our minds into the future and final state, and mark what goes on within them there. We ought often to enter this mysterious realm, and become habituated to its mental processes, and by a wise anticipation become prepared for the reality itself.

I. The human mind, in eternity, will have a distinct and unvarying perception of the character of God. And that one particular attribute in this character, respecting which the cognition will be of the most luminous quality, is the Divine holiness. In eternity, the immaculateness of the Deity will penetrate the consciousness of every rational creature with the subtlety and the thoroughness of fire. God's essence is infinitely pure, and intensely antagonistic to sin, but it is not until there is a direct contact between it and the human mind, that man understands it and feels it. "I have heard of Thee by the hearing of the ear, but now mine eye seeth Thee, and I abhor myself." Even the best of men know but "in part" concerning the holiness of God. Yet it is noticeable how the apprehension of it grows upon the ripening Christian, as he draws nearer to the time of his departure. The vision of the cherubim themselves seems to dawn upon the soul of a Leighton and an Edwards, and though it does not in the least disturb their saintly and seraphic peace, because they are sheltered in the clefts of the Rock of Ages, as the brightness passes by them, it does yet bring out from their comparatively holy and spiritual hearts the utterance, "Behold I am vile; infinite upon, infinite is my sin." But what shall be said of the common and ordinary knowledge of mankind, upon this subject! Except at certain infrequent times, the natural man does not know even "in part," respecting the holiness of God, and hence goes on in transgression without anxiety or terror. It is the very first work of prevenient grace, to disclose to the human mind something of the Divine purity; and whoever, at any moment, is startled by a more than common sense of God's holy character, should regard it and cherish it as a token of benevolence and care for his soul.

Now, in eternity this species of knowledge must exist in the very highest degree. The human soul will be encircled by the character and attributes of God. It cannot look in any direction without beholding it. It is not so here. Here, in this life, man may and does avert his eye, and refuse to look at the sheen and the splendor that pains his organ. He fastens his glance upon the farm, or the merchandise, or the book, and perseveringly determines not to see the purity of God that rebukes him. And here he can succeed. He can and does live days and months without so much as a momentary glimpse of his Maker, and, as the apostle says, is "without God" in this world. And yet such men do have, now and then, a view of the face of God. It may be for an instant only. It may be merely a thought, a gleam, a flash; and yet, like that quick flash of lightning, of which our Lord speaks, that lighteneth out of the one part of heaven, and shineth unto the other part, that cometh out of the East and shineth even unto the West,—like that swift momentary flash which runs round the whole horizon in the twinkling of an eye, this swift thought and gleam of God's purity fills the whole guilty soul full of light. What spiritual distress seizes the man in such moments, and of what a penetrating perception of the Divine character is he possessed for an instant! It is a distinct and an accurate knowledge, but, unlike the cognition of the future state, it is not yet an inevitable and unintermittent one. He can expel it, and become again an ignorant and indifferent being, as he was before. He knows but "in part" at the very best, and this only temporarily.

But carry this rational and accountable creature into eternity, denude him of the body of sense, and take him out of the busy and noisy world of sense into the silent world of spirits, and into the immediate presence of God, and then he will know upon this subject even as he is known. That sight and perception of God's purity which he had here for a brief instant, and which was so painful because he was not in sympathy with it, has now become everlasting. That distinct and accurate knowledge of God's character has now become his only knowledge. That flash of lightning has become light,—fixed, steady, permanent as the orb of day. The rational spirit cannot for an instant rid itself of the idea of God. Never for a moment, in the endless cycles, can it look away from its Maker; for in His presence what other object is there to look at? Time itself, with its pursuits and its objects of thought and feeling, is no longer, for the angel hath sworn it by Him who liveth for ever and ever. There is nothing left, then, to occupy and engross the attention but the character and attributes of God; and, now, the immortal mind, created for such a purpose, must yield itself up to that contemplation which in this life it dreaded and avoided. The future state of every man is to be an open and unavoidable vision of God. If he delights in the view, he will be blessed; if he loathes it, he will be miserable. This is the substance of heaven and hell. This is the key to the eternal destiny of every human soul. If a man love God, he shall gaze at him and adore; if he hate God, he shall gaze at him and gnaw his tongue for pain.

The subject, as thus far unfolded, teaches the following lessons:

14

1. In the first place, it shows that a false theory of the future state will not protect a man from future misery. For, we have seen that the eternal world, by its very structure and influences, throws a flood of light upon the Divine character, causing it to appear in its ineffable purity and splendor, and compels every creature to stand out in that light. There is no darkness in which man can hide himself, when he leaves this world of shadows. A false theory, therefore, respecting God, can no more protect a man from the reality, the actual matter of fact, than a false theory of gravitation will preserve a man from falling from a precipice into a bottomless abyss. Do you come to us with the theory that every human creature will be happy in another life, and that the doctrine of future misery is false? We tell you, in reply, that God is holy, beyond dispute or controversy; that He cannot endure the sight of sin; and that in the future world every one of His creatures must see Him precisely as He is, and know Him in the real and eternal qualities of His nature. The man, therefore, who is full of sin, whose heart is earthly, sensual, selfish, must, when he approaches that pure Presence, find that his theory of future happiness shrivels up like the heavens themselves, before the majesty and glory of God. He now stands face to face with a Being whose character has never dawned upon him with such a dazzling purity, and to dispute the reality would be like disputing the fierce splendor of the noonday sun. Theory must give way to fact, and the deluded mortal must submit to its awful force.

In this lies the irresistible power of death, judgment, and eternity, to alter the views of men. Up to these points they can dispute and argue, because there is no ocular demonstration. It is possible to debate the question this side of the tomb, because we are none of us face to face with God, and front to front with eternity. In the days of Noah, before the flood came, there was skepticism, and many theories concerning the threatened deluge. So long as the sky was clear, and the green earth smiled under the warm sunlight, it was not difficult for the unbeliever to maintain an argument in opposition to the preacher of righteousness. But when the sky was rent with lightnings, and the earth was scarred with thunderbolts, and the fountains of the great deep were broken up, where was the skepticism? where were the theories? where were the arguments? When God teaches, "Where is the wise? where is the scribe? where is the disputer of this world?" They then knew as they were known; they stood face to face with the facts.

It is this inevitableness of the demonstration upon which we would fasten attention. We are not always to live in this world of shadows. We are going individually into the very face and eyes of Jehovah, and whatever notions we may have adopted and maintained must all disappear, except as they shall be actually verified by what we shall see and know in that period of our existence when we shall perceive with the accuracy and clearness of God Himself. Our most darling theories, by which we may have sought to solace our souls in reference to our future destiny, if false, will be all ruthlessly torn away, and we must see what verily and eternally is. All mankind come upon one doctrinal platform when they enter eternity. They all have one creed there. There is not a skeptic even in hell. The devils believe and tremble. The demonstration that God is holy is so irrefragable, so complete and absolute, that doubt or denial is impossible in any spirit that has passed the line between time and eternity.

2. In the second place, this subject shows that indifference and carelessness respecting the future life will not protect the soul from future misery. There may be no false theory adopted, and yet if there be no thoughtful preparation to meet God, the result will be all the same. I may not dispute the Newtonian theory of gravitation, yet if I pay no heed to it, if I simply forget it, as I clamber up mountains, and walk by the side of precipices, my body will as surely be dashed to pieces as if I were a theoretical skeptic upon the subject of gravitation.

The creature's indifference can no more alter the immutable nature of God, than can the creature's false reasoning, or false theorizing. That which is settled in heaven, that which is fixed and eternal, stands the same stern, relentless fact under all circumstances. We see the operation of this sometimes here upon earth, in a very impressive manner. A youth or a man simply neglects the laws and conditions of physical well-being. He does not dispute them. He merely pays no attention to them. A. few years pass by, and disease and torturing pain become his portion. He comes now into the awful presence of the powers and the facts which the Creator has inlaid in the world, of physical existence. He knows now even as he is known. And the laws are stern. He finds no place of repentance in them, though he seek it carefully with tears. The laws never repent, never change their mind. The principles of physical life and growth which he has never disputed, but which he has never regarded, now crush him into the ground in their relentless march and motion.

Precisely so will it be in the moral world, and with reference to the holiness of God. That man who simply neglects to prepare himself to see a holy God, though he never denies that there is such a Being, will find the vision just as unendurable to him, as it is to the most determined of earthly skeptics. So far as the final result in the other world is concerned, it matters little whether a man adds unbelief to his carelessness, or not. The carelessness will ruin his soul, whether with or without skepticism. Orthodoxy is valuable only as it inspires the hope that it will end in timely and practical attention to the concerns of the soul. But if you show me a man who you infallibly know will go through life careless and indifferent, I will show you a man who will not be prepared to meet God face to face, even though his theology be as accurate as that of St. Paul himself. Nay, we have seen that there is a time coming when all skeptics will become believers like the devils themselves, and will tremble at the ocular demonstration of truths which they have heretofore denied. Theoretical unbelief must be a temporary affair in every man; for it can last only until he dies. Death will make all the world theoretically orthodox, and bring them all to one and the same creed. But death will not bring them all to one and the same happy experience of the truth, and lave of the creed. For those who have made preparation for the vision of God and the ocular demonstration of Divine truth, these will rise upon their view with a blessed and glorious light. But for those who have remained sinful and careless, these eternal truths and facts will be a vision of terror and despair. They will not alter. No man will find any place of repentance in them, though, like Esau, he seek it carefully and with tears.

3. In the third place, this subject shows that only faith in Christ and a new heart can protect the soul from future misery. The nature and character of God cannot be altered, and therefore the change must be wrought in man's soul. The disposition and affections of the heart must be brought into such sweet sympathy and harmony with God's holiness, that when in the next world that holiness shall be revealed as it is to the seraphim, it will fall in upon the soul like the rays of a vernal sun, starting every thing into cheerful life and joy. If the Divine holiness does not make this impression, it produces exactly the contrary effect. If the sun's rays do not start the bud in the spring, they kill it. If the vision of a holy God is not our heaven, then it must be our hell. Look then directly into your heart, and tell us which is the impression for you. Can you say with David, "We give thanks and rejoice, at the remembrance of Thy holiness?" Are you glad that there is such a pure and immaculate Being upon the throne, and when His excellence abashes you, and rebukes your corruption and sin, do you say, "Let the righteous One smite me, it shall be a kindness?" Do you love God's holy character? If so, you are a new creature, and are ready for the vision of God, face to face. For you, to know God even as you are known by Him will not be a terror, but a glory and a joy. You are in sympathy with Him. You have been reconciled to Him by the blood of atonement, and brought into harmony with Him by the washing of regeneration. For you, as a believer in Christ, and a new man in Christ Jesus, all is well. The more you see of God, the more you desire to see of Him; and the more you know of Him, the more you long to know.

But if this is not your experience, then all is ill with you. We say experience. You must feel in this manner toward God, or you cannot endure the vision which is surely to break upon you after death. You must love this holiness without which no man can see the Lord. You may approve of it, you may praise it in other men, but if there is no affectionate going out of your own heart toward, the holy God, you are not in right relations to Him. You have the carnal mind, and that is enmity, and enmity is misery.

Look these facts in the eye, and act accordingly. "Make the tree good, and his fruit good," says Christ. Begin at the beginning. Aim at nothing less than a change of disposition and affections. Ask for nothing less, seek for nothing less. If you become inwardly holy as God is holy; if you become a friend of God, reconciled to Him by the blood of Christ; then your nature will be like God's nature, your character like God's character. Then, when you shall know God even as you are known by Him, and shall see Him as He is, the knowledge and the vision will be everlasting joy.

[Note 1:
"She has seen the mystery hid,
Under Egypt's pyramid;
By those eyelids pale and close,
Now she knows what Rhamses knows."
                    - ELIZABETH BROWNING: On the Death of a Child.]

II - The Future State A Self-Conscious State.

1 COR. xiii. 12.—*"Now I know in part; but then shall I know even as also I am known."*

In the preceding discourse, we found in these words the principal characteristic of our future existence. The world beyond the tomb is a world of clear and conscious knowledge. When, at death, I shall leave this region of time and sense and enter eternity, my knowledge, the apostle Paul tells me instead of being diminished or extinguished by the dissolution, of the body, will not only be continued to me, but will be even greater and clearer than before. He assures me that the kind and style of my cognition will be like that of God himself. I am to know as I am known. My intelligence will coincide with that of Deity.

By this we are not to understand that the creature's knowledge, in the future state, will be as extensive as that of the Omniscient One; or that it will be as profound and exhaustive as His. The infinitude of things can be known only by the Infinite Mind; and the creature will forever be making new acquisitions, and never reaching the final limit of truths and facts. But upon certain moral subjects, the perception of the creature will be like that of his Maker and Judge, so far as the kind or quality of the apprehension is concerned. Every man in eternity, for illustration, will see sin to be an odious and abominable thing, contrary to the holy nature of God, and awakening in that nature the most holy and awful displeasure. His knowledge upon this subject will be so identical with that of God, that he will be unable to palliate or excuse his transgressions, as he does in this world. He will see them precisely as God sees them. He must know them as God knows them, because he will "know even as he is known."

II. In continuing the examination of this solemn subject, we remark as a second and further characteristic of the knowledge which every man will possess in eternity, that he will know himself even as he is known by God. His knowledge of God we have found to be direct, accurate, and unceasing; his knowledge of his own heart will be so likewise. This follows from the relation of the two species of cognition to each other. The true knowledge of God involves the true knowledge of self. The instant that any one obtains a clear view of the holy nature of his Maker, he obtains a clear view of his own sinful nature. Philosophers tell us, that our consciousness of God and our consciousness of self mutually involve and imply each other[1]; in other words, that we cannot know God without immediately knowing ourselves, any more than we can know light without knowing darkness, any more than we can have the idea of right without having the idea of wrong. And it is certainly true that so soon as any being can intelligently say, "God is holy," he can and must say, "I am holy," or, "I am unholy," as the fact may be. Indeed, the only way in which man can truly know himself is to contrast himself with his Maker; and the most exhaustive self-knowledge and self-consciousness is to be found, not in the schools of secular philosophy but, in the searchings of the Christian heart,—in the "Confessions" of Augustine; in the labyrinthine windings of Edwards "On the Affections." Hence the frequent exhortations in the Bible to look at the character of God, in order that we may know ourselves and be abased by the contrast. In eternity, therefore, if we must have a clear and constant perception of God's character, we must necessarily have a distinct and unvarying knowledge of our own. It is not so here. Here in this world, man knows himself but "in part." Even when he endeavors to look within, prejudice and passion often affect his judgment; but more often, the fear of what he shall discover in the secret places of his soul deters him from making the attempt at self-examination. For it is a surprising truth that the transgressor dares not bring out into the light that which is most truly his own, that which he himself has originated, and which he loves and cherishes with all his strength and might. He is afraid of his own heart! Even when God forces the vision of it upon him, he would shut his eyes; or if this be not possible, he would look through distorting media and see it with a false form and coloring.

> "But 'tis not so above;
> There is no shuffling; there the action lies
> In his true nature: and we ourselves compelled,
> Even to the teeth and forehead of our faults,
> To give in evidence." [2]

The spirit that has come into the immediate presence of God, and beholds Him face to face, cannot deceive Him, and therefore cannot deceive itself. It cannot remain ignorant of God's character any longer, and therefore cannot remain ignorant of its own.

We do not sufficiently consider and ponder the elements of anguish that are sleeping in the fact that in eternity a sinner must know God's character, and therefore must know his own. It is owing to their neglect of such subjects, that mankind so little understand what an awful power there is in the distinct perception of the Divine purity, and the allied consciousness of sin. Lord Bacon tells us that the knowledge acquired in the schools is power; but it is weakness itself, if compared with that form and species of cognition which is given to the mind of man by the workings of conscience in the light of the Divine countenance. If a transgressor knew clearly what disclosures of God's immaculateness and of his own character must be made to him in eternity, he would fear them, if unprepared, far more than physical sufferings. If he understood what capabilities for distress the rational spirit possesses in its own mysterious constitution, if when brought into contact with the Divine purity it has no sympathy with it, but on the contrary an intense hostility; if he knew how violent will be the antagonism between God's holiness and man's sin when, the two are finally brought together, the assertion that there is no external source of anguish in hell, even if it were true, would afford him no relief. Whoever goes into the presence of God with a corrupt heart carries thither a source of sorrow that is inexhaustible, simply because that corrupt heart must be distinctly known, and perpetually understood by its possessor, in that Presence. The thoughtless man may never know while upon earth, even "in part," the depth and the bitterness of this fountain,—he may go through this life for the most part self-ignorant and undistressed,—but he must know in that other, final, world the immense fulness of its woe, as it unceasingly wells up into everlasting death. One theory of future punishment is, that our globe will become a penal orb of fire, and the wicked with material bodies, miraculously preserved by Omnipotence, will burn forever in it. But what is this compared with the suffering soul? The spirit itself, thus alienated from God's purity and conscious that it is, wicked, and knowing that it is wicked, becomes an "orb of fire." "It is,"—says John Howe, who was no fanatic, but one of the most thoughtful and philosophic of Christians,—"it is a throwing hell into hell, when a wicked man comes to hell; for he was his own hell before."[3]

It must ever be borne in mind, that the principal source and seat of future torment will be the sinner's sin. We must never harbor the thought, or fall into the notion, that the retributions of eternity are a wanton and arbitrary infliction upon the part of God. Some men seem to suppose, or at any rate they represent, that the woes of hell are a species of undeserved suffering; that God, having certain helpless and innocent creatures in His power, visits them with wrath, in the exercise of an arbitrary sovereignty. But this is not Christ's doctrine of endless punishment. There is no suffering inflicted, here or hereafter, upon any thing but sin,—unrepented, incorrigible sin,—and if you will show me a sinless creature, I will show you one who will never feel the least twinge or pang through all eternity. Death is the wages of sin. The substance of the wretchedness of the lost will issue right out of their own character. They will see their own wickedness steadily and clearly, and this will make them miserable. It will be the carrying out of the same principle that operates here in time, and in our own daily experience. Suppose that by some method, all the sin of my heart, and all the sins of my outward conduct, were made clear to my own view; suppose that for four-and-twenty hours continuously I were compelled to look at my wickedness intently, just as I would look intently into a burning furnace of fire; suppose that for this length of time I should see nothing, and hear nothing, and experience nothing of the world, about me, but should be absorbed in the vision of my own disobedience of God's good law, think you that (setting aside the work of Christ) I should be happy? On the contrary, should I not be the most wretched of mortals? Would not this self-knowledge be pure living torment? And yet the misery springs entirely out of the sin. There is nothing arbitrary or wanton in the suffering. It is not brought in upon me from the outside. It comes out of myself. And, while I was writhing under the sense and power of my transgressions, would you mock me, by telling me that I was a poor innocent struggling in the hands of omnipotent malice; that the suffering was unjust, and that if there were any justice in the universe, I should be delivered from it? No, we shall suffer in the future world only as we are sinners, and because we are sinners. There will be weeping and wailing and gnashing of teeth, only because the sinful creature will be compelled to look at himself; to know his sin in the same manner that it is known by the Infinite Intelligence. And is there any injustice in this? If a sinful being cannot bear the sight of himself, would you have the holy Deity step in between him and his sins, so that he should not see them, and so that he might be happy in them? Away with such folly and such wickedness. For it is the height of wickedness to desire that some method should be invented, and introduced into the universe of God, whereby the wages of sin shall be life and joy; whereby a sinner can look into his own wicked heart and be happy.

III. A third characteristic of the knowledge which every man will possess in eternity will be a clear understanding of the nature and wants of the soul. Man has that in his constitution, which needs God, and which cannot be at rest except in God. A state of sin is a state of alienation and separation from the Creator. It is, consequently, in its intrinsic nature, a state of restlessness and dissatisfaction. "There is no peace saith my God to the wicked; the wicked are like the troubled sea." In order to know this, it is only necessary to bring an apostate creature, like man, to a consciousness of the original requirements and necessities of his being.

But upon this subject, man while upon earth most certainly knows only "in part." Most men are wholly ignorant of the constitutional needs of a rational spirit, and are not aware that it is as impossible for the creature, when in eternity, to live happily out of God, as it is for the body to live at all in the element of fire. Most men, while here upon earth, do not know upon this subject as they are known. God knows that the whole created universe cannot satisfy the desires of an immortal being, but impenitent men do not know this fact with a clear perception, and they will not until they die and go into another world.

And the reason is this. So long as the worldly natural man lives upon earth, he can find a sort of substitute for God. He has a capacity for loving, and he satisfies it to a certain degree by loving himself; by loving fame, wealth, pleasure, or some form of creature-good. He has a capacity for thinking, and he gratifies it in a certain manner by pondering the thoughts of other minds, or by original speculations of his own. And so we might go through with the list of man's capacities, and we should find, that he contrives, while here upon earth, to meet these appetences of his nature, after a sort, by the objects of time and sense, and to give his soul a species of satisfaction short of God, and away from God. Fame, wealth, and pleasure; the lust of the flesh, the lust of the eye, and the pride of life; become a substitute for the Creator, in his search, for happiness. As a consequence, the unregenerate man knows but "in part" respecting the primitive and constitutional necessities of his being. He is feeding them with a false and unhealthy food, and in this way manages to stifle for a season their true and deep cravings. But this cannot last forever. When a man dies and goes into eternity, he takes nothing with him but his character and his moral affinities. "We brought nothing into this world, and it is certain that we can carry nothing out." The original requirements and necessities of his soul are not destroyed by death, but the earthly objects by which he sought to meet them, and by which he did meet them after a sort, are totally destroyed. He still has a capacity for loving; but in eternity where is the fame, the wealth, the pleasure upon which he has hitherto expended it? He still has a capacity for thinking; but where are the farm, the merchandise, the libraries, the works of art, the human literatures, and the human philosophies, upon which he has heretofore employed it? The instant you cut off a creature who seeks his good in the world, and not in God, from intercourse with the world, you cause him to know even as he is known respecting the true and proper portion of his soul. Deprived of his accustomed and his false object of love and support, he immediately begins to reach out in all directions for something to love, something to think of, something to trust in, and finds nothing. Like that insect in our gardens which spins a slender thread by which to guide itself in its meanderings, and which when the clew is cut thrusts out its head in every direction, but does not venture to advance, the human creature who has suddenly been cut off by death from his accustomed objects of support and pleasure stretches out in every direction for something to take their place. And the misery of his case is, that when in his reachings out he sees God, or comes into contact with God, he starts back like the little insect when you present a coal of fire to it. He needs as much as ever, to love some being or some thing. But he has no heart to love God and there is no other being and no other thing in eternity to love. He needs, as much as ever, to think of some object or some subject. But to think of

God is a distress to him; to reflect upon divine and holy things is weariness and woe. He is a carnal, earthly-minded man, and therefore cannot find enjoyment in such meditations. Before he can take relish in such objects and such thinking, he must be born again; he must become a new creature. But there is no new-birth of the soul in eternity. The disposition and character which a man takes along with him when he dies remains eternally unchanged. The constitutional wants still continue. The man must love, and must think. But the only object in eternity upon which such capability can be expended is God; and the carnal mind, saith the Scripture, is enmity against God, and is not subject to the law of God, neither indeed can be.

Now, whatever may be the course of a man in this life; whether he becomes aware of these created imperatives, and constitutional necessities of his immortal spirit or not; whether he hears its reproaches and rebukes because he is feeding them with the husks of earth, instead of the bread of heaven, or not; it is certain that in the eternal world they will be continually awake and perpetually heard. For that spiritual world will be fitted up for nothing but a rational spirit. There will be nothing material, nothing like earth, in its arrangements. Flesh and blood cannot inherit either the kingdom of God or the kingdom of Satan. The enjoyments and occupations of this sensuous and material state will be found neither in heaven nor in hell. Eternity is a spiritual region, and all its objects, and all its provisions, will have reference solely to the original capacities and destination of a spiritual creature. They will, therefore, all be terribly reminiscent of apostasy; only serving to remind the soul of what it was originally designed to be, and of what it has now lost by worshipping and loving the creature more than the Creator. How wretched then must man be, when, with the awakening of this restlessness and dissatisfaction of an immortal spirit, and with the bright pattern of what he ought to be continually before his eye, there is united an intensity of self-love and enmity toward God, that drives him anywhere and everywhere but to his Maker, for peace and comfort. How full of woe must the lost creature be, when his immortal necessities are awakened and demand their proper food, but cannot obtain it, because of the aversion of the heart toward the only Being who can satisfy them. For, the same hatred of holiness, and disinclination toward spiritual things, which prevents a man from choosing God for his portion here, will prevent him hereafter. It is the bold fancy of an imaginative thinker,[4] that the material forces which lie beneath external nature are conscious of being bound down and confined under the crust of the earth, like the giant Enceladus under Mt. Etna, and that there are times when they roar from the depths where they are in bondage, and call aloud for freedom; when they rise in their might, and manifest themselves in the earthquake and the volcano. It will be a more fearful and terrific struggle, when the powers of an apostate being are roused in eternity; when the then eternal sin and guilt has its hour of triumph, and the eternal reason and conscience have their hour of judgment and remorse; when the inner world of man's spirit, by this schism and antagonism within it, has a devastation and a ruin spread over it more awful than that of earthquakes and volcanic eruptions.

We have thus, in this and the preceding discourse, considered the kind and quality of that knowledge which every human being will possess in the eternal world. He will know God, and he will know himself, with a distinct, and accurate, and unceasing intelligence like that of the Deity. It is one of the most solemn and startling themes that can be presented to the human mind. We have not been occupied with what will be around a creature, what will be outside of a man, in the life to come; but we have been examining what will be within him. We have been considering what he will think of beyond the tomb; what his own feelings will be when he meets God face to face. But a man's immediate consciousness determines his happiness or his misery. As a man thinketh in his heart so is he. We must not delude ourselves with the notion, that the mere arrangements and circumstances of the spiritual world will decide our weal or our woe, irrespective of the tenor of our thoughts and affections; that if we are only placed in pleasant gardens or in golden streets, all will be well. As a man thinketh in his heart, so will he be in his experience. This vision of God, and of our own hearts, will be either the substance of heaven, or the substance of hell. The great future is a world of open vision. Now, we see through a glass darkly, but then, face to face. The vision for every human creature will be beatific, if he is prepared for it; will be terrific, if he is unprepared.

Does not the subject, then, speak with solemn warning to every one who knows that he is not prepared for the coming revelations that will be made to him when he dies; for this clear and accurate knowledge of God, and of his own character? Do you believe that there is an eternal world, and that the general features of this mode of existence have been scripturally depicted? Do you suppose that your present knowledge of the holiness of God, and of your own sinful nature, is equal to what it will be when your spirit returns to God who gave it? Are you prepared for the impending and inevitable disclosures and revelations of the day of judgment? Do you believe that Jesus Christ is the Eternal Son of God, who came forth from eternity eighteen centuries since, and went back into eternity, leaving upon record for human instruction an unexaggerated description of that invisible world, founded upon the personal knowledge of an eye-witness?

Whoever thus believes, concerning the record which Christ and His apostles have left for the information of dim-eyed mortals who see only "through a glass darkly," and who know only "in part," ought immediately to adopt their descriptions and ponder them long and well. We have already observed, that the great reason why the future state exerts so little influence over worldly men lies in the fact, that they do not bring it into distinct view. They live absorbed in the interests and occupations of earth, and their future abode throws in upon them none of its solemn shadows and warnings. A clear luminous perception of the nature and characteristics of that invisible world which is soon to receive them, would make them thoughtful and anxious for their souls; for they would become aware of their utter unfitness, their entire lack of preparation, to see God face to face. Still, live and act as sinful men may, eternity is over and around them all, even as the firmament is bent over the globe. If theirs were a penitent and a believing eye, they would look up with adoration into its serene depths, and joyfully behold the soft gleam of its stars, and it would send down upon them the sweet influences of its constellations. They may shut their eyes upon all this glory, and feel only earthly influences, and continue to be "of the earth, earthy." But there is a time coming when they cannot but look at eternity; when this firmament will throw them into consternation by the livid glare of its lightnings, and will compel them to hear the quick rattle and peal of its thunder; when it will not afford them a vision of glory and joy, as it will the redeemed and the holy, but one of despair and destruction.

There is only one shelter from this storm; there is only one covert from this tempest. He, and only he, who trusts in Christ's blood of atonement, will be able to look into the holy countenance of God, and upon the dread record of his own sins, without either trembling or despair. The merits and righteousness of Christ so clothe the guilty soul, that it can endure the otherwise intolerable brightness of God's pure throne and presence.

"Jesus! Thy blood and righteousness,
My beauty are, my glorious dress;
Mid flaming worlds, in these arrayed,
With joy shall I lift up my head."

Amidst those great visions that are to dawn upon every human creature, those souls will be in perfect peace who trust in the Great Propitiation. In those great tempests that are to shake down the earth and the sky, those hearts will be calm and happy who are hid in the clefts of the Rock of Ages. Flee then to Christ, ye prisoners of hope. Make preparation to know even as you are known, by repentance toward God and faith in the Lord Jesus Christ. A voice comes to you out of the cloud, saying, "This is my beloved Son, in whom I am well pleased; hear ye Him." Remember, and forget not, that this knowledge of God and your own heart is inevitable. At death, it will all of it flash upon the soul like lightning at midnight. It will fill the whole horizon of your being full of light. If you are in Christ Jesus, the light will not harm you. But if you are out of Christ, it will blast you. No sinful mortal can endure such a vision an instant, except as he is sprinkled with atoning blood, and clothed in the righteousness of the great Substitute and Surety for guilty man. Flee then to CHRIST, and so be prepared to know God and your own heart, even as you are known.

[Note 1: Noverim me, noverim Te.—BERNARD.]
[Note 2: Shakespeare: Hamlet, Act III., Sc. 4.]
[Note 3: Howe: On Regeneration. Sermon xliii.]
[Note 4: Bookschammer: On the Will.]

III - God's Exhaustive Knowledge of Man.

PSALM cxxxix. I-6.—*"O Lord, thou hast searched me, and known me. Thou knowest my down-sitting and mine uprising, thou understandest my thought afar off. Thou compassest my path and my lying down, and art acquainted with, all my ways. For there is not a word in my tongue, but, lo, O Lord, thou knowest it altogether. Thou, hast beset me behind and before, and laid thine hand upon me. Such knowledge is too wonderful for me; it is high, I cannot attain unto it."*

One of the most remarkable characteristics of a rational being is the power of self-inspection. The brute creation possesses many attributes that are common to human nature, but it has no faculty that bears even the remotest resemblance to that of self-examination. Instinctive action, undoubtedly, approaches the nearest of any to human action. That wonderful power by which the bee builds up a structure that is not exceeded in accuracy, and regularity, and economy of space, by the best geometry of Athens or of Rome; by which the beaver, after having chosen the very best possible location for it on the stream, constructs a dam that outlasts the work of the human engineer; by which the faithful dog contrives to perform many acts of affection, in spite of obstacles, and in the face of unexpected discouragements,—the instinct, we say, of the brute creation, as exhibited in a remarkably wide range of action and contrivance, and in a very varied and oftentimes perplexing conjuncture of circumstances, seems to bring man and beast very near to each other, and to furnish some ground for the theory of the materialist, that there is no essential difference between the two species of existences. But when we pass beyond the mere power of acting, to the additional power of surveying or inspecting an act, and of forming an estimate of its relations to moral law, we find a faculty in man that makes him differ in kind from the brute. No brute animal, however high up the scale, however ingenious and sagacious he may be, can ever look back and think of what he has done, "his thoughts the meanwhile accusing or else excusing him."

The mere power of performance, is, after all, not the highest power. It is the superadded power of calmly looking over the performance, and seeing what has been done, that marks the higher agency, and denotes a loftier order of existence than that of the animal or of material nature. If the mere ability to work with energy, and produce results, constituted the highest species of power, the force of gravitation would be the loftiest energy in the universe. Its range of execution is wider than that of any other created principle. But it is one of the lower and least important of agencies, because it is blind. It is destitute of the power of self-inspection. It does not know what it does, or why. "Man," says Pascal,[1] "is but a reed, and the weakest in all nature; yet he is a reed that thinks. The whole material universe does not need to arm itself, in order to crush him. A vapor, a drop of water is enough to destroy him. But if the whole universe of matter should combine to crush him, man would be more noble than that which destroyed him. For he would be conscious that he was dying, while, of the advantage which the material universe had obtained over him, that universe would know nothing." The action of a little child is altogether nothing and vanity compared with the energy of the earthquake or the lightning, so far as the exhibition of force and the mere power to act is concerned; but, on the other hand, it is more solemn than centuries of merely natural processes, and more momentous than all the material phenomena that have ever filled the celestial spaces, when we remember that it is the act of a thinking agent, and a self-conscious creature. The power to survey the act, when united with the power to act, sets mind infinitely above matter, and places the action of instinct, wonderful as it is, infinitely below the action of self-consciousness. The proud words of one of the characters in the old drama are strictly true:

"I am a nobler substance than the stars,
Or are they better since they are bigger?

I have a will and faculties of choice,
To do or not to do; and reason why
I do or not do this: the stars have none.
They know not why they shine, more than this taper,
Nor how they, work, nor what." [2]

But this characteristic of a rational being, though thus distinctive and common to every man that lives, is exceedingly marvellous. Like the air we breathe, like the light we see, it involves a mystery that no man has ever solved. Self-consciousness has been the problem and the thorn of the philosophic mind in all ages; and the mystery is not yet unravelled. Is not that a wonderful process by which a man knows, not some other thing but, himself? Is not that a strange act by which he, for a time, duplicates his own unity, and sets himself to look at himself? All other acts of consciousness are comparatively plain and explicable. When we look at an object other than ourselves,—when we behold a tree or the sky,—the act of knowledge is much more simple and easy to be explained. For then there is something outside of us, and in front of us, and another thing than we are, at which we look, and which we behold. But in this act of self-inspection there is no second thing, external, and extant to us, which we contemplate. That which is seen is one and the same identical object with that which sees. The act of knowledge which in all other instances requires the existence of two things,— a thing to be known and a thing to know,—in this instance is performed with only one. It is the individual soul that sees, and it is that very same individual soul that is seen. It is the individual man that knows, and it is that very identical man that is known. The eyeball looks at the eyeball.

And when this power of self-inspection is connected with the power of memory, the mystery of human existence becomes yet more complicated, and its explanation still more baffling. Is it not exceedingly wonderful, that we are able to re-exhibit our own thoughts and feelings; that we can call back what has gone clear by in our experience, and steadily look at it once more? Is it not a mystery that we can summon before our mind's eye feelings, purposes, desires, and thoughts, which occurred in the soul long years ago, and which, perhaps, until this moment, we have not thought of for years? Is it not a marvel, that they come up with all the vividness with which they first took origin in our experience, and that the lapse of time has deprived them of none of their first outlines or colors? Is it not strange, that we can recall that one particular feeling of hatred toward a fellow-man which, rankled in the heart twenty years ago; that we can now eye it, and see it as plainly as if it were still throbbing within us; that we can feel guilty for it once more, as if we were still cherishing it? If it were not so common, would it not be surprising, that we can reflect upon acts of disobedience toward God which we committed in the days of childhood, and far back in the dim twilights of moral agency; that we can re-act them, as it were, in our memory, and fill ourselves again with the shame and distress that attended their original commission? Is it not one of those mysteries which overhang human existence, and from which that of the brute is wholly free, that man can live his life, and act his agency, over, and over, and over again, indefinitely and forever, in his self-consciousness; that he can cause all his deeds to pass and re-pass before his self-reflection, and be filled through and through with the agony of self-knowledge? Truly such knowledge is too wonderful for me; it is high, I cannot attain unto it. Whither shall I go from my own spirit, and whither shall I flee from my own presence. If I ascend up into heaven, it is there looking at me. If I make my bed in hell, behold it is there torturing me. If I take the wings of the morning and dwell in the uttermost parts of the sea, even there must I know myself, and acquit or condemn myself.

But if that knowledge whereby man knows himself is mysterious, then certainly that whereby God knows him is far more so. That act whereby another being knows my secret thoughts, and inmost feelings, is most certainly inexplicable. That cognition whereby another person understands what takes place in the corners of my heart, and sees the minutest movements of my spirit, is surely high; most surely I cannot attain unto it.

And yet, it is a truth of revelation that God searches the heart of man; that He knows his down-sitting and uprising, and understands his thought afar off; that He compasses his path and his lying-down, and is acquainted with all his ways. And yet, it is a deduction of reason, also, that because God is the creator of the human mind, He must perfectly understand its secret agencies; that He in whose Essence man lives and moves and has his being, must behold every motion, and feel every stirring of the human spirit. "He that planted the ear, shall He not hear? He that formed the eye, shall He not see?" Let us, then, ponder the fact of God's exhaustive knowledge of man's soul, that we may realize it, and thereby come under its solemn power and impression. For all religion, all holy and reverential fear of God, rises and sets, as in an atmosphere, in the thought: "Thou God seest me."

I. In analyzing and estimating the Divine knowledge of the human soul, we find, in the first place, that God accurately and exhaustively knows all that man knows of himself.

Every man in a Christian land, who is in the habit of frequenting the house of God, possesses more or less of that self-knowledge of which we have spoken. He thinks of the moral character of some of his own thoughts. He reflects upon the moral quality of some of his own feelings. He considers the ultimate tendency of some of his own actions. In other words, there is a part of his inward and his outward life with which he is uncommonly well acquainted; of which he has a distinct perception. There are some thoughts of his mind, at which he blushes at the very time of their origin, because he is vividly aware what they are, and what they mean. There are some emotions of his heart, at which he trembles and recoils at the very moment of their uprising, because he perceives clearly that they involve a very malignant depravity. There are some actings of his will, of whose wickedness he is painfully conscious at the very instant of their rush and movement. We are not called upon, here, to say how many of a man's thoughts, feelings, and determinations, are thus subjected to his self-inspection at the very time of their origin, and are known in the clear light of self-knowledge. We are not concerned, at this point, with the amount of this man's self-inspection and self-knowledge. We are only saying that there is some experience such as this in his personal history, and that he does know something of himself, at the very

27

time of action, with a clearness and a distinctness that makes him start, or blush, or fear.

Now we say, that in reference to all this intimate self-knowledge, all this best part of a man's information respecting himself, he is not superior to God. He may be certain that in no particular does he know more of himself than the Searcher of hearts knows. He may be an uncommonly thoughtful person, and little of what is done within his soul may escape his notice,—nay, we will make the extreme supposition that he arrests every thought as it rises, and looks at it, that he analyzes every sentiment as it swells his heart, that he scrutinizes every purpose as it determines his will,—even if he should have such a thorough and profound self-knowledge as this, God knows him equally profoundly, and equally thoroughly. Nay more, this process of self-inspection may go on indefinitely, and the man may grow more and more thoughtful, and obtain an everlastingly augmenting knowledge of what he is and what he does, so that it shall seem to him that he is going down so far along that path which the vulture's eye hath not seen, is penetrating so deeply into those dim and shadowy regions of consciousness where the external life takes its very first start, as to be beyond the reach of any eye, and the ken of any intelligence but his own, and then he may be sure that God understands the thought that is afar off, and deep down, and that at this lowest range and plane in his experience He besets him behind and before.

O, this man, like the most of mankind, may be an unreflecting person. Then, in this case, thoughts, feelings, and purposes are continually rising up within his soul like the clouds and exhalations of an evaporating deluge, and at the time of their rise he subjects them to no scrutiny of conscience, and is not pained in the least by their moral character and significance. He lacks self-knowledge altogether, at these points in his history. But, notice that the fact that he is not self-inspecting at these points cannot destroy the fact that he is acting at them. The fact that he is not a spectator of his own transgression, does not alter the fact that he is the author of it. If this man, for instance, thinks over his worldly affairs on God's holy day, and perhaps in God's holy house, with such an absorption and such a pleasure that he entirely drowns the voice of conscience while he is so doing, and self-inspection is banished for the time, it will not do for him to plead this absence of a distinct and painful consciousness of what his mind was actually doing in the house of God, and upon the Lord's day, as the palliative and excuse of his wrong thoughts. If this man, again, indulges in an envious or a sensual emotion, with such an energy and entireness, as for the time being to preclude all action of the higher powers of reason and self-reflection, so that for the time being he is not in the least troubled by a sense of his wickedness, it will be no excuse for him at the eternal bar, that he was not thinking of his envy or his lust at the time when he felt it. And therefore it is, that accountableness covers the whole field of human agency, and God holds us responsible for our thoughtless sin, as well as for our deliberate transgression.

In the instance, then, of the thoughtless man; in the case where there is little or no self-examination; God unquestionably knows the man as well as the man knows himself. The Omniscient One is certainly possessed of an amount of knowledge equal to that small modicum which is all that a rational and immortal soul can boast of in reference to itself. But the vast majority of mankind fall into

28

this class. The self-examiners are very few, in comparison with the millions who possess the power to look into their hearts, but who rarely or never do so. The great God our Judge, then, surely knows the mass of men, in their down-sitting and uprising, with a knowledge that is equal to their own. And thus do we establish our first position, that God knows all that the man knows; God's knowledge is equal to the very best part of man's knowledge.

In concluding this part of the discussion, we turn to consider some practical lessons suggested by it.

1. In the first place, the subject reminds us that we are fearfully and wonderfully made. When we take a solar microscope and examine even the commonest object—a bit of sand, or a hair of our heads-we are amazed at the revelation that is made to us. We had no previous conception of the wonders that are contained in the structure of even such ordinary things as these. But, if we should obtain a corresponding view of our own mental and moral structure; if we could subject our immortal natures to a microscopic self-examination; we should not only be surprised, but we should be terrified. This explains, in part, the consternation with which a criminal is filled, as soon as he begins to understand the nature of his crime. His wicked act is perceived in its relation to his own mental powers and faculties. He knows, now, what a hazardous thing it is to possess a free-will; what an awful thing it is to own a conscience. He feels, as he never did before, that he is fearfully and wonderfully made, and cries out: "O that I had never been born! O that I had never been created a responsible being! these terrible faculties of reason, and will, and conscience, are too heavy for me to wield; would that I had been created a worm, and no man, then, I should not have incurred the hazards under which I have sinned and ruined myself."

The constitution of the human soul is indeed a wonderful one; and such a meditation as that which we have just devoted to its functions of self-examination and memory, brief though it be, is enough to convince us of it. And remember, that this constitution is not peculiar to you and to me. It belongs to every human creature on the globe. The imbruted pagan in the fiery centre of Africa, who never saw a Bible, or heard of the Redeemer; the equally imbruted man, woman, or child, who dwells in the slime of our own civilization, not a mile from where we sit, and hear the tidings of mercy; the filthy savage, and the yet filthier profligate, are both of them alike with ourselves possessed of these awful powers of self-knowledge and of memory.

Think of this, ye earnest and faithful laborers in the vineyard of the Lord. There is not a child that you allure into your Sabbath Schools, and your Mission Schools, that is not fearfully and wonderfully made; and whose marvellous powers you are doing much to render to their possessor a blessing, instead of a curse. When Sir Humphrey Davy, in answer to an inquiry that had been made of him respecting the number and series of his discoveries in chemistry, had gone through with the list, he added: "But the greatest of my discoveries is Michael Faraday." This Michael Faraday was a poor boy employed in the menial services of the laboratory where Davy made those wonderful discoveries by which he revolutionized the science of chemistry, and whose chemical genius he detected, elicited, and encouraged, until he finally took the place of his teacher and patron, and acquired a name that is now one of the influences of England. Well might he say: "My greatest discovery was when I detected the wonderful powers of Michael Faraday." And never will you make a greater and more beneficent discovery, than when, under the thick scurf of pauperism and vice, you detect the human soul that is fearfully and wonderfully made; than when you elicit its powers of self-consciousness and of memory, and, instrumentally, dedicate them to the service of Christ and the Church.

2. In the second place, we see from the subject, that thoughtlessness in sin will never excuse sin. There are degrees in sin. A deliberate, self-conscious act of sin is the most intense form of moral evil. When a man has an active conscience; when he distinctly thinks over the nature of the transgression which he is tempted to commit; when he sees clearly that it is a direct violation of a command of God which he is about to engage in; when he says, "I know that this is positively forbidden by my Maker and Judge, but I will do it,"—we have an instance of the most heaven-daring sin. This is deliberate and wilful transgression. The servant knows his lord's will and does it not, and he shall be beaten with "many stripes," says Christ.

But, such sin as this is not the usual form. Most of human transgressions are not accompanied with such a distinct apprehension, and such a deliberate determination. The sin of ignorance and thoughtlessness is the species which is most common. Men, generally, do not first think of what they are about to do, and then proceed to do it; but they first proceed to do it, and then think nothing at all about it. But, thoughtlessness will not excuse sin; though, it is a somewhat less extreme form of it, than deliberate transgression. Under the Levitical law, the sin of ignorance, as it was called, was to be expiated by a somewhat different sacrifice from that offered for the wilful and deliberate sin; but it must be expiated. A victim must be offered for it. It was guilt before God, and needed atonement. Our Lord, in His prayer for His murderers, said, "Father forgive them, for they know not what they do." The act of crucifying the Lord of glory was certainly a sin, and one of an awful nature. But the authors of it were not fully aware of its import. They did not understand the dreadful significance of the crucifixion of the Son of God, as we now understand it, in the light of eighteen centuries. Our Lord alludes to this, as a species of mitigation; while yet He teaches, by the very prayer which He puts up for them, that this ignorance did not excuse His murderers. He asks that they may be forgiven. But where there is absolutely no sin there is no need of forgiveness. It is one of our Lord's assertions, that it will be more tolerable for Sodom and Gomorrah, in the day of judgment, than it will be for those inhabitants of Palestine who would not hear the words of His apostles,—because the sin of the former was less deliberate and wilful than that of the latter. But He would not have us infer from this, that Sodom and Gomorrah are not to be punished for sin. And, finally, He sums up the whole doctrine upon this point, in the declaration, that "he who knew his master's will and did it not shall be beaten with many stripes; but he who knew not his master's will and did it not shall be beaten with few stripes." The sin of thoughtlessness shall be beaten with fewer stripes than the sin of deliberation,—but it shall be beaten, and therefore it is sin.

The almost universal indifference and thoughtlessness with which men live on in a worldly and selfish life, will not excuse them in the day of accurate accounts.

And the reason is, that they are capable of thinking upon the law of God; of thinking upon their duties; of thinking upon their sins. They possess the wonderful faculties of self-inspection and memory, and therefore they are capable of bringing their actions into light. It is the command of God to every man, and to every rational spirit everywhere, to walk in the light, and to be a child of the light. We ought to examine ourselves; to understand our ruling motives and abiding purposes; to scrutinize our feelings and conduct. But if we do little or nothing of this, we must not expect that in the day of judgment we can plead our thoughtless ignorance of what we were, and what we did, here upon earth, as an excuse for our disobedience. God expects, and demands, that every one of His rational creatures should be all that he is capable of being. He gave man wonderful faculties and endowments,—ten talents, five talents, two talents,—and He will require the whole original sum given, together with a faithful use and improvement of it. The very thoughtlessness then, particularly under the Gospel dispensation,—the very neglect and non-use of the power of self-inspection,—will go in to constitute a part of the sin that will be punished. Instead of being an excuse, it will be an element of the condemnation itself.

3. In the third place, even the sinner himself ought to rejoice in the fact that God is the Searcher of the heart. It is instinctive and natural, that a transgressor should attempt to conceal his character from his Maker; but next to his sin itself, it would be the greatest injury that he could do to himself, should he succeed in his attempt. Even after the commission of sin, there is every reason for desiring that God should compass our path and lying down, and be acquainted with all our ways. For, He is the only being who can forgive sin; the only one who can renew and sanctify the heart. There is the same motive for having the disease of the soul understood by God, that there is for having the disease of the body examined by a skilful physician. Nothing is gained, but every thing is lost, by ignorance.

The sinner, therefore, has the strongest of motives for rejoicing in the truth that God sees him. It ought not to be an unwelcome fact even to him. For how can his sin be pardoned, unless it is clearly understood by the pardoning power? How can his soul be purified from its inward corruption, unless it is searched by the Spirit of all holiness?

Instead, therefore, of being repelled by such a solemn truth as that which we have been discussing, even the natural man should be allured by it. For it teaches him that there is help for him in God. His own knowledge of his own heart, as we have seen, is very imperfect and very inadequate. But the Divine knowledge is thoroughly adequate. He may, therefore, devolve his case with confidence upon the unerring One. Let him take words upon his lips, and cry unto Him: "Search me, O God, and try me; and see what evil ways there are in me, and lead me in the way everlasting." Let him endeavor to come into possession of the Divine knowledge. There is no presumption in this. God desires that he should know himself as He knows him; that he should get possession of His views upon this point; that he should see himself as He sees him. One of the principal sins which God has to charge upon the sinner is, that his apprehensions respecting his own character are in conflict with the Divine. Nothing would more certainly meet the approbation of God, than a renunciation of human estimates of human nature, and the adoption of those contained in the inspired word. Endeavor, therefore, to obtain the very same knowledge of your heart which God Himself possesses. And in this endeavor, He will assist you. The influences of the Holy Spirit to enlighten are most positively promised and proffered. Therefore be not repelled by the truth; but be drawn by it to a deeper, truer knowledge of your heart. Lift up your soul in prayer, and beseech God to impart to you a profound knowledge of yourself, and then to sprinkle all your discovered guilt, and all your undiscovered guilt, with atoning blood. This is salvation; first to know yourself, and then to know Christ as your Prophet, Priest, and King.

*[**Note 1:** PENSÉES: Grandeur de l'homme, 6. Ed. Wetstein.]*
*[**Note 2:** CHAPMAN: Byron's Conspiracy.]*

IV - God's Exhaustive Knowledge of Man. (continued)

PSALM cxxxix. 1—6.— *"O Lord, thou hast searched me, and known me. Thou knowest my down-sitting and mine uprising; thou understandest my thought afar off. Thou compassest my path and my lying down, and art acquainted with all my ways. For there is not a word in my tongue, but lo, O Lord, thou knowest it altogether. Thou hast beset me behind and before, and laid thy hand upon me. Such knowledge is too wonderful for me; it is high, I cannot attain unto it."*

In the preceding discourse upon this text, we directed attention to the fact that man is possessed of the power of self-knowledge, and that he cannot ultimately escape from using it. He cannot forever flee from his own presence; he cannot, through all eternity, go away from his own spirit. If he take the wings of the morning and dwell in the uttermost parts of the earth, he must, sooner or later, know himself, and acquit or condemn himself.

Our attention was then directed to the fact, that God's knowledge of man is certainly equal to man's knowledge of himself. No man knows more of his own heart than the Searcher of hearts knows. Up to this point, certainly, the truth of the text is incontrovertible. God knows all that man knows.

II. We come now to the second position: That God accurately and exhaustively knows all that man might, but does not, know of himself.

Although the Creator designed that every man should thoroughly understand his own heart, and gave him the power of self-inspection that he might use it faithfully, and apply it constantly, yet man is extremely ignorant of himself. Mankind, says an old writer, are nowhere less at home, than at home. Very few persons practise serious self-examination at all; and none employ the power of self-inspection with that carefulness and sedulity with which they ought. Hence men generally, and unrenewed men always, are unacquainted with much that goes on within their own minds and hearts. Though it is sin and self-will, though it is thought and feeling and purpose and desire, that is going on and taking place during all these years of religious indifference, yet the agent himself, so far as a sober reflection upon the moral character of the process, and a distinct perception of the dreadful issue of it, are concerned, is much of the time as destitute of self-knowledge as an irrational brute itself. For, were sinful men constantly self-examining, they would be constantly in torment. Men can be happy in sin, only so long as they can sin without thinking of it. The instant they begin to perceive and understand what they are doing, they begin to feel the fang of the worm. If the frivolous wicked world, which now takes so much pleasure in its wickedness, could be forced to do here what it will be forced to do hereafter, namely, to eye its sin while it commits it, to think of what it is doing while it does it, the billows of the lake of fire would roll in upon time, and from gay Paris and luxurious Vienna there would instantaneously ascend the wailing cry of Pandemonium.

But it is not so at present. Men here upon earth are continually thinking sinful thoughts and cherishing sinful feelings, and yet they are not continually in hell. On the contrary, "they are not in trouble as other men are, neither are they plagued like other men. Their eyes stand out with fatness; they have more than heart could wish." This proves that they are self-ignorant; that they know neither their sin nor its bitter end. They sin without the consciousness of sin, and hence are happy in it. Is it not so in our own personal experience? Have there not been in the past ten years of our own mental history long trains of thought,—sinful thought,—and vast processions of feelings and imaginings,—sinful feelings and imaginings,—that have trailed over the spaces of the soul, but which have been as unwatched and unseen by the self-inspecting eye of conscience, as the caravans of the African desert have been, during the same period, by the eye of our sense? We have not felt a pang of guilt every single time that we have thought a wrong thought; yet we should have felt one inevitably, had we scrutinized every such single thought. Our face has not flushed with crimson in every particular instance in which we have exercised a lustful emotion; yet it would have done so had we carefully noted every such emotion. A distinct self-knowledge has by no means run parallel with all our sinful activity; has by no means been co-extensive with it. We perform vastly more than we inspect. We have sinned vastly more than we have been aware of at the time.

Even the Christian, in whom this unreflecting species of life and conduct has given way, somewhat, to a thoughtful and vigilant life, knows and acknowledges that perfection is not yet come. As he casts his eye over even his regenerate and illuminated life, and sees what a small amount of sin has been distinctly detected, keenly felt, and heartily confessed, in comparison with that large amount of sin which he knows he must have committed, during this long period of incessant action of mind, heart, and limbs, he finds no repose for his misgivings with respect to the filial examination and account, except by enveloping himself yet more entirely in the ample folds of his Redeemer's righteousness; except by hiding himself yet more profoundly in the cleft of that Rock of Ages which protects the chief of sinners from the unsufferable splendors and terrors of the Divine glory and holiness as it passes by. Even the Christian knows that he must have committed many sins in thoughtless moments and hours,—many sins of which he was not deliberately thinking at the time of their commission,—and must pray with David, "Cleanse thou me from secret faults." The functions and operations of memory evince that such is the case. Are we not sometimes, in our serious hours when memory is busy, convinced of sins which, at the time of their commission, were wholly unaccompanied with a sense of their sinfulness? The act in this instance was performed blindly, without self-inspection, and therefore without self-conviction. Ten years, we will say, have intervened,—years of new activity, and immensely varied experiences. And now the magic power of recollection sets us back, once more, at that point of responsible action, and bids do what we did not do at the time,—analyze our performance and feel consciously guilty, experience the first sensation of remorse, for what we did ten years ago. Have we not, sometimes, been vividly reminded that upon such an occasion, and at such a time, we were angry, or proud, but at the time when the emotion was swelling our veins were not filled with, that clear and painful sense of its turpitude which now attends the recollection of it? The re-exhibition of an action in memory, as in a mirror, is often accompanied with a distinct apprehension of its moral character that formed no part of the experience of the agent while absorbed in the hot and hasty original action itself. And when we remember how immense are the stores of memory, and what an amount of sin has been committed in hours of thoughtlessness and moral indifference, what prayer is more natural and warm than the supplication: "Search me O God, and try me, and see what evil ways there are within me, and lead me in the way everlasting."

But the careless, unenlightened man, as we have before remarked, leads a life almost entirely destitute of self-inspection, and self-knowledge. He sins constantly. He does only evil, and that continually, as did man before the deluge. For he is constantly acting. A living self-moving soul, like his, cannot cease action if it would. And yet the current is all one way. Day after day sends up its clouds of sensual, worldly, selfish thoughts. Week after week pours onward its stream of low-born, corrupt, unspiritual feelings. Year after year accumulates that hardening mass of carnal-mindedness, and distaste for religion, which is sometimes a more insuperable obstacle to the truth, than positive faults and vices which startle and shock the conscience. And yet the man thinks nothing about all this action of his mind and heart. He does not subject it to any self-inspection. If he should, for but a single hour, be lifted up to the eminence from which all this current of self-will, and moral agency, may be seen and surveyed in its real character and significance, he would start back as if brought to the brink of hell. But he is not thus lifted up. He continues to use and abuse his mental and his moral faculties, but, for most of his probation, with all the blindness and heedlessness of a mere animal instinct.

There is, then, a vast amount of sin committed without self-inspection; and, consequently, without any distinct perception, at the time, that it is sin. The Christian will find himself feeling guilty, for the first time, for a transgression that occurred far back in the past, and will need a fresh application of atoning blood. The sinner will find, at some period or other, that remorse is fastening its tooth in his conscience for a vast amount of sinful thought, feeling, desire, and motive, that took origin in the unembarrassed days of religious thoughtlessness and worldly enjoyment.

For, think you that the insensible sinner is always to be thus insensible,—that this power of self-inspection is eternally to "rust unused?" What a tremendous revelation will one day be made to an unreflecting transgressor, simply because he is a man and not a brute, has lived a human life, and is endowed with the power of self-knowledge, whether he has used it or not! What a terrific vision it will be for him, when the limitless line of his sins which he has not yet distinctly examined, and thought of, and repented of, shall be made to pass in slow procession before that inward eye which he has wickedly kept shut so long! Tell us not of the disclosures that shall be made when the sea shall give up the dead that are in it, and the graves shall open and surrender their dead; what are these material disclosures, when compared with the revelations of self-knowledge! What is all this external display, sombre and terrible as it will be to the outward eye, when compared with all that internal revealing that will be made to a hitherto thoughtless soul, when, of a sudden, in the day of judgment, its deepest caverns shall heave in unison with the material convulsions of the day, and shall send forth to judgment their long slumbering, and hidden iniquity; when the sepulchres of its own memory shall burst open, and give up the sin that has long lain buried there, in needless and guilty forgetfulness, awaiting this second resurrection!

For (to come back to the unfolding of the subject, and the movement of the argument), God perfectly knows all that man might, but does not, know of himself. Though the transgressor is ignorant of much of his sin, because at the time of its commission he sins blindly as well as wilfully, and unreflectingly as well as freely; and though the transgressor has forgotten much of that small amount of sin of which he was conscious, and by which he was pained, at the time of its perpetration; though on the side of man the powers of self-inspection and memory have accomplished so little towards the preservation of man's sin, yet God knows it all, and remembers it all. He compasseth man's path, and his lying-down, and is acquainted with all his ways. "There is nothing covered, therefore, that shall not be revealed, neither hid that shall not be known. Whatsoever ye have spoken in darkness shall be heard in the light; and that which ye have spoken in the ear in closets shall be proclaimed upon the house-tops." The Creator of the human mind has control over its powers of self-inspection, and of memory; and when the proper time comes He will compel these endowments to perform their legitimate functions, and do their appointed work. The torturing self-survey will begin, never more to end. The awful recollection will commence, endlessly to go on.

One principal reason why the Biblical representations of human sinfulness exert so little influence over men, and, generally speaking, seem to them to be greatly exaggerated and untrue, lies in the fact that the Divine knowledge of human character is in advance of the human knowledge. God's consciousness and cognition upon this subject is exhaustive; while man's self-knowledge is superficial and shallow. The two forms of knowledge, consequently, when placed side by side, do not agree, but conflict. There would be less difficulty, and less contradiction, if mankind generally were possessed of even as much self-knowledge as the Christian is possessed of. There would be no difficulty, and no contradiction, if the knowledge of the judgment-day could be anticipated, and the self-inspection of that occasion could commence here and now. But such is not the fact. The Bible labors, therefore, under the difficulty of possessing an advanced knowledge; the difficulty of being addressed to a mind that is almost entirely unacquainted with the subject treated of. The Word of God knows man exhaustively, as God knows him; and hence all its descriptions of human character are founded upon such a knowledge. But man, in his self-ignorance, does not perceive their awful truth. He has not yet attained the internal correspondent to the Biblical statement,—that apprehension of total depravity, that knowledge of the plague of the heart, which always and ever says "yea" to the most vivid description of human sinfulness, and "amen" to God's heaviest malediction upon it. Nothing deprives the Word of its nerve and influence, more than this general lack of self-inspection and self-knowledge. For, only that which is perceived to be true exerts an influence upon the human mind. The doctrine of human sinfulness is preached to men, year after year, to whom it does not come home with the demonstration of the Spirit and with power, because the sinfulness which is really within them is as yet unknown, and because not one of a thousand of their transgressions has ever been scanned in the light of self-examination. But is the Bible untrue, because the man is ignorant? Is the sun black, because the eye is shut?

However ignorant man may be, and may desire and strive to be, of himself, God knows him altogether, and knows that the representations of His word, respecting the character and necessities of human nature, are the unexaggerated, sober, and actual fact. Though most of the sinner's life of alienation from God, and of disobedience, has been a blind and a reckless agency, unaccompanied with self-scrutiny, and to a great extent passed from his memory, yet it has all of it been looked at, as it welled, up from the living centres of free agency and responsibility, by the calm and dreadful eye of retributive Justice, and has all of it been indelibly written down in the book of God's sure memory, with a pen of iron, and the point of a diamond.

And here, let us for a moment look upon the bright, as well as the dark side of this subject. For if God's exhaustive knowledge of the human heart waken dread in one of its aspects, it starts infinite hope in another. If that Being has gone down into these depths of human depravity, and seen it with a more abhorring glance than could ever shoot from a finite eye, and yet has returned with a cordial offer to forgive it all, and a hearty proffer to cleanse it all away, then we can lift up the eye in adoration and in hope. There has been an infinite forbearance and condescension. The worst has been seen, and that too by the holiest of Beings, and yet eternal glory is offered to us! God knows, from personal examination, the worthlessness of human character, with a thoroughness and intensity of knowledge of which man has no conception; and yet, in the light of this knowledge, in the very flame of this intuition, He has devised a plan of mercy and redemption. Do not think, then, because of your present ignorance of your guilt and corruption, that the incarnation and death of the Son of God was unnecessary, and that that costly blood of atonement which you are treading under foot wet the rocks of Calvary for a peccadillo. Could you, but for a moment only, know yourself altogether and exhaustively, as the Author of this Redemption knows you, you would cry out, in the words of a far holier man than you are, "I am undone." If you could but see guilt as God sees it, you would also see with Him that nothing but an infinite Passion can expiate it. If you could but fathom the human heart as God fathoms it, you would know as He knows, that nothing less than regeneration can purify its fountains of uncleanness, and cleanse it from its ingrain corruption.

Thus have we seen that God knows man altogether,—that He knows all that man knows of himself, and all that man might but does not yet know of himself. The Searcher of hearts knows all the thoughts that we have thought upon, all the reflections that we have reflected upon, all the experience that we have ourselves analyzed and inspected. And He also knows that far larger part of our life which we have not yet subjected to the scrutiny of self-examination,—all those thoughts, feelings, desires, and motives, innumerable as they are, of which we took no heed at the time of their origin and existence, and which we suppose, perhaps, we shall hear no more of again. Whither then shall we go from God's spirit? or whither shall we flee from His presence and His knowledge? If we ascend up into heaven, He is there, and knows us perfectly. If we make our bed in hell, behold He is there, and reads the secret thoughts and feelings of our heart. The darkness hideth not from Him; our ignorance does not affect His knowledge; the night shineth as the day; the darkness and the light are both alike to Him.

This great truth which we have been considering obtains a yet more serious emphasis, and a yet more solemn power over the mind, when we take into view the character of the Being who thus searches our hearts, and is acquainted with all our ways. Who of us would not be filled with uneasiness, if he knew that an imperfect fellow-creature were looking constantly into his soul? Would not the flush of shame often burn upon our cheek, if we knew that a sinful man like ourselves were watching all the feelings and thoughts that are rising within us? Should we not be more circumspect than we are, if men were able mutually to search each other's hearts? How often does a man change his course of conduct, when he discovers, accidentally, that his neighbor knows what he is doing.

But it is not an imperfect fellow-man, it is not a perfect angel, who besets us behind and before, and is acquainted with, all our ways. It is the immaculate God himself. It is He before whom archangels veil their faces, and the burning seraphim cry, "Holy." It is He, in whose sight the pure cerulean heavens are not clean, and whose eyes are a flame of fire devouring all iniquity. We are beheld, in all this process of sin, be it blind or be it intelligent, by infinite Purity. We are not, therefore, to suppose that God contemplates this our life of sin with the dull indifference of an Epicurean deity; that He looks into our souls, all this while, from mere curiosity, and with no moral emotion towards us. The God who knows us altogether is the Holy One of Israel, whose wrath is both real, and revealed, against all unrighteousness.

If, therefore, we connect the holy nature and pure essence of God with all this unceasing and unerring inspection of the human soul, does not the truth which, we have been considering speak with a bolder emphasis, and acquire an additional power to impress and solemnize the mind? When we realize that the Being who is watching us at every instant, and in every act and element of our existence, is the very same Being who revealed himself amidst the lightenings of Sinai as hating sin and not clearing the thoughtless guilty, do not our prospects at the bar of justice look dark and fearful? For, who of the race of man is holy enough to stand such an inspection? Who of the sons of men will prove pure in such a furnace?

Are we not, then, brought by this truth close up to the central doctrine of Christianity, and made to see our need of the atonement and righteousness of the

Redeemer? How can we endure such a scrutiny as God is instituting into our character and conduct? What can we say, in the day of reckoning, when the Searcher of hearts shall make known, to us all that He knows of us? What can we do, in that day which shall reveal the thoughts and the estimates of the Holy One respecting us?

It is perfectly plain, from the elevated central point of view where we now stand, and in the focal light in which we now see, that no man can be justified before God upon the ground of personal character; for that character, when subjected to God's exhaustive scrutiny, withers and shrinks away. A man may possibly be just before his neighbor, or his friend, or society, or human laws, but he is miserably self-deceived who supposes that his heart will appear righteous under such a scrutiny and in such a Presence as we have been considering.[1] However it may be before other tribunals, the apostle is correct when he asserts that "every mouth, must be stopped, and the whole world plead guilty before God." Before the Searcher of hearts, all mankind must appeal to mere and sovereign mercy. Justice, in this reference, is out of the question.

Now, in this condition of things, God so loved the world that He gave His only-begotten Son, that whosoever believeth in Him might not perish, but have everlasting life. The Divine mercy has been manifested in a mode that does not permit even the guiltiest to doubt its reality, its sufficiency, or its sincerity. The argument is this. "If when, we were yet sinners," and known to be such, in the perfect and exhaustive manner that has been described, "Christ died for us, much more, being now justified by His blood, shall we be saved from Wrath through Him." Appropriating this atonement which the Searcher of hearts has Himself provided for this very exigency, and which He knows to be thoroughly adequate, no man, however guilty, need fear the most complete disclosures which the Divine Omniscience will have to make of human character in the day of doom. If the guilt is "infinite upon infinite," so is the sacrifice of the God-man. Who is he that condemmeth? it is the Son of God that died for sin. Who shall lay anything to God's elect? it is God that justifieth. And as God shall, in the last day, summon up from the deep places of our souls all of our sins, and bring us to a strict account for everything, even to the idle words that we have spoken, we can look Him full in the eye, without a thought of fear, and with love unutterable, if we are really relying upon the atoning sacrifice of Christ for justification. Even in that awful Presence, and under that Omniscient scrutiny, "there is no condemnation to them that are in Christ Jesus."

The great lesson, then, taught by the text and its unfolding, is the importance of attaining self-knowledge here upon earth, and while there remaineth a sacrifice for sins. The duty and wisdom of every man is, to anticipate the revelations of the judgment day; to find out the sin of his soul, while it is an accepted time and a day of salvation. For we have seen that this self-inspection cannot ultimately be escaped. Man was made to know himself, and he must sooner or later come to it. Self-knowledge is as certain, in the end, as death. The utmost that can be done, is to postpone it for a few days, or years. The article of death and the exchange of worlds will pour it all in, like a deluge, upon every man, whether he will or not. And he who does not wake up to a knowledge of his heart, until he enters eternity, wakes up not to pardon but to despair.

The simple question, then, which, meets us is: Wilt thou know thyself here and now, that thou mayest accept and feel God's pity in Christ's blood, or wilt thou keep within the screen, and not know thyself until beyond the grave, and then feel God's judicial wrath? The self-knowledge, remember, must come in the one way or the other. It is a simple question of time; a simple question whether it shall come here in this world, where the blood of Christ "freely flows," or in the future world, where "there remaineth no more sacrifice for sin." Turn the matter as we will, this is the sum and substance,—a sinful man must either come to a thorough self-knowledge, with a hearty repentance and a joyful pardon, in this life; or he must come to a thorough, self-knowledge, with a total despair and an eternal damnation, in the other. God is not mocked. God's great pity in the blood of Christ must not be trifled with. He who refuses, or neglects, to institute that self-examination which leads to the sense of sin, and the felt need of Christ's work, by this very fact proves that he does not desire to know his own heart, and that he has no wish to repent of sin. But he who will not even look at his sin,— what does not he deserve from that Being who poured out His own blood for it? He who refuses even to open his eyes upon that bleeding Lamb of God,—what must not he expect from the Lion of the tribe of Judah, in the day of judgment? He who by a life of apathy, and indifference to sin, puts himself out of all relations to the Divine pity,—what must he experience in eternity, but the operations of stark, unmitigated law?

Find out your sin, then. God will forgive all that is found. Though your sins be as scarlet, they shall be as white as snow. The great God delights to forgive, and is waiting to forgive. But, sin must be seen by the sinner, before it can be pardoned by the Judge. If you refuse at this point; if you hide yourself from yourself; if you preclude all feeling and conviction upon the subject of sin, by remaining ignorant of it; if you continue to live an easy, thoughtless life in sin, then you cannot be forgiven, and the measure of God's love with which He would have blessed you, had you searched yourself and repented, will be the measure of God's righteous wrath with which He will search you, and condemn you, because you have not.

[**Note 1:** "It is easy,"—says one of the keenest and most incisive of theologians,—"for any one in the cloisters of the schools to indulge himself in idle speculations on the merit of works to justify men; but when he comes into the presence of God, he must bid farewell to these amusements, for there the business is transacted with seriousness. To this point must our attention be directed, if we wish to make any useful inquiry concerning true righteousness: How we can answer the celestial Judge when He shall call us to an account? Let us place that Judge before our eyes, not according to the inadequate imaginations of our minds, but according to the descriptions given of him in the Scriptures, which represent him as one whose refulgence eclipses the stars, whose purity makes all things appear polluted, and who searches the inmost soul of his creatures,—let us so conceive of the Judge of all the earth, and every one must present himself as a criminal before Him, and voluntarily prostrate and humble himself in deep solicitude concerning; his absolution." CALVIN: Institutes, iii. 12.]

V - All Mankind Guilty; Or, Every Man Knows More Than He Practises

ROMANS i. 24.—*"When they knew God, they glorified him not as God."*

The idea of God is the most important and comprehensive of all the ideas of which the human mind is possessed. It is the foundation of religion; of all right doctrine, and all right conduct. A correct intuition of it leads to correct religious theories and practice; while any erroneous or defective view of the Supreme Being will pervade the whole province of religion, and exert a most pernicious influence upon the entire character and conduct of men.

In proof of this, we have only to turn to the opening chapters of St. Paul's Epistle to the Romans. Here we find a profound and accurate account of the process by which human nature becomes corrupt, and runs its downward career of unbelief, vice, and sensuality. The apostle traces back the horrible depravity of the heathen world, which he depicts with a pen as sharp as that of Juvenal, but with none of Juvenal's bitterness and vitriolic sarcasm, to a distorted and false conception of the being and attributes of God. He does not, for an instant, concede that this distorted and false conception is founded in the original structure and constitution of the human soul, and that this moral ignorance is necessary and inevitable. This mutilated idea of the Supreme Being was not inlaid in the rational creature on the morning of creation, when God said, "Let us make man in our image, after our likeness." On the contrary, the apostle affirms that the Creator originally gave all mankind, in the moral constitution of a rational soul and in the works of creation and providence, the media to a correct idea of Himself, and asserts, by implication, that if they had always employed these media they would have always possessed this idea. "The wrath of God," he says, "is revealed from heaven against all ungodliness and unrighteousness of men who hold the truth in unrighteousness; because that which may be known of God is manifest in them, for God hath shewed it unto them. For the invisible things of him, even his eternal power and Godhead, are clearly seen from the creation of the world, being understood by the things that are made, so that they are without excuse; because that when they knew God, they glorified him not as God" (Rom. i. 18-21). From this, it appears that the mind of man has not kept what was committed to its charge. It has not employed the moral instrumentalities, nor elicited the moral ideas, with which it has been furnished. And, notice that the apostle does not confine this statement to those who live within the pale of Revelation. His description is unlimited and universal. The affirmation of the text, that "when man knew God he glorified him not as God," applies to the Gentile as well as to the Jew. Nay, the primary reference of these statements was to the pagan world. It was respecting the millions of idolaters in cultivated Greece and Rome, and the millions of idolaters in barbarous India and China,—it was respecting the whole world lying in wickedness, that St. Paul remarked: "The invisible things of God, even his eternal power and Godhead, are clearly seen from the creation of the world down to the present moment, being understood by the things that are made; so that they are without excuse."

When Napoleon was returning from his campaign in Egypt and Syria, he was seated one night upon the deck of the vessel, under the open canopy of the heavens, surrounded by his captains and generals. The conversation had taken a skeptical direction, and most of the party had combated the doctrine of the Divine existence. Napoleon had sat silent and musing, apparently taking no interest in the discussion, when suddenly raising his hand, and pointing at the crystalline firmament crowded with its mildly shining planets and its keen glittering stars, he broke out, in those startling tones that so often electrified a million of men: "Gentlemen, who made all that?" The eternal power and Godhead of the Creator are impressed by the things that are made, and these words of Napoleon to his atheistic captains silenced them. And the same impression is made the world over. Go to-day into the heart of Africa, or into the centre of New Holland; select the most imbruted pagan that can be found; take him out under a clear star-lit heaven and ask him who made all that, and the idea of a Superior Being,— superior to all his fetishes and idols,—possessing eternal power and supremacy ([Greek: theotaes]) immediately emerges in his consciousness. The instant the missionary takes this lustful idolater away from the circle of his idols, and brings him face to face with the heavens and the earth, as Napoleon brought his captains, the constitutional idea dawns again, and the pagan trembles before the unseen Power.[1]

But it will be objected that it is a very dim, and inadequate idea of the Deity that thus rises in the pagan's mind, and that therefore the apostle's affirmation that he is "without excuse" for being an idolater and a sensualist requires some qualification. This imbruted creature, says the objector, does not possess the metaphysical conception of God as a Spirit, and of all his various attributes and qualities, like the dweller in Christendom. How then can he be brought in guilty before the same eternal bar, and be condemned to the same eternal punishment, with the nominal Christian? The answer is plain, and decisive, and derivable out of the apostle's own statements. In order to establish the guiltiness of a rational creature before the bar of justice, it is not necessary to show that he has lived in the seventh heavens, and under a blaze of moral intelligence like that of the archangel Gabriel. It is only necessary to show that he has enjoyed some degree of moral light, and that he has not lived up to it. Any creature who knows more than he practises is a guilty creature. If the light in the pagan's intellect concerning God and the moral law, small though it be, is yet actually in advance of the inclination and affections of his heart and the actions of his life, he deserves to be punished, like any and every other creature, under the Divine government, of whom the same thing is true. Grades of knowledge vary indefinitely. No two men upon the planet, no two men in Christendom, possess precisely the same degree of moral intelligence. There are men walking the streets of this city to-day, under the full light of the Christian revelation, whose notions respecting God and law are exceedingly dim and inadequate; and there are others whose views are clear and correct in a high degree. But there is not a person in this city, young or old, rich or poor, ignorant or cultivated, in the purlieus of vice or the saloons of wealth, whose knowledge of God is not in advance of his own character and conduct. Every man, whatever be the grade of his intelligence, knows more than he puts in practice. Ask the young thief, in the subterranean haunts of vice and crime, if he does not know that it is wicked to steal, and if he renders an honest answer, it is in the affirmative. Ask the most besotted soul, immersed and petrified in sensuality, if his course of life upon earth has been in accordance with his own knowledge and conviction of what is right, and required by his Maker, and he will answer No, if he answers truly. The grade of knowledge in the Christian land is almost infinitely various; but in every instance the amount of knowledge is greater than the amount of virtue. Whether he knows little or much, the man knows more than he performs; and therefore his mouth must be stopped in the judgment, and he must plead guilty before God. He will not be condemned for not possessing that ethereal vision of God possessed by the seraphim; but he will be condemned because his perception of the holiness and the holy requirements of God was sufficient, at any moment, to rebuke his disregard of them; because when he knew God in some degree, he glorified him not as God up to that degree.

And this principle will be applied to the pagan world. It is so applied by the apostle Paul. He himself concedes that the Gentile has not enjoyed all the advantages of the Jew, and argues that the ungodly Jew will be visited with a more severe punishment than the ungodly Gentile. But he expressly affirms that the pagan is under law, and knows that he is; that he shows the work of the law that is written on the heart, in the operations of an accusing and condemning conscience. But the knowledge of law involves the knowledge of God in an equal degree. Who can feel himself amenable to a moral law, without at the same time thinking of its Author? The law and the Lawgiver are inseparable. The one is the mirror and index of the other. If the eye opens dimly upon the commandment, it opens dimly upon the Sovereign; if it perceives eternal right and law with clear and celestial vision, it then looks directly into the face of God. Law and God are correlative to each other; and just so far, consequently, as the heathen understands the law that is written on the heart does he apprehend the Being who sitteth upon the circle of the heavens, and who impinges Himself upon the consciousness of men. This being so, it is plain that we can confront the ungodly pagan with the same statements with which we confront the ungodly nominal Christian. We can tell him with positiveness, wherever we find him, be it upon the burning sands of Africa or in the frozen home of the Esquimaux, that he knows more than he puts in practice. We will concede to him that the quantum of his moral knowledge is very stinted and meagre; but in the same breath we will remind him that small as it is, he has not lived up to it; that he too has "come short"; that he too, knowing God in the dimmest, faintest degree, has yet not glorified him as God in the slightest, faintest manner. The Bible sends the ungodly and licentious pagan to hell, upon the same principle that it sends the ungodly and licentious nominal Christian. It is the principle enunciated by our Lord Christ, the judge of quick and dead, when he says, "He who knew his master's will [clearly], and did it not, shall be beaten with many stripes; and he who knew not his master's will [clearly, but knew it dimly,] and did it not, shall be beaten with few stripes." It is the just principle enunciated by St. Paul, that "as many as have sinned without [written] law shall also perish without [written] law."[2] And this is right and righteous; and let all the universe say, Amen.

The doctrine taught in the text, that no human creature, in any country or grade of civilization, has ever glorified God to the extent of his knowledge of God, is very fertile in solemn and startling inferences, to some of which we now invite attention.

1. In the first place, it follows from this affirmation of the apostle Paul, that the entire heathen world is in a state of condemnation and perdition. He himself draws this inference, in saying that in the judgment "every mouth must be stopped, and the whole world become guilty before God."

The present and future condition of the heathen world is a subject that has always enlisted the interest of two very different classes of men. The Church of God has pondered, and labored, and prayed over this subject, and will continue to do so until the millennium. And the disbeliever in Revelation has also turned his mind to the consideration of this black mass of ignorance and misery, which welters upon the globe like a chaotic ocean; these teeming millions of barbarians and savages who render the aspect of the world so sad and so dark. The Church, we need not say, have accepted the Biblical theory, and have traced the lost condition of the pagan world, as the apostle Paul does, to their sin and transgression. They have held that every pagan is a rational being, and by virtue of this fact has known something of the moral law; and that to the extent of the knowledge he has had, he is as guilty for the transgression of law, and as really under its condemnation, as the dweller under the light of revelation and civilization. They have maintained that every human creature has enjoyed sufficient light, in the workings of natural reason and conscience, and in the impressions that are made by the glory and the terror of the natural world above and around him, to render him guilty before the Everlasting Judge. For this reason, the Church has denied that the pagan is an innocent creature, or that he can stand in the judgment before the Searcher of hearts. For this reason, the Church has believed the declaration of the apostle John, that "the whole world lieth in wickedness" (1 John v. 19), and has endeavored to obey the command of Him who came to redeem pagans as much as nominal Christians, to go and preach the gospel to every creature, because every creature is a lost creature.

But the disbeliever in Revelation adopts the theory of human innocency, and looks upon all the wretchedness and ignorance of paganism, as he looks upon suffering, decay, and death, in the vegetable and animal worlds. Temporary evil is the necessary condition, he asserts, of all finite existence; and as decay and death in the vegetable and animal worlds only result in a more luxuriant vegetation, and an increased multiplication of living creatures, so the evil and woe of the hundreds of generations, and the millions of individuals, during the sixty centuries that have elapsed since the origin of man, will all of it minister to the ultimate and everlasting weal of the entire race. There is no need therefore, he affirms, of endeavoring to save such feeble and ignorant beings from judicial condemnation and eternal penalty. Such finiteness and helplessness cannot be put into relations to such an awful attribute as the eternal nemesis of God. Can it be,—he asks,—that the millions upon millions that have been born, lived their brief hour, enjoyed their little joys and suffered their sharp sorrows, and then dropped into "the dark backward and abysm of time," have really been guilty creatures, and have gone down to an endless hell?

But what does all this reasoning and querying imply? Will the objector really take the position and stand to it, that the pagan man is not a rational and responsible creature? that he does not possess sufficient knowledge of moral truth, to justify his being brought to the bar of judgment? Will he say that the population that knew enough to build the pyramids did not know enough to break the law of God? Will he affirm that the civilization of Babylon and Nineveh, of Greece and Rome, did not contain within it enough of moral intelligence to constitute a foundation for rewards and punishments? Will he tell us that the people of Sodom and Gomorrah stood upon the same plane with the brutes that perish, and the trees of the field that rot and die, having no idea of God, knowing nothing of the distinction between right and wrong, and never feeling the pains of an accusing conscience? Will he maintain that the populations of India, in the midst of whom one of the most subtile and ingenious systems of pantheism has sprung up with the luxuriance and involutions of one of their own jungles, and has enervated the whole religious sentiment of the Hindoo race as opium has enervated their physical frame,—will he maintain that such an untiring and persistent mental activity as this is incapable of apprehending the first principles of ethics and natural religion, which, in comparison with the complicated and obscure ratiocinations of Boodhism, are clear as water, and lucid as atmospheric air? In other connections, this theorist does not speak in this style. In other connections, and for the purpose of exaggerating natural religion and disparaging revealed, he enlarges upon the dignity of man, of every man, and eulogizes the power of reason which so exalts him in the scale of being. With Hamlet, he dilates in proud and swelling phrase: "What a piece of work is man! How noble in reason! how infinite in faculties! in form and moving, how express and admirable! in action how like an angel! in apprehension how like a god! the beauty of the world! the paragon of animals!" It is from that very class of theorizers who deny that the heathen are in danger of eternal perdition, and who represent the whole missionary enterprise as a work of supererogation, that we receive the most extravagant accounts of the natural powers and gifts of man. Now if these powers and gifts do belong to human nature by its constitution, they certainly lay a foundation for responsibility; and all such theorists must either be able to show that the pagan man has made a right use of them, and has walked according to this large amount of truth and reason with which, according to their own statement, he is endowed, or else they consign him, as St. Paul does, to "the wrath of God which is revealed from heaven against all ungodliness, and unrighteousness of men who hold the truth in unrighteousness." If you assert that the pagan man has had no talents at all committed to him, and can prove your assertion, and will stand by it, you are consistent in denying that he can be summoned to the bar of God, and be tried for eternal life or death. But if you concede that he has had one talent, or two talents, committed to his charge; and still more, if you exaggerate his gifts and endow him with five or ten talents, then it is impossible for you to save him from the judgment to come, except you can prove a perfect administration and use of the trust.[3]

2. In the second place, it follows from the doctrine of the text, that the degraded and brutalized population of large cities is in a state of condemnation and perdition.

There are heathen near our own doors whose religious condition is as sad, and hopeless, as that of the heathen of Patagonia or New Zealand. The vice and crime that nestles and riots in the large cities of Christendom has become a common theme, and has lost much of its interest for the worldly mind by losing its novelty. The manners and way of life of the outcast population of London and Paris have been depicted by the novelist, and wakened a momentary emotion in the readers of fiction. But the reality is stern and dreadful, beyond imagination or conception. There is in the cess-pools of the great capitals of Christendom a mass of human creatures who are born, who live, and who die, in moral putrefaction. Their existence is a continued career of sin and woe. Body and soul, mind and heart, are given up to earth, to sense, to corruption. They emerge for a brief season into the light of day, run their swift and fiery career of sin, and then disappear. Dante, in that wonderful Vision which embodies so much of true ethics and theology, represents the wrathful and gloomy class as sinking down under the miry waters and continuing to breathe in a convulsive, suffocating manner, sending up bubbles to the surface, that mark the place where they are drawing out their lingering existence.[4] Something like this, is the wretched life of a vicious population. As we look in upon the fermenting mass, the only signs of life that meet our view indicate that the life is feverish, spasmodic, and suffocating. The bubbles rising to the dark and turbid surface reveal that it is a life in death.

But this, too, is the result of sin. Take the atoms one by one that constitute this mass of pollution and misery, and you will find that each one of them is a self-moving and an unforced will. Not one of these millions of individuals has been necessitated by Almighty God, or by any of God's arrangements, to do wrong. Each one of them is a moral agent, equally with you and me. Each one of them is self-willed and self-determined in sin. He does not like to retain religious truth in his mind, or to obey it in his heart. Go into the lowest haunt of vice and select out the most imbruted person there; bring to his remembrance that class of truths with which he is already acquainted by virtue of his rational nature, and add to them that other class of truths taught in Revelation, and you will find that he is predetermined against them. He takes sides, with all the depth and intensity of his being, with that sinfulness which is common to man, and which it is the aim of both ethics and the gospel to remove. This vicious and imbruted man loves the sin which is forbidden, more than he loves the holiness that is commanded. He inclines to the sin which so easily besets him, precisely as you and I incline to the bosom-sin which so easily besets us. We grant that the temptations that assail him are very powerful; but are not some of the temptations that beset you and me very powerful? We grant that this wretched slave of vice and pollution cannot break off his sins by righteousness, without the renewing and assisting grace of God; but neither can you or I. It is the action of his own will that has made him a slave. He loves his chains and his bondage, even as you and I naturally love ours; and this proves that his moral corruption, though assuming an outwardly more repulsive form than ours, is yet the same thing in principle. It is the rooted aversion of the human heart, the utter disinclination of the human will, towards the purity and holiness of God; it is "the carnal mind which is enmity against God; for it is not subject to the law of God, neither indeed can be" (Rom. viii. 7).

But there is no more convincing proof of the position, that the degraded creature of whom we are speaking is a self-deciding and unforced sinner, than the fact that he resists efforts to reclaim him. Ask these faithful and benevolent missionaries who go down into these dens of vice and pollution, to pour more light into the mind, and to induce these outcasts to leave their drunkenness and their debauchery,—ask them if they find that human nature is any different there from what it is elsewhere, so far as yielding to the claims of God and law is concerned. Do they tell you that they are uniformly successful in inducing these sinners to leave their sins? that they never find any self-will, any determined opposition to the holy law of purity, any preference of a life of licence with its woes here upon earth and hereafter in hell, to a life of self-denial with its joys eternal? On the contrary, they testify that the old maxim upon which so many millions of the human family have acted: "Enjoy the present and jump the life to come," is the rule for this mass of population, of whom so very few can be persuaded to leave their cups and their orgies. Like the people of Israel, when expostulated with by the prophet Jeremiah for their idolatry and pollution, the majority of the degraded population of whom we are speaking, when endeavors have been made to reclaim them, have said to the philanthropist and the missionary: "There is no hope: no; for I have loved strangers, and after them I will go" (Jer. ii. 25). There is not a single individual of them all who does not love the sin that is destroying him, more than he loves the holiness that would save him. Notwithstanding all the horrible accompaniments of sin—the filth, the disease, the poverty, the sickness, the pain of both body and mind,—the wretched creature prefers to enjoy the pleasures of sin for a season, rather than come out and separate himself from the unclean thing, and begin that holy warfare and obedience to which his God and his Saviour invite him. This, we repeat, proves that the sin is not forced upon this creature. For if he hated his sin, nay if he felt weary and heavy laden in the least degree because of it, he might leave it. There is a free grace, and a proffered assistance of the Holy Ghost, of which he might avail himself at any moment. Had he the feeling of the weary and penitent prodigal, the same father's house is ever open for his return; and the same father seeing him on his return, though still a great way off, would run and fall upon his neck and kiss him. But the heart is hard, and the spirit is utterly selfish, and the will is perverse and determined, and therefore the natural knowledge of God and his law which this sinner possesses by his very constitution, and the added knowledge which his birth in a Christian land and the efforts of benevolent Christians have imparted to him, are not strong enough to overcome his inclination, and his preference, and induce him to break off his sins by righteousness. To him, also, as well as to every sin-loving man, these solemn words will be spoken in the day of final adjudication: "The wrath of God is revealed from heaven against all ungodliness, and unrighteousness, of men who hold down ([Greek: katechein]) the truth in unrighteousness; because that which may be known of God is manifest within them; for God hath shewed it unto them. For the invisible things of him, even his eternal power and Godhead, are clearly seen from the creation of the world, being understood by the things that are made; so that they are without excuse, because that when they knew God. they glorified him not as God."

3. In the third and last place, it follows from this doctrine of the apostle Paul, as thus unfolded, that that portion of the enlightened and cultivated population of Christian lands who have not believed on the Lord Jesus Christ, and repented of sin, are in the deepest state of condemnation and perdition.

"Behold thou art called a Jew, and restest in the law, and makest thy boast of God, and knowest his will, and approvest the things that are more excellent, being instructed out of the law, and art confident that thou thyself art a guide of the blind, a light of them which are in darkness: an instructor of the foolish, a teacher of babes: which hast the form of knowledge, and of the truth, in the law: thou therefore that teachest another teachest thou not thyself? thou that makest thy boast of the law, through breaking the law dishonored thou God?"

If it be true that the pagan knows more of God and the moral law than he has ever put in practice; if it be true that the imbruted child of vice and pollution knows more of God and the moral law than he has ever put in practice; how much more fearfully true is it that the dweller in a Christian home, the visitant of the house of God, the possessor of the written Word, the listener to prayer and oftentimes the subject of it, possesses an amount of knowledge respecting his origin, his duty, and his destiny, that infinitely outruns his character and his conduct. If eternal punishment will come down upon those classes of mankind who know but comparatively little, because they have been unfaithful in that which is least, surely eternal punishment will come down upon that more favored class who know comparatively much, because they have been unfaithful in that which is much. "If these things are done in the green tree, what shall be done in the dry?"

The great charge that will rest against the creature when he stands before the final bar will be, that "when he knew God, he glorified Him not as God." And this will rest heaviest against those whose knowledge was the clearest. It is a great prerogative to be able to know the infinite and glorious Creator; but it brings with it a most solemn responsibility. That blessed Being, of right, challenges the homage and obedience of His creature. What he asks of the angel, that he asks of man; that he should glorify God in his body and spirit which are His, and should thereby enjoy God forever and forever. This is the condemnation, under which man, and especially enlightened and cultivated man, rests, that while he knows God he neither glorifies Him nor enjoys Him. Our Redeemer saw this with all the clearness of the Divine Mind; and to deliver the creature from the dreadful guilt, of his self-idolatry, of his disposition to worship and love the creature more than the Creator, He became incarnate, suffered and died. It cannot be a small crime, that necessitated, such an apparatus of atonement and Divine influences as that of Christ and His redemption. Estimate the guilt of coming short of the glory of God, which is the same as the guilt of idolatry and creature-worship, by the nature of the provision that has been made to cancel it. If you do not actually feel that this crime is great, then argue yourself towards a juster view, by the consideration that it cost the blood of Christ to expiate it. If you do not actually feel that the guilt is great, then argue yourself towards a juster view, by the reflection that you have known God to be supremely great, supremely good, and supremely excellent, and yet you have never, in a single feeling of your heart, or a single thought of your mind, or a single purpose of your will, honored Him. It is honor, reverence, worship, and love that He requires. These you have never rendered; and there is an infinity of guilt in the fact. That guilt will be forgiven for Christ's sake, if you ask for forgiveness. But if you do not ask, then it will stand recorded against you for eternal ages: "When he, a rational and immortal creature, knew God, he glorified Him not as God."

[**Note 1:** *The early Fathers, in their defence of the Christian doctrine of one God, against the objections of the pagan advocate of the popular mythologies, contend that the better pagan writers themselves agree with the new religion, in teaching that there is one Supreme Being. LACTANTIUS (Institutiones i. 5), after quoting the Orphic poets, Hesiod, Virgil, and Ovid, in proof that the heathen poets taught the unity of the Supreme Deity, proceeds to show that the better pagan philosophers, also, agree with them in this. "Aristotle," he says, "although he disagrees with himself, and says many things that are self-contradictory, yet testifies that one Supreme Mind rules over the world. Plato, who is regarded as the wisest philosopher of them all, plainly and openly defends the doctrine of a divine monarchy, and denominates the Supreme Being; not ether, nor reason, nor nature, but, as he is, God; and asserts that by him this perfect and admirable world was made. And Cicero follows Plato, frequently confessing the Deity, and calls him the Supreme Being, in his treatise on the Laws." TERTULLIAN (De Test. An. c. 1; Adv. Marc. i. 10; Ad. Scap. c. 2; Apol. c. 17), than whom no one of the Christian Fathers was more vehemently opposed to the philosophizing of the schools, earnestly contends that the doctrine of the unity of God is constitutional to the human mind. "God," he says, "proves himself to be God, and the one only God, by the very fact that He is known to all nations; for the existence of any other deity than He would first have to be demonstrated. The God of the Jews is the one whom the souls of men call their God. We worship one God, the one whom ye all naturally know, at whose lightnings and thunders ye tremble, at whose benefits ye rejoice. Will ye that we prove the Divine existence by the witness of the soul itself, which, although confined by the prison of the body, although circumscribed by bad training, although enervated by lusts and passions, although made the servant of false gods, yet when it recovers itself as from a surfeit, as from a slumber, as from some infirmity, and is in its proper condition of soundness, calls God by this name only, because it is the proper name of the true God. 'Great God,' 'good God,' and 'God grant' [deus, not dii], are words in every mouth. The soul also witnesses that He is its judge, when it says, 'God sees,' 'I commend to God,' 'God shall recompense me.' O testimony of a soul naturally Christian [i.e., monotheistic]! Finally, in pronouncing these words, it looks not to the Roman capitol, but to heaven; for it knows the dwelling-place of the true God: from Him and from thence it descended." CALVIN (Inst. i. 10) seems to have had these statements in his eye, in the following remarks: "In almost all ages, religion has been generally corrupted. It is true, indeed, that the name of one Supreme God has been universally known and celebrated. For those who used to worship a multitude of deities, whenever they spake according to the genuine sense of nature, used simply the name of God in the singular number, as though they were contented with one God. And this was wisely remarked by Justin Martyr, who for this purpose wrote a book 'On the Monarchy of God,' in which he demonstrates, from numerous testimonies, that the unity of God is a principle universally impressed on the hearts of men. Tertullian (De Idololatria) also proves the same point, from the common phraseology. But since all men, without exception, have become vain in their understandings, all their natural perception of the Divine Unity has only served to render them inexcusable." In consonance with these views, the Presbyterian CONFESSION OF FAITH (ch. i.) affirms that "the light of nature, and the works of creation and providence, do so far manifest the goodness, wisdom, and power of God, as to leave men inexcusable."]*

[**Note 2:** *The word [Greek: apolountai], in Rom. ii. 12, is opposed to the [Greek: sotaeria] spoken of in Rom. i. 16, and therefore signifies eternal perdition, as that signifies eternal salvation.-Those theorists who reject revealed religion, and remand man back to the first principles of ethics and morality as the only religion that he needs, send him to a tribunal that damns him. "Tell me," says St. Paul, "ye that desire to be under the law, do ye not hear the law? The law is not of faith, but the man that doeth them shall live by them. Circumcision* *verily profiteth if thou keep the law; but if thou be a breaker of the law, thy circumcision is made uncircumcision." If man had been true to all the principles and precepts of natural religion, it would indeed be religion enough for him. But he has not been thus true. The entire list of vices and sins recited by St. Paul, in the first chapter of Romans, is as contrary to natural religion, as it is to revealed. And it is precisely because the pagan world has not obeyed the principles of natural religion, and is under a curse and a bondage therefor, that it is in perishing need of the truths of revealed religion. Little do those know what they are saying, when they propose to find a salvation for the pagan in the mere light of natural reason and conscience. What pagan has ever realized the truths of natural conscience, in his inward character and his outward life? What pagan is there in all the generations that will not be found guilty before the bar of natural religion? What heathen will not need an atonement, for his failure to live up even to the light of nature? Nay, what is the entire sacrificial cultus of heathenism, but a confession that the whole heathen world finds and feels itself to be guilty at the bar of natural reason and conscience? The accusing voice within them wakes their forebodings and fearful looking-for of Divine judgment, and they endeavor to propitiate the offended Power by their offerings and sacrifices.]*

*[**Note 3:** Infidelity is constantly changing its ground. In the 18th century, the skeptic very generally took the position of Lord Herbert of Cherbury, and maintained that the light of reason is very clear, and is adequate to all the religious needs of the soul. In the 19th century, he is now passing to the other extreme, and contending that man is kindred to the ape, and within the sphere of paganism does not possess sufficient moral intelligence to constitute him responsible. Like Luther's drunken beggar on horseback, the opponent of Revelation sways from the position that man is a god, to the position that he is a chimpanzee.]*

*[**Note 4:** DANTE: Inferno, vii. 100-130.]*

VI - Sin in The Heart the Source of Error in The Head

ROMANS i. 28.—*"As they did not like to retain God in their knowledge, God gave them over to a reprobate mind."*

In the opening of the most logical and systematic treatise in the New Testament, the Epistle to the Romans, the apostle Paul enters upon a line of argument to demonstrate the ill-desert of every human creature without exception. In order to this, he shows that no excuse can be urged upon the ground of moral ignorance. He explicitly teaches that the pagan knows that there is one Supreme God (Rom. i. 20); that He is a spirit (Rom. i. 23); that He is holy and sin-hating (Rom. i. 18); that He is worthy to be worshipped (Rom. i. 21, 25); and that men ought to be thankful for His benefits (Rom. i. 21). He affirms that the heathen knows that an idol is a lie (Rom. i. 25); that licentiousness is a sin (Rom. i. 26, 32); that envy, malice, and deceit are wicked (Rom. i. 29, 32); and that those who practise such sins deserve eternal punishment (Rom. i. 32).

In these teachings and assertions, the apostle has attributed no small amount and degree of moral knowledge to man as man,—to man outside of Revelation, as well as under its shining light. The question very naturally arises: How comes it to pass that this knowledge which Divine inspiration postulates, and affirms to be innate and constitutional to the human mind, should become so vitiated? The majority of mankind are idolaters and polytheists, and have been for thousands of years. Can it be that the truth that there is only one God is native to the human spirit, and that the pagan "knows" this God? The majority of men are earthly and sensual, and have been for thousands of years. Can it be that there is a moral law written upon their hearts forbidding such carnality, and enjoining purity and holiness?

Some theorizers argue that because the pagan man has not obeyed the law, therefore he does not know the law; and that because he has not revered and worshipped the one Supreme Deity, therefore he does not possess the idea of any such Being. They look out upon the heathen populations and see them bowing down to stocks and stones, and witness their immersion in the abominations of heathenism, and conclude that these millions of human beings really know no better, and that therefore it is unjust to hold them responsible for their polytheism and their moral corruption. But why do they confine this species of reasoning to the pagan world? Why do they not bring it into nominal Christendom, and apply it there? Why does not this theorist go into the midst of European civilization, into the heart of London or Paris, and gauge the moral knowledge of the sensualist by the moral character of the sensualist? Why does he not tell us that because this civilized man acts no better, therefore he knows no better? Why does he not maintain that because this voluptuary breaks all the commandments in the decalogue, therefore he must be ignorant of all the commandments in the decalogue? that because he neither fears nor loves the one only God, therefore he does not know that there is any such Being?

It will never do to estimate man's moral knowledge by man's moral character. He knows more than he practises. And there is not so much difference in this particular between some men in nominal Christendom, and some men in Heathendom, as is sometimes imagined. The moral knowledge of those who lie in the lower strata of Christian civilization, and those who lie in the higher strata of Paganism, is probably not so very far apart. Place the imbruted outcasts of our metropolitan population beside the Indian hunter, with his belief in the Great Spirit, and his worship without images or pictorial representations;[1] beside the stalwart Mandingo of the high table-lands of Central Africa, with his active and enterprising spirit, carrying on manufactures and trade with all the keenness of any civilized worldling; beside the native merchants and lawyers of Calcutta, who still cling to their ancestral Boodhism, or else substitute French infidelity in its place; place the lowest of the highest beside the highest of the lowest, and tell us if the difference is so very marked. Sin, like holiness, is a mighty leveler. The "dislike to retain God" in the consciousness, the aversion of the heart towards the purity of the moral law, vitiates the native perceptions alike in Christendom and Paganism.

The theory that the pagan is possessed of such an amount and degree of moral knowledge as has been specified has awakened some apprehension in the minds of some Christian theologians, and has led them, unintentionally to foster the opposite theory, which, if strictly adhered to, would lift off all responsibility from the pagan world, would bring them in innocent at the bar of God, and would render the whole enterprise of Christian missions a superfluity and an absurdity. Their motive has been good. They have feared to attribute any degree of accurate knowledge of God and the moral law, to the pagan world, lest they should thereby conflict with the doctrine of total depravity. They have mistakenly supposed,

50

that if they should concede to every man, by virtue of his moral constitution, some correct apprehensions of ethics and natural religion, it would follow that there is some native goodness in him. But light in the intellect is very different from life in the heart. It is one thing to know the law of God, and quite another thing to be conformed to it. Even if we should concede to the degraded pagan, or the degraded dweller in the haunts of vice in Christian lands, all the intellectual knowledge of God and the moral law that is possessed by the ruined archangel himself, we should not be adding a particle to his moral character or his moral excellence. There is nothing of a holy quality in the mere intellectual perception that there is one Supreme Deity, and that He has issued a pure and holy law for the guidance of all rational beings. The mere doctrine of the Divine Unity will save no man. "Thou believest," says St. James, "that there is one God; thou doest well, the devils also believe and tremble." Satan himself is a monotheist, and knows very clearly all the commandments of God; but his heart and will are in demoniacal antagonism with them. And so it is, only in a lower degree, in the instance of the pagan, and of the natural man, in every age, and in every clime. He knows more than he practises. This intellectual perception therefore, this inborn constitutional apprehension, instead of lifting up man into a higher and more favorable position before the eternal bar, casts him down to perdition. If he knew nothing at all of his Maker and his duty, he could not be held responsible, and could, not be summoned to judgment. As St. Paul affirms: "Where there is no law there is no transgression." But if, when he knew God in some degree, he glorified him not as God to that degree; and if, when the moral law was written upon the heart he went counter to its requirements, and heard the accusing voice of his own conscience; then his mouth must be stopped, and he must become guilty before his Judge, like any and every other disobedient creature.

It is this serious and damning fact in the history of man upon the globe, that St. Paul brings to view, in the passage which we have selected as the foundation of this discourse. He accounts for all the idolatry and sensuality, all the darkness and vain imaginations of paganism, by referring to the aversion of the natural heart towards the one only holy God. "Men," he says,—these pagan men—"did not like to retain God in their knowledge." The primary difficulty was in their affections, and not in their understandings. They knew too much for their own comfort in sin. The contrast between the Divine purity that was mirrored in their conscience, and the sinfulness that was wrought into their heart and will, rendered this inborn constitutional idea of God a very painful one. It was a fire in the bones. If the Psalmist, a renewed man, yet not entirely free from human corruption, could say: "I thought of God and was troubled," much more must the totally depraved man of paganism be filled with terror when, in the thoughts of his heart, in the hour when the accusing conscience was at work, he brought to mind the one great God of gods whom he did not glorify, and whom he had offended. It was no wonder, therefore, that he did not like to retain the idea of such a Being in his consciousness, and that he adopted all possible expedients to get rid of it. The apostle informs us that the pagan actually called in his imagination to his aid, in order to extirpate, if possible, all his native and rational ideas and convictions upon religious subjects. He became vain in his imaginations, and his foolish heart as a consequence was darkened, and he changed the glory of the incorruptible God, the spiritual unity of the Deity, into an image made like to corruptible man, and to birds, and four-footed beasts, and creeping things (Rom. i. 21-23). He invented idolatry, and all those "gay religions full of pomp and gold," in order to blunt the edge of that sharp spiritual conception of God which was continually cutting and lacerating his wicked and sensual heart. Hiding himself amidst the columns of his idolatrous temples, and under the smoke of his idolatrous incense, he thought like Adam to escape from the view and inspection of that Infinite One who, from the creation of the world downward, makes known to all men his eternal power and godhead; who, as St. Paul taught the philosophers of Athens, is not far from anyone of his rational creatures (Acts xvii. 27); and who, as the same apostle taught the pagan Lycaonians, though in times past he suffered all nations to walk in their own ways, yet left not himself without witness, in that he did good, and gave them rain from heaven, and fruitful seasons, filling their hearts with food and gladness. (Acts xiv. 16, 17).

The first step in the process of mutilating the original idea of God, as a unity and an unseen Spirit, is seen in those pantheistic religions which lie behind all the mythologies of the ancient world, like a nebulous vapor out of which the more distinct idols and images of paganism are struggling. Here the notion of the Divine unity is still preserved; but the Divine personality and holiness are lost. God becomes a vague impersonal Power, with no moral qualities, and no religious attributes; and it is difficult to say which is worst in its moral influence, this pantheism which while retaining the doctrine of the Divine unity yet denudes the Deity of all that renders him an object of either love or reverence, or the grosser idolatries that succeeded it. For man cannot love, with all his mind and heart and soul and strength, a vast impersonal force working blindly through infinite space and everlasting time.

And the second and last stage in this process of vitiating the true idea of God appears in that polytheism in the midst of which St. Paul lived, and labored, and preached, and died; in that seductive and beautiful paganism, that classical idolatry, which still addresses the human taste in such a fascinating manner, in the Venus de Medici, and the Apollo Belvidere. The idea of the unity of God is now mangled and cut up into the "gods many" and the "lords many," into the thirty thousand divinities of the pagan pantheon. This completes the process. God now gives his guilty creature over to these vain imaginations of naturalism, materialism, and idolatry, and to an increasingly darkening mind, until in the lowest forms of heathenism he so distorts and suppresses the concreated idea of the Deity that some speculatists assert that it does not belong to his constitution, and that his Maker never endowed him with it. How is the gold become dim! How is the most fine gold changed!

But it will be objected that all this lies in the past. This is the account of a process that has required centuries, yea millenniums, to bring about. A hundred generations have been engaged in transmuting the monotheism with which the human race started, into the pantheism and polytheism in which the great majority of it is now involved. How do you establish the guilt of those at the end of the line? How can you charge upon the present generation of pagans the same culpability that Paul imputed to their ancestors eighteen centuries ago, and that Noah the preacher of righteousness denounced, upon the antediluvian pagan? As the deteriorating process advances, does not the guilt diminish? and now, in these ends of the ages, and in these dark habitations of cruelty, has not the culpability run down to a minimum, which God in the day of judgment will "wink at?"

We answer No: Because the structure of the human mind is precisely the same that it was when the Sodomites held down the truth in unrighteousness, and the Roman populace turned up their thumbs that they might see the last drops of blood ebb slowly from the red gash in the dying gladiator's side. Man, in his deepest degradation, in his most hardened depravity, is still a rational intelligence; and though he should continue to sin on indefinitely, through cycles of time as long as those of geology, he cannot unmake himself; he cannot unmould his immortal essence, and absolutely eradicate all his moral ideas. Paganism itself has its fluctuations of moral knowledge. The early Roman, in the days of Numa, was highly ethical in his views of the Deity, and his conceptions of moral law. Varro informs us that for a period of one hundred and seventy years the Romans worshipped their gods without any images;[2] and Sallust denominates these pristine Romans "*religiosissimi mortales.*" And how often does the missionary discover a tribe or a race, whose moral intelligence is higher than that of the average of paganism. Nay, the same race, or tribe, passes from one phase of polytheism to another; in one instance exhibiting many of the elements and truths of natural religion, and in another almost entirely suppressing them. These facts prove that the pagan man is under supervision; that he is under the righteous despotism of moral ideas and convictions; that God is not far from him; that he lives and moves and has his being in his Maker; and that God does not leave himself without witness in his constitutional structure. Therefore it is, that this sea of rational intelligence thus surges and sways in the masses of paganism; sometimes dashing the creature up the heights, and sometimes sending him down into the depths.

But while this subject has this general application to mankind outside of Revelation; while it throws so much light upon the question of the heathens' responsibility and guilt; while it tends to deepen our interest in the work of Christian missions, and to stimulate us to obey our Redeemer's command to go and preach the gospel to them, in order to save them from the wrath of God which abideth upon them as it does upon ourselves; while this subject has these profound and far-reaching applications, it also presses with sharpness and energy upon the case, and the position, of millions of men in Christendom. And to this more particular aspect of the theme, we ask attention for a moment.

This same process of corruption, and vitiation of a correct knowledge of God, which we have seen to go on upon a large scale in the instance of the heathen world, also often goes on in the instance of a single individual under the light of Revelation itself. Have you never known a person to have been well educated in childhood and youth respecting the character and government of God, and yet in middle life and old age to have altered and corrupted all his early and accurate apprehensions, by the gradual adoption of contrary views and sentiments? In his childhood, and youth, he believed that God distinguishes between the righteous and the wicked, that he rewards the one and punishes the other, and hence he cherished a salutary fear of his Maker that agreed well with the dictates of his unsophisticated reason, and the teachings of nature and revelation. But when, he became a man, he put away these childish things, in a far different sense from that of the Apostle. As the years rolled, along, he succeeded, by a career of worldliness and of sensuality, in expelling this stock of religious knowledge, this right way of conceiving of God, from his mind, and now at the close of life and upon the very brink of eternity and of doom, this very same person is as unbelieving respecting the moral attributes of Jehovah, and as unfearing with regard to them, as if the entire experience and creed of his childhood and youth were a delusion and a lie. This rational and immortal creature in the morning of his existence looked up into the clear sky with reverence, being impressed by the eternal power and godhead that are there, and when he had committed a sin he felt remorseful and guilty; but the very same person now sins recklessly and with flinty hardness of heart, casts sullen or scowling glances upward, and says: "There is no God." Compare the Edward Gibbon whose childhood expanded under the teachings of a beloved Christian matron trained in the school of the devout William Law, and whose youth exhibited unwonted religions sensibility,—compare this Edward Gibbon with the Edward Gibbon whose manhood was saturated with utter unbelief, and whose departure into the dread hereafter was, in his own phrase, "a leap in the dark." Compare the Aaron Burr whose blood was deduced from one of the most saintly lineages in the history of the American church, and all of whose early life was embosomed in ancestral piety,—compare this Aaron Burr with the Aaron Burr whose middle life and prolonged old age was unimpressible as marble to all religious ideas and influences. In both of these instances, it was the aversion of the heart that for a season (not for eternity, be it remembered) quenched out the light in the head. These men, like the pagan of whom St. Paul speaks, did not like to retain a holy God in their knowledge, and He gave them over to a reprobate mind.

These fluctuations and changes in doctrinal belief, both in the general and the individual mind, furnish materials for deep reflection by both the philosopher and the Christian; and such an one will often be led to notice the exact parallel and similarity there is between religious deterioration in races, and religious deterioration in individuals. The dislike to retain a knowledge already furnished, because it is painful, because it rebukes worldliness and sin, is that which ruins both mankind in general, and the man in particular. Were the heart only conformed to the truth, the truth never would be corrupted, never would be even temporarily darkened in the human soul. Should the pagan, himself, actually obey the dictates of his own reason and conscience, he would find the light that was in him growing still clearer and brighter. God himself, the author of his rational mind, and the Light that lighteth every man that cometh into the world, would reward him for his obedience by granting him yet more knowledge. We cannot say in what particular mode the Divine providence would bring it about, but it is as certain as that God lives, that if the pagan world should act up to the degree of light which they enjoy, they would be conducted ultimately to the truth as it is in Jesus, and would be saved by the Redeemer of the world. The instance of the Roman centurion Cornelius is a case in point. This was a thoughtful and serious pagan. It is indeed very probable that his military residence in Palestine had cleared up, to some degree, his natural intuitions of moral truth; but we know that he was ignorant of the way of salvation through Christ, from the fact that the apostle Peter was instructed in a vision to go and preach it unto him. The sincere endeavor of this Gentile, this then pagan in reference to Christianity, to improve the little knowledge which he had, met with the Divine approbation, and was crowned with a saving acquaintance with the redemption that is in Christ Jesus. Peter himself testified to this, when, after hearing from the lips of Cornelius the account of his previous life, and of the way in which God had led him, "he opened his mouth and said, Of a truth I perceive that God is no respecter of persons: but in every nation, he that feareth him and worketh righteousness is accepted with him" (Acts x. 34, 35).[3]

But such instances as this of Cornelius are not one in millions upon millions. The light shines in the darkness that comprehends it not. Almost without an exception, so far as the human eye can see, the unevangelized world holds the truth in unrighteousness, and does not like to retain the idea of a holy God, and a holy law, in its knowledge. Therefore the knowledge continually diminishes; the light of natural reason and conscience grows dimmer and dimmer; and the soul sinks down in the mire of sin and sensuality, apparently devoid of all the higher ideas of God, and law, and immortal life.

We have thus considered the truth which St. Paul teaches in the text, that the ultimate source of all human error is in the character of the human heart. Mankind do not like to retain God in their knowledge, and therefore they come to possess a reprobate mind. The origin of idolatry, and of infidelity, is not in the original constitution with which the Creator endowed the creature, but in that evil heart of unbelief by which he departed from the living God. Sinful man shapes his creed in accordance with his wishes, and not in accordance with the unbiased decisions of his reason and conscience. He does not like to think of a holy God, and therefore he denies that God is holy. He does not like to think of the eternal punishment of sin, and therefore he denies that punishment is eternal. He does not like to be pardoned through the substituted sufferings of the Son of God, and therefore he denies the doctrine of atonement. He does not like the truth that man is so totally alienated from God that he needs to be renewed in the spirit of his mind by the Holy Ghost, and therefore he denies the doctrines of depravity and regeneration. Run through the creed which the Church has lived by and died by, and you will discover that the only obstacle to its reception is the aversion of the human heart. It is a rational creed in all its parts and combinations. It has outlived the collisions and conflicts of a hundred schools of infidelity that have had their brief day, and died with their devotees. A hundred systems of philosophy falsely so called have come and gone, but the one old religion of the patriarchs, and the prophets, and the apostles, holds on its way through the centuries, conquering and to conquer. Can it be that sheer imposture and error have such a tenacious vitality as this? If reason is upon the side of infidelity, why does not infidelity remain one and the same unchanging thing, like Christianity, from age to age, and subdue all men unto it? If Christianity is a delusion and a lie, why does it not die out, and disappear? The difficulty is not upon the side of the human reason, but of the human heart. Skeptical men do not like the religion of the New Testament, these doctrines of sin and grace, and therefore they shape their creed by their sympathies and antipathies; by what they wish to have true; by their heart rather than by their head. As the Founder of Christianity said to the Jews, so he says to every man who rejects His doctrine of grace and redemption: "Ye will not come unto me that ye might have life." It is an inclination of the will, and not a conviction of the reason, that prevents the reception of the Christian religion.

Among the many reflections that are suggested by this subject and its discussion, our limits permit only the following:

1. It betokens deep wickedness, in any man, to change the truth of God into a lie,—to substitute a false theory in religion for the true one. "Woe unto them," says the prophet, "that call evil good, and good evil; that put darkness for light, and light for darkness; that put bitter for sweet, and sweet for bitter." There is no form of moral evil that is more hateful in the sight of Infinite Truth, than that intellectual depravity which does not like to retain a holy God in its knowledge, and therefore mutilates the very idea of the Deity, and attempts to make him other than he is. There is no sinner that will be visited with a heavier vengeance than that cool and calculating man, who, because he dislikes the unyielding purity of the moral law, and the awful sanctions by which it is accompanied, deliberately alters it to suit his wishes and his self-indulgence. If a person is tempted and falls into sin, and yet does not change his religious creed in order to escape the reproaches of conscience and the fear of retribution, there is hope that the orthodoxy of his head may result, by God's blessing upon his own truth, in sorrow for the sin and a forsaking thereof. A man, for instance, who amidst all his temptations and transgressions still retains the truth taught him from the Scriptures, at his mother's knees, that a finally impenitent sinner will go down to eternal torment, feels a powerful check upon his passions, and is often kept from outward and actual transgressions by his creed. But if he deliberately, and by an act of will, says in his heart: "There is no hell;" if he substitutes for the theory that renders the commission of sin dangerous and fearful, a theory that relieves it from all danger and all fear, there is no hope that he will ever cease from sinning. On the contrary, having brought his head into harmony with his heart; having adjusted his theory to his practice; having shaped his creed by his passions; having changed the truth of God into a lie; he then plunges into sin with an abandonment and a momentum that is awful. In the phrase of the prophet, he "draws iniquity with cords of vanity, and sin as it were with a cart-rope."

It is here that we see the deep guilt of those, who, by false theories of God and man and law and penalty, tempt the young or the old to their eternal destruction. It is sad and fearful, when the weak physical nature is plied with all the enticements of earth and sense; but it is yet sadder and more fearful, when the intellectual nature is sought to be perverted and ensnared by specious theories that annihilate the distinction between virtue and vice, that take away all holy fear of God, and reverence for His law, that represent the everlasting future either as an everlasting elysium for all, or else as an eternal sleep. The demoralization, in this instance, is central and radical. It is in the brain, in the very understanding itself. If the foundations themselves of morals and religion are destroyed, what can be done for the salvation of the creature? A heavy woe is denounced against any and every one who tempts a fellow-being. Temptation implies malice. It is Satanic. It betokens a desire to ruin an immortal spirit. When therefore the siren

56

would allure a human creature from the path of virtue, the inspiration of God utters a deep and bitter curse against her. But when the cold-blooded Mephistopheles endeavors to sophisticate the reason, to debauch the judgment, to sear the conscience; when the temptation is addressed to the intellect, and the desire of the tempter is to overthrow the entire religious creed of a human being,—perhaps a youth just entering upon that hazardous enterprise of life in which he needs every jot and tittle of eternal truth to guide and protect him,—when the enticement assumes this purely mental form and aspect, it betokens the most malignant and heaven-daring guilt in the tempter. And we may be certain that the retribution that will be meted out to it, by Him who is true and The Truth; who abhors all falsehood and all lies with an infinite intensity; will be terrible beyond conception. "Woe unto you ye blind guides! Ye serpents, ye generation of vipers, how can ye escape the damnation of hell! If any man shall add unto these things, God shall add unto him the plagues that are written in this book. And if any man shall take away from the words of the book of this prophecy, God shall take away his part out of the book of life, and out of the holy city, and from the things that are written in this book."

2. In the second place, we perceive, in the light of this subject, the great danger of not reducing religious truth to practice. There are two fatal hazards in not obeying the doctrines of the Bible while yet there is an intellectual assent to them. The first is, that these doctrines shall themselves become diluted and corrupted. So long as the affectionate submission of the heart is not yielded to their authority; so long as there is any dislike towards their holy claims; there is great danger that, as in the instance of the pagan, they will not be retained in the knowledge. The sinful man becomes weary of a form of doctrine that continually rebukes him, and gradually changes it into one that is less truthful and restraining. But a second and equally alarming danger is, that the heart shall become accustomed to the truth, and grow hard and indifferent towards it. There are a multitude of persons who hear the word of God and never dream of disputing it, who yet, alas, never dream of obeying it. To such the living truth of the gospel becomes a petrifaction, and a savor of death unto death.

We urge you, therefore, ye who know the doctrines of the law and the doctrines of the gospel, to give an affectionate and hearty assent to them both. When the divine Word asserts that you are guilty, and that you cannot stand in the judgment before God, make answer: "It is so, it is so." Practically and deeply acknowledge the doctrine of human guilt and corruption. Let it no longer be a theory in the head, but a humbling salutary consciousness in the heart. And when the divine Word affirms that God so loved the world that he gave his Only-Begotten Son to redeem it, make a quick and joyful response: "It is so, it is so." Instead of changing the truth of God into a lie, as the guilty world have been doing for six thousand years, change it into a blessed consciousness of the soul. Believe_ what you know; and then what you know will be the wisdom of God to your salvation.

[**Note 1:** "There are no profane words in the (Iowa) Indian language: no light or profane way of speaking of the 'Great Spirit.'"—FOREIGN MISSIONARY: May, 1863, p. 337.]
[**Note 2:** PLUTARCH: Numa, 8; AUGUSTINE: De Civitate, iv. 31.]

[*Note 3:* It should be noticed that Cornelius was not prepared for another life, by the moral virtue which he had practised before meeting with Peter, but by his penitence for sin and faith in Jesus Christ, whom Peter preached to him as the Saviour from sin (Acts x. 43). Good works can no more prepare a pagan for eternity than they can a nominal Christian. Epictetus and Marcus Aurelius could no more be justified by their personal character, than Saul of Tarsus could be. First, because the virtue is imperfect, at the best: and, secondly, it does not begin at the beginning of existence upon earth, and continue unintermittently to the end of it. A sense of sin is a far more hopeful indication, in the instance of a heathen, than a sense of virtue. The utter absence of humility and sorrow in the "Meditations" of the philosophic Emperor, and the omnipresence in them of pride and self-satisfaction, place him out of all relations to the Divine mercy. In trying to judge of the final condition of a pagan outside of revelation, we must ask the question: Was he penitent? rather than the question: Was he virtuous?]

VII - The Necessity of Divine Influences

LUKE xi. 13.—*"If ye then, being evil, know how to give good gifts unto your children; how much more shall your heavenly Father give the Holy Spirit to them that ask him?"*

The reality, and necessity, of the operation of the Holy Spirit upon the human heart, is a doctrine very frequently taught in the Scriptures. Our Lord, in the passage from which the text is taken, speaks of the third Person in the Trinity in such a manner as to convey the impression that His agency is as indispensable, in order to spiritual life, as food is in order to physical; that sinful man as much needs the influences of the Holy Ghost as he does his daily bread. "If a son shall ask bread of any of you that is a father, will he give him a stone?" If this is not at all supposable, in the case of an affectionate earthly parent, much less is it supposable that God the heavenly Father will refuse renewing and sanctifying influences to them that ask for them. By employing such a significant comparison as this, our Lord implies that there is as pressing need of the gift in the one instance as in the other. For, he does not compare spiritual influences with the mere luxuries of life,—with wealth, fame, or power,—but with the very staff of life itself. He selects the very bread by which the human body lives, to illustrate the helpless sinner's need of the Holy Ghost. When God, by his prophet, would teach His people that he would at some future time bestow a rich and remarkable blessing upon them, He says: "I will pour out my Spirit upon all flesh." When our Saviour was about to leave his disciples, and was sending them forth as the ministers of his religion, he promised them a direct and supernatural agency that should "reprove the world of sin, of righteousness, and of judgment."

And the history of Christianity evinces both the necessity and reality of Divine influences. God the Spirit has actually been present by a special and peculiar agency, in this sinful and hardened world, and hence the heart of flesh and the spread of vital religion. God the Spirit has actually been absent, so far as concerns his special and peculiar agency, and hence the continuance of the heart of stone, and the decline, and sometimes the extinction of vital religion. Where the Holy Spirit has been, specially and peculiarly, there the true Church of Christ has been, and where the Holy Spirit has not been, specially and peculiarly, there, the

Church of Christ has not been; however carefully, or imposingly, the externals of a church organization may have been maintained.

But there is no stronger, or more effective proof of the need of the presence and agency of the Holy Spirit, than that which is derived from the nature of the case, as it appears in the individual. Just in proportion as we come to know our own moral condition, and our own moral necessities, shall we see and feel that the origin and growth of holiness within our earthly and alienated souls, without the agency of God the Holy Spirit, is an utter impossibility. Let us then look into the argument from the nature of the case, and consider this doctrine of a direct Divine operation, in its relations to ourselves personally. Why, then, does every man need these influences of the Holy Spirit which are so cordially offered in the text?

1. He needs them, in the first place, in order that he may be convinced of the reality of the eternal world.

There is such a world. It has as actual an existence as Europe or Asia. Though not an object for any one of the five senses, the invisible world is as substantial as the great globe itself, and will be standing when the elements shall have been melted with fervent heat, and the heavens are no more. This eternal world, furthermore, is not only real, but it is filled with realities that are yet more solemn. God inhabits it. The judgment-seat of Christ is set up in it. Heaven is in it. Hell is in it. Myriads of myriads of holy and happy spirits are there. Myriads of sinful and wretched spirits are there. Nay, this unseen world is the only real world, and the objects in it the only real objects, if we remember that only that which is immutable deserves the name of real. If we employ the eternal as the measure of real being, then all that is outside of eternity is unreal and a vanity. This material world acquires impressiveness for man, by virtue of the objects that fill it. His farm is in it, his houses are upon it, solid mountains rise up from it, great rivers run through it, and the old rolling heavens are bent over it. But what is the transient reality of these objects, these morning vapors, compared with the everlasting reality of such beings as God and the soul, of such facts as holiness and sin, of such states as heaven and hell? Here, then, we have in the unseen and eternal world a most solemn and real object of knowledge; but where, among mankind, is the solemn and vivid knowledge itself? Knowledge is the union of a fact with a feeling. There may be a stone in the street, but unless I smite it with my foot, or smite it with my eye, I have no knowledge of the stone. So, too, there is an invisible world, outstanding and awfully impressive; but unless I feel its influences, and stand with awe beneath its shadows, it is as though it were not. Here is an orb that has risen up into the horizon, but all eyes are shut.

For, no thoughtful observer fails to perceive that an earthly, and unspiritual mode of thought and feeling is the prevalent one among men. No one who has ever endeavored to arrest the attention of a fellow-man, and give his thoughts an upward tendency towards eternity, will say that the effort is easily and generally successful. On the contrary, if an ethereal and holy inhabitant of heaven were to go up and down our earth, and witness man's immersion in sense and time, the earthliness of his views and aims, his neglect of spiritual objects and interests, his absorption in this existence, and his forgetfulness of the other, it would be difficult to convince him that he was among beings made in the image of God, and was mingling with a race having an immortal destination beyond the grave.

In this first feature of the case, then, as we find it in ourselves, and see it in all our fellow-men, we have the first evidence of the need of awakening influences from on high. Since man, naturally, is destitute of a solemn sense of eternal things, it is plain that there can be no moral change produced in him, unless he is first wakened from this drowze. He cannot become the subject of that new birth without which he cannot see the kingdom of God, unless his torpor respecting the Unseen is removed. Entirely satisfied as he now is with this mode of exist-ence, and thinking little or nothing about another, the first necessity in his case is a startle, and an alarm. Difficult as he now finds it to be, to bring the invisible world before his mind in a way to affect his feelings, he needs to have it loom upon his inward vision with such power and impressiveness that he cannot take his eye off, if he would. Lethargic as he now is, respecting his own immortality, it is impossible for him to live and act with constant reference to it, unless he is wakened to its significance. Is it not self-evident, that if the sinner's present in-difference towards the invisible world, and his failure to feel its solemn reality, continues through life, he will certainly enter that state of existence with his pre-sent character? Looking into the human spirit, and seeing how dead it is towards God and the future, must we not say, that if this deadness to eternity lasts until the death of the body, it will certainly be the death of the soul?

But, in what way can man be made to realize that there is an eternal world, to which he is rapidly tending, and realities there, with which, by the very constitu-tion of his spirit, he is forever and indissolubly connected either for bliss or woe? How shall thoughtless and earthly man, as he treads these streets, and transacts all this business, and enjoys life, be made to feel with misgiving, foreboding, and alarm, that there is an eternity, and that he must soon enter it, as other men do, either as a heaven or a hell for his soul? The answer to this question, so often asked in sadness and sorrow by the preacher of the word, drives us back to the throne of God and to a mightier agency than that of man.

For one thing is certain, that this apathy and deadness will never of itself gen-erate sensibility and life. Satan never casts out Satan. If this slumberer be left to himself, he is lost. Should any man be given over to the natural inclination of his heart, he would never be awakened. Should his earthly mind receive no check, and his corrupt heart take its own way, he would never realize that there is an-other world than this, until he entered it. For, the worldly mind and the corrupt heart busy themselves solely and happily with this existence. They find pleasure in the things of this life, and therefore never look beyond them. Worldly men do not interfere with their own present actual enjoyment. Who of this class volun-tarily makes himself unhappy, by thinking of subjects that are gloomy to his mind? What man of the world starts up from his sweet sleep and his pleasant dreams, and of his own accord looks the stern realities of death and the judg-ment in the eye? No natural man begins to wound himself, that he may be healed. No earthly man begins to slay himself, that he may be made alive. Even when the natural heart is roused and wakened by some foreign agency; some startling providence of God or some Divine operation in the conscience, how soon, if left to its own motion and tendency, does it relapse into its old slumber and sleep.

The needle has received a shock, but after a slight trembling and vibration it soon settles again upon its axis, ever and steady to the north. It is plain, that the sinner's worldly mind and apathetic nature will never conduct him to a proper sense of Divine things.

The awakening, then, of the human soul, to an effectual apprehension of eternal realities, must take its first issue from some other Being than the drowsy and slumbering creature himself. We are not speaking of a few serious thoughts that now and then fleet across the human mind, like meteors at midnight, and are seen no more. We are speaking of that permanent, that everlasting dawning of eternity, with its terrors and its splendors, upon the human soul, which allows it no more repose, until it is prepared for eternity upon good grounds and foundations; and with reference to such a profound consciousness of the future state as this, we say with confidence, that the awakening must proceed from some Being who is far more alive to the solemnity and significance of eternal duration than earthly man is. Without impulses from on high, the sinner never rouses up to attend to the subject of religion. He lives on indifferent to his religious interests, until God, who is more merciful to his deathless soul than he himself is, by His providence startles him, or by His Spirit in his conscience alarms him. Never, until God interferes to disturb his dreams, and break up his slumber, does he profoundly and permanently feel that he was made for another world, and is fast going into it. How often does God say to the careless man: "Arise, O sleeper, and Christ shall give thee light;" and how often does he disregard the warning voice! How often does God stimulate his conscience, and flare light into his mind; and how often does he stifle down these inward convictions, and suffer the light to shine in the darkness that comprehends it not! These facts in the personal history of every sin-loving man show, that the human soul does not of its own isolated action wake up to the realities of eternity. They also show that God is very merciful to the human soul, in positively and powerfully interfering for its welfare; but that man, in infinite folly and wickedness, loves the sleep, and inclines to remain in it. The Holy Spirit strives, but the human spirit resists.

II. In the second place, man needs the influences of the Holy Spirit that he may be convinced of sin.

Man universally is a sinner, and yet he needs in every single instance to be made aware of it. "There is none good, no, not one;" and yet out of the millions of the race how very few feel this truth! Not only does man sin, but he adds to his guilt by remaining ignorant of it. The criminal in this instance also, as in our courts of law, feels and confesses his crime no faster than it is proved to him. Through what blindness of mind, and hardness of heart, and insensibility of conscience, is the Holy Spirit obliged to force His way, before there is a sincere acknowledgment of sin before God! The careful investigations, the persevering questionings and cross-questionings, by which, before a human tribunal, the wilful and unrepenting criminal is forced to see and acknowledge his wickedness, are but faint emblems of that thorough work that must be wrought by the Holy Ghost, before the human soul, at a higher tribunal, forsaking its refuges of lies, and desisting from its subterfuges and palliations, smites upon the breast, and cries, "God be merciful to me a sinner!" Think how much of our sin has occurred in total apathy, and indifference, and how unwilling we are to have any distinct consciousness upon this subject. It is only now and then that we feel ourselves to be sinners; but it is by no means only now and then that we are sinners. We sin habitually; we are conscious of sin rarely. Our affections and inclinations and motives are evil, and only evil, continually; but our experimental knowledge that they are so comes not often into our mind, and what is worse stays not long, because we dislike it.

The conviction of sin, with what it includes and leads to, is of more worth to man than all other convictions. Conviction of any sort,—a living practical consciousness of any kind,—is of great value, because it is only this species of knowledge that moves mankind. Convince a man, that is, give him a consciousness, of the truth of a principle in politics, in trade, or in religion, and you actuate him politically, commercially, or religiously. Convince a criminal of his crime, that is, endue him with a conscious feeling of his criminality, and you make him burn with electric fire. A convicted man is a man thoroughly conscious; and a thoroughly conscious man is a deeply moved one. And this is true, with emphasis, of the conviction of sin. This consciousness produces a deeper and more lasting effect than all others. Convince a community of the justice or injustice of a certain class of political principles, and you stir it very deeply, and broadly, as the history of all democracies clearly shows; but let society be once convinced of sin before the holy and righteous God, and deep calleth unto deep, all the waters are moved. Never is a mass of human beings so centrally stirred, as when the Spirit of God is poured out upon it, and from no movement in human society do such lasting and blessed consequences flow, as from a genuine revival of religion.

But here again, as in reference to the eternal state, there is no realizing sense. Conviction of sin is not a characteristic of mankind at large. Men generally will acknowledge in words that they are sinners, but they wait for some far-distant day to come, when they shall be pricked in the heart, and feel the truth of what they say. Men generally are not conscious of the dreadful reality of sin, any more than they are of the solemn reality of eternity. A deep insensibility, in this respect also, precludes a practical knowledge of that guilt in the soul, which, if unpardoned and unremoved, will just as surely ruin it as God lives and the soul is immortal. Since, then, if man be left to his own inclination, he never will be convinced of sin, it is plain that some Agent who has the power must overcome his aversion to self-knowledge, and bring him to consciousness upon this unwelcome subject. If any one of us, for the remainder of our days, should be given over to that ordinary indifference towards sin with which we walk these streets, and transact business, and enjoy life; if God's truth should never again in this world stab the conscience, and God's Spirit should never again make us anxious; is it not infallibly certain that the future would be as the past, and that we should go through this "accepted time and day of salvation" unconvicted and therefore unconverted?

But besides this destitution of the experimental sense of sin, another ground of the need of Divine agency is found in the blindness of the natural mind. Man's vision of spiritual things, even when they are set before his eyes, is dim and inadequate. The Christian ministry is greatly hindered, because it cannot illuminate the human understanding, and impart the power of a keen spiritual insight. It is compelled to present the objects of sight, but it cannot give the eye to see them. Vision depends altogether upon the condition of the organ. The eye sees only what it brings the means of seeing. The scaled eye of a worldling, or a deb-auchee, or a self-righteous man, cannot see that sin of the heart, that "spiritual wickedness," at which men like Paul and Isaiah stood aghast. These were men whose character compared with that of the worldling was saintly; men whose shoes' latchets the worldling is not worthy to stoop down and unloose. And yet they saw a depravity within their own hearts which he does not see in his; a de-pravity which he cannot see, and which he steadily denies to exist, until he is enlightened by the Holy Ghost.

But the preacher has no power to impart this clear spiritual discernment. He cannot arm the eye of the natural man with that magnifying and microscopic power, by which hatred shall be seen to be murder, and lust, adultery, and the least swelling of pride, the sin of Lucifer. He is compelled, by the testimony of the Bible, of the wise and the holy of all time, and of his own consciousness, to tell every unregenerate man that he is no better than his race; that he certainly is no better than the Christian Church which continually confesses and mourns over indwelling sin. The faithful preacher of the word is obliged to insist that there is no radical difference among men, and that the depravity of the man of irre-proachable morals but unrenewed heart is as total as was that of the great preacher to the Gentiles,—a man of perfectly irreproachable morals, but who confessed that he was the chief of sinners, and feared lest he should be a cast-away. But the preacher of this unwelcome message has no power to open the blind eye. He cannot endow the self-ignorant and incredulous man before him, with that consciousness of the "plague of the heart" which says "yea" to the most vivid description of human sinfulness, and "amen" to God's heaviest malediction upon it. The preacher's position would be far easier, if there might be a transfer of experience; if some of that bitter painful sense of sin with which the struggling Christian is burdened might flow over into the easy, unvexed, and thoughtless souls of the men of this world. Would that the consciousness upon this subject of sin, of a Paul or a Luther, might deluge that large multitude of men who doubt or deny the doctrine of human depravity. The materials for that consciousness, the items that go to make up that experience, exist as really and as plentifully in your moral state and character, as they do in that of the mourning and self-reproaching Christian who sits by your side,—your devout father, your saintly mother, or sister,—whom you know, and who you know is a better being than you are. Why should they be weary and heavy-laden with a sense of their un-worthiness before God, and you go through life indifferent and light-hearted? Are they deluded in respect to the doctrine of human depravity, and are you in the right? Think you that the deathbed and the day of judgment will prove this to be the fact? No! if you shall ever know anything of the Christian struggle with innate corruption; if you shall ever, in the expressive phrase of Scripture, have your senses exercised as in a gymnasium [1] to discern good and evil, and see yourself with self-abhorrence; your views will harmonize most profoundly and exactly with theirs. And, furthermore, you will not in the process create any new sinfulness. You will merely see the existing depravity of the human heart. You will simply see what is,—is now, in your heart, and in all human hearts, and has been from the beginning.

But all this is the work of a more powerful and spiritual agency than that of man. The truth may be exhibited with perfect transparency and plainness, the hearer himself may do his utmost to have it penetrate and tell; and yet, there be no vivid and vital consciousness of sin. How often does the serious and alarmed man say to us: "I know it, but I do not feel it." How long and wearily, sometimes, does the anxious man struggle after an inward sense of these spiritual things, without success, until he learns that an inward sense, an experimental consciousness, respecting religious truth, is as purely a gift and product of God the Spirit as the breath of life in his nostrils. Considering, then, the natural apathy of man respecting the sin that is in his own heart, and the exceeding blindness of his mental vision, even when his attention has been directed to it, is it not perfectly plain that there must be the exertion of a Divine agency, in order that he may pass through even the first and lowest stages of the religious experience?

In view of the subject, as thus far unfolded, we remark:

1. First, that it is the duty of every one, to take the facts in respect to man's character as he finds them. Nothing is gained, in any province of human thought or action, by disputing actual verities. They are stubborn things, and will not yield to the wishes and prejudices of the natural heart. This is especially true in regard to the facts in man's moral and religious condition. The testimony of Revelation is explicit, that "the carnal mind is enmity against God, for it is not subject to the law of God, neither indeed can be;" and also, that "the natural man receiveth not the things of the Spirit, neither can he know them, because they are spiritually discerned." According to this Biblical statement, there is corruption and blindness together. The human heart is at once sinful, and ignorant that it is so. It is, therefore, the very worst form of evil; a fatal disease unknown to the patient, and accompanied with the belief that there is perfect health; sin and guilt without any just and proper sense of it. This is the testimony, and the assertion, of that Being who needs not that any should testify to Him of man, for he knows what is in man. And this is the testimony, also, of every mind that has attained a profound self-knowledge. For it is indisputable, that in proportion as a man is introspective, and accustoms himself to the scrutiny of his motives and feelings, he discovers that "the whole head is sick, and the whole heart is faint."

It is, therefore, the duty and wisdom of every one to set to his seal that God is true,—to have this as his motto. Though, as yet, he is destitute of a clear conviction of sin, and a godly sorrow for it, still he should presume the fact of human depravity. Good men in every age have found it to be a fact, and the infallible Word of God declares that it is a fact. What, then, is gained, by proposing another than the Biblical theory of human nature? Is the evil removed by denying its existence? Will the mere calling men good at heart, and by nature, make them such?

"Who can hold a fire in his hand,
By thinking on the frosty Caucasus?
Or cloy the hungry edge of appetite,
By bare imagination of a feast?
Or wallow naked in December snow,
By thinking on fantastic summer heat?" [2]

2. In the second place, we remark that it is the duty of every one, not to be discouraged by these facts and truths relative to the moral condition of man. For, one fact conducts to the next one. One truth prepares for a second. If it is a solemn and sad fact that men are sinners, and blind and dead in their trespasses and sin, it is also a cheering fact that the Holy Spirit can enlighten the darkest understanding, and enliven the most torpid and indifferent soul; and it is a still further, and most encouraging truth and fact, that the Holy Spirit is given to those who ask for it, with more readiness than a father gives bread to his hungry child. Here, then, we have the fact of sin, and of blindness and apathy in sin; the fact of a mighty power in God to convince of sin, of righteousness, and of judgment; and the blessed fact that this power is accessible to prayer. Let us put these three facts together, all of them, and act accordingly. Then we shall be taught by the Spirit, and shall come to a salutary consciousness of sin; and then shall be verified in our own experience the words of God: "I dwell in the high and holy place, and with him also that is of a contrite and humble spirit, to revive the spirit of the humble, and to revive the heart of the contrite ones."

*[**Note 1:** [Greek: Ta aisthaeria gegurasmena.] Heb. v. 14.]*
*[**Note 2:** SHAKSPEARE: Richard II. Act i. Sc. 3.]*

VIII - The Necessity of Divine Influences. (continued)

Luke xi. 13.—"If ye, then, being evil, know how to give good gifts unto your children; how much more shall your heavenly Father give the Holy Spirit to them that ask him."

In expounding the doctrine of these words, in the preceding discourse, the argument for the necessity of Divine influences had reference to the more general aspects of man's character and condition. We were concerned with the origin of seriousness in view of a future life, and the production of a sense of moral corruption and unfitness to enter eternity. We have now to consider the work of the Spirit, in its relations, first, to that more distinct sense of sin which is denominated the consciousness of guilt, and secondly, to that saving act of faith by which the atonement of Christ is appropriated by the soul.

I. Sin is not man's misfortune, but his fault; and any view that falls short of this fact is radically defective. Sin not only brings a corruption and bondage, but also a condemnation and penalty, upon the self-will that originates it. Sin not only renders man unfit for rewards, font also deserving of punishment. As one who has disobeyed law of his own determination, he is liable not merely to the negative loss of blessings, but also to the positive infliction of retribution. It is not enough that a transgressor be merely let alone; he must be taken in hand and punished. He is not simply a diseased man; he is a criminal. His sin, therefore, requires not a removal merely, but also an expiation.

This relation and reference of transgression to law and justice is a fundamental one; and yet it is very liable to be overlooked, or at least to be inadequately apprehended. The sense of ill-desert is too apt to be confused and shallow, in the human soul. Man is comparatively ready to acknowledge the misery of sin, while he is slow to confess the guilt of it. When the word of God asserts he is poor, and blind, and wretched, he is comparatively forward to assent; but when, in addition, it asserts that he deserves to be punished everlastingly, he reluctates. Mankind are willing to acknowledge their wretchedness, and be pitied; but they are not willing to acknowledge their guiltiness, and stand condemned before law.

And yet, guilt is the very essence of sin. Extinguish the criminality, and you extinguish the inmost core and heart of moral evil. We may have felt that sin is bondage, that it is inward dissension and disharmony, that it takes away the true dignity of our nature, but if we have not also felt that it is iniquity and merits penalty, we have not become conscious of its most essential quality. It is not enough that we come before God, saying: "I am wretched in my soul; I am weary of my bondage; I long for deliverance." We must also say, as we look up into that holy Eye: "I am guilty; O my God I deserve thy judgments." In brief, the human mind must recognize all the Divine attributes. The entire Divine character, in both its justice and its love, must rise full-orbed before the soul, when thus seeking salvation. It is not enough, that we ask God to free us from disquietude, and give us repose. Before we do this, and that we may do it successfully, we must employ the language of David, while under the stings of guilt: "O Lord rebuke me not in thy wrath: neither chasten me in thy hot displeasure. Be merciful unto me, O God be merciful unto me."

What is needed is, more consideration of sin in its objective, and less in its subjective relations; more sense of it in its reference to the being and attributes of God, and less sense of it in its reference to our own happiness or misery, or even to the harmony of our own powers and faculties. The adorable being and attributes of God are of more importance than any human soul, immortal though it be; and what is required in the religious experience is, more anxiety lest the Divine glory should be tarnished, and less fear that a worm of the dust be made miserable by his transgressions. And whatever may be our theory of the matter, "to this complexion must we come at last," even in order to our own peace of mind. We must lose our life, in order to find it. Even in order to our own inward repose of conscience and of heart, there must come a point and period in our mental history, when we do actually sink self out of sight, and think of sin in its relation to the character and government of the great and holy God,—when we do see it to be guilt, as well as corruption.

For guilt is a distinct, and a distinguishable quality. It is a thing by itself, like the Platonic idea of Beauty.[1] It is sin stripped of its accompaniments,—the restlessness, the dissatisfaction, and the unhappiness which it produces,—and perceived in its pure odiousness and ill-desert. And when thus seen, it does not permit the mind to think of any thing but the righteous law, and the Divine character. In the hour of thorough conviction, the sinful spirit is lost in the feeling of guiltiness: wholly engrossed in the reflection that it has incurred the condemnation of the Best Being in the universe. It is in distress, not because an Almighty Being can make it miserable but, because a Holy and Good Being has reason to be displeased with it. When it gives utterance to its emotion, it says to its Sovereign and its Judge: "I am in anguish, more because Thou the Holy and the Good art unreconciled with me, than because Thou the Omnipotent canst punish me forever. I refuse not to The punished; I deserve the inflictions of Thy justice; only forgive, and Thou mayest do what Thou wilt unto me." A soul that is truly penitent has no desire to escape penalty, at the expense of principle and law. It says with David: "Thou desirest not sacrifice;" such atonement as I can make is inadequate; "else would I give it." It expresses its approbation of the pure justice of God, in the language of the gentlest and sweetest of Mystics:

"Thou hast no lightnings, O Thou Just!
Or I their force should know;
And if Thou strike me into dust,
My soul approves the blow.
The heart that values less its ease,
Than it adores Thy ways;
In Thine avenging anger, sees
A subject of its praise.
Pleased I could lie, concealed and lost,
In shades of central night;
Not to avoid Thy wrath, Thou know'st,
But lest I grieve Thy sight.
Smite me, O Thou whom I provoke!
And I will love Thee still;
The well deserved and righteous stroke
Shall please me, though it kill." [2]

Now, it is only when the human spirit is under the illuminating, and discriminating influences of the Holy Ghost, that it possesses this pure and genuine sense of guilt. Worldly losses, trials, warnings by God's providence, may rouse the sinner, and make him solemn; but unless the Spirit of Grace enters his heart he does not feel that he is ill-deserving. He is sad and fearful, respecting the future life, and perhaps supposes that this state of mind is one of true conviction, and wonders that it does not end in conversion, and the joy of pardon. But if he would examine it, he would discover that it is full of the lust of self. He would find that he is merely unhappy, and restless, and afraid to die. If he should examine the workings of his heart, he would discover that they are only another form of self-love; that instead of being anxious about self in the present world, he has become anxious about self in the future world; that instead of looking out for his happiness here, he has begun to look out for it hereafter; that in fact he has merely transferred sin, from time and its relations, to eternity and its relations. Such sorrow as this needs to be sorrowed for, and such repentance as this needs to be repented of. Such conviction as this needs to be laid open, and have its defect shown. After a course of wrongdoing, it is not sufficient for man to come before the Holy One, making mention of his wretchedness, and desire for happiness, but making no mention of his culpability, and desert of righteous and holy judgments. It is not enough for the criminal to plead for life, however earnestly, while he avoids the acknowledgment that death is his just due. For silence in such a connection as this, is denial. The impenitent thief upon the cross was clamorous for life and happiness, saying, "If thou be the Christ, save thyself and us." He said nothing concerning the crime that had brought him to a malefactor's death, and thereby showed that it did not weigh heavy upon his conscience. But the real penitent rebuked him, saying: "Dost thou not fear God, seeing thou art in the same condemnation? And we indeed justly; for we receive the due reward of our deeds." And then followed that meek and broken-hearted supplication: "Lord remember me," which drew forth the world-renowned answer: "This day shalt thou be with me in paradise."

In the fact, then, that man's experience of sin is so liable to be defective upon the side of guilt, we find another necessity for the teaching of the Holy Spirit; for a spiritual agency that cannot be deceived, which pierces to the dividing asunder of the soul and spirit, and is a discerner of the real intent and feeling of the heart.

II. In the second place, man needs the influences of the Holy Spirit, in order that he may actually appropriate Christ's atonement for sin.

The feeling of ill-desert, of which we have spoken, requires an expiation, in order to its extinction, precisely as the burning sensation of thirst needs the cup of cold water, in order that it may be allayed, the sense of guilt is awakened in its pure and genuine form, by the Holy Spirit's operation, the soul craves the atonement,—it wants the dying Lamb of God. We often speak of a believer's longings after purity, after peace, after joy. There is an appetency for them. In like manner, there is in the illuminated and guilt-smitten conscience an appetency for the piacular work of Christ, as that which alone can give it pacification. Contemplated from this point of view, there is not a more rational doctrine within the whole Christian system, than that of the Atonement. Anything that ministers to a distinct and legitimate craving in man is reasonable, and necessary. That theorist, therefore, who would evince the unreasonableness of the atoning work of the Redeemer, must first evince the unreasonableness of the consciousness of guilt, and of the judicial craving of the conscience. He must show the groundlessness of that fundamental and organic feeling which imparts such a blood-red color to all the religions of the globe; be they Pagan, Jewish, or Christian. Whenever, therefore, this sensation of ill-desert is elicited, and the soul feels consciously criminal before the Everlasting Judge, the difficulties that beset the doctrine of the Cross all vanish in the craving, in the appetency, of the conscience, for acquittal through the substituted sufferings of the Son of God. He who has been taught by the Spirit respecting the iniquity of sin, and views it in its relations to the Divine holiness, has no wish to be pardoned at the expense of justice. His conscience is now jealous for the majesty of God, and the dignity of His government. He now experimentally understands that great truth which has its foundation in the nature of guilt, and consequently in the method of Redemption,—the great ethical truth, that after an accountable agent has stained himself with crime, there is from the necessity of the case no remission without the satisfaction of law.

But it is one thing to acknowledge this in theory, and even to feel the need of Christ's atonement, and still another thing to really appropriate it. Unbelief and despair have great power over a guilt-stricken mind; and were it not for that Spirit who "takes of the things of Christ and shows them to the soul," sinful man would in every instance succumb under their awful paralysis. For, if the truth and Spirit of God should merely convince the sinner of his guilt, but never apply the atoning blood of the Redeemer, hell would be in him and he would be in hell.

If God, coming forth as He justly might only in His judicial character, should confine Himself to a convicting operation in the conscience,—should make the transgressor feel his guilt, and then leave him to the feeling and with the feeling, forevermore,—this would be eternal death. And if, as any man shall lie down upon his death-bed, he shall find that owing to his past quenching of the Spirit the illuminating energy of God is searching him, and revealing him to himself, but does not assist him to look up to the Saviour of sinners; and if, in the day of judgment, as he draws near the bar of an eternal doom, he shall discover that the sense of guilt grows deeper and deeper, while the atoning blood is not applied,— if this shall be the experience of any one upon his death-bed, and in the day of judgment, will he need to be told what he is and whither he is going?

Now it is with reference to these disclosures that come in like a deluge upon him, that man needs the aids and operation of the Holy Spirit. Ordinarily, nearly the whole of his guilt is latent within him. He is, commonly, undisturbed by conscience; but it would be a fatal error to infer that therefore he has a clear and innocent conscience. There is a vast amount of undeveloped guilt within every impenitent soul. It is slumbering there, as surely as magnetism is in the magnet, and the electric fluid is in the piled-up thunder-cloud. For there are moments when the sinful soul feels this hidden criminality, as there are moments when the magnet shows its power, and the thunder-cloud darts its nimble and forked lightnings. Else, why do these pangs and fears shoot and flash through it, every now and then? Why does the drowning man instinctively ask for God's mercy? Were his conscience pure and clear from guilt, like that of the angel or the seraph,—were there no latent crime within him,—he would sink into the unfathomed depths of the sea, without the thought of such a cry. When the traveller in South America sees the smoke and flame of the volcano, here and there, as he passes along, he is justified in inferring that a vast central fire is burning beneath the whole region. In like manner, when man discovers, as he watches the phenomena of his conscience, that guilt every now and then emerges like a flash of flame into consciousness, filling him with fear and distress,—when he finds that he has no security against this invasion, but that in an hour when he thinks not, and commonly when he is weakest and faintest, in his moments of danger or death, it stings him and wounds him, he is justified in inferring, and he must infer, that the deep places of his spirit, the whole potentiality of his soul is full of crime.

Now, in no condition of the soul is there greater need of the agency of the Comforter (O well named the Comforter), than when all this latency is suddenly manifested to a man. When this deluge of discovery comes in, all the billows of doubt, fear, terror, and despair roll over the soul, and it sinks in the deep waters. The sense of guilt,—that awful guilt, which the man has carried about with him for many long years, and which he has trifled with,—now proves too great for him to control. It seizes him like a strong-armed man. If he could only believe that the blood of the Lamb of God expiates all this crime which is so appalling to his mind, he would be at peace instantaneously. But he is unable to believe this. His sin, which heretofore looked too small to be noticed, now appears too great to be forgiven. Other men may be pardoned, but not he. He despairs of mercy; and if he should be left to the natural workings of his own mind; if he should not be taught and assisted by the Holy Ghost, in this critical moment, to behold the Lamb of God; he would despair forever. For this sense of ill-desert, this fearful looking-for of judgment and fiery indignation, with which he is wrestling, is organic to the conscience, and the human will has no more power over it than it has over the sympathetic nerve. Only as he is taught by the Divine Spirit, is he able with perfect calmness to look up from this brink of despair, and say: "There is no condemnation to them that are in Christ Jesus. The blood of Jesus Christ cleanseth from all sin. Therefore, being justified by faith we have peace with God through our Lord Jesus Christ. I know whom I have believed, and am persuaded that he is able to keep that which I have committed unto him against that day."

In view of the truths which we have now considered, it is worthy of observation:

1. First, that the Holy Spirit constitutes the tie, and bond of connection, between man and God. The third Person in the Godhead is very often regarded as more distant from the human soul, than either the Father or the Son. In the history of the doctrine of the Trinity, the definition of the Holy Spirit, and the discrimination of His relations in the economy of the Godhead, was not settled until after the doctrine of the first and second Persons had been established. Something analogous to this appears in the individual experience. God the Father and God the Son are more in the thoughts of many believers, than God the Holy Ghost. And yet, we have seen that in the economy of Redemption, and from the very nature of the case, the soul is brought as close to the Spirit, as to the Father and Son. Nay, it is only through the inward operations of the former, that the latter are made real to the heart and mind of man. Not until the third Person enlightens, are the second and first Persons beheld. "No man," says St. Paul, "can say that Jesus is the Lord, but by the Holy Ghost."

The sinful soul is entirely dependent upon the Divine Spirit, and from first to last it is in most intimate communication with Him during the process of salvation. It is enlightened by His influence; it is enlivened by Him; it is empowered by Him to the act of faith in Christ's Person and Work; it is supported and assisted by Him, in every step of the Christian race; it is comforted by Him in all trials and tribulations; and, lastly, it is perfected in holiness, and fitted for the immediate presence of God, by Him. Certainly, then, the believer should have as full faith in the distinct personality, and immediate efficiency, of the third Person, as he has in that of the first and second. His most affectionate feeling should centre upon that Blessed Agent, through whom he appropriates the blessings that have been provided for sinners by the Father and Son, and without whose influence the Father would have planned the Redemptive scheme, and the Son have executed it, in vain.

2. In the second place, it is deserving of very careful notice that the influences of the Holy Spirit may be obtained by asking for them. This is the only condition to be complied with. And this gift, furthermore, is peculiar, in that it is invariably bestowed whenever it is sincerely implored. There are other gifts of God which may be asked for with deep and agonizing desire, and it is not certain that they will be granted. This is the case with temporal blessings. A sick man may turn his face to the wall, with Hezekiah, and pray in the bitterness of his soul, for the prolongation of his life, and yet not obtain the answer which Hezekiah received. But no man ever supplicated in the earnestness of his soul for the influences of the Holy Spirit, and was ultimately refused. For this is a gift which it is always safe to grant. It involves a spiritual and everlasting good. It is the gift of righteousness, of the fear and love of God in the heart. There is no danger in such a bestowment. It inevitably promotes the glory of God. Hence our Lord, after bidding his hearers to "ask," to "seek," and to "knock," adds, as the encouraging reason why they should do so: "For, every one that asketh receiveth; and he that seeketh, [always] findeth; and to him that knocketh, it shall [certainly] be opened." This is a reason that cannot be assigned in the instance of other prayers. Our Lord commands his disciples to pray for their daily bread; and we know that the children of God do generally find their wants supplied. Still, it would not be true that every one who in the sincerity of his soul has asked for daily bread has received it. The children of God have sometimes died of hunger. But no soul that has ever hungered for the bread of heaven, and supplicated for it, has been sent empty away. Nay more: Whoever finds it in his heart to ask for the Holy Spirit may know, from this very fact, that the Holy Spirit has anticipated him, and has prompted the very prayer itself. And think you that God will not grant a request which He himself has inspired? And therefore, again, it is, that every one who asks invariably receives.

3. The third remark suggested by the subject we have been considering is, that it is exceedingly hazardous to resist Divine influences. "Quench not the Spirit" is one of the most imperative of the Apostolic injunctions. Our Lord, after saying that a word spoken against Himself is pardonable, adds that he that blasphemes against the Holy Ghost shall never be forgiven, neither in this world nor in the world to come. The New Testament surrounds the subject of Divine influences with very great solemnity. It represents the resisting of the Holy Ghost to be as heinous, and dangerous, as the trampling upon Christ's blood.

There is a reason for this. We have seen that in this operation upon the mind and heart, God comes as near, and as close to man, as it is possible for Him to come. Now to grieve or oppose such a merciful, and such an inward agency as this, is to offer the highest possible affront to the majesty and the mercy of God. It is a great sin to slight the gifts of Divine providence,—to misuse health, strength, wealth, talents. It is a deep sin to contemn the truths of Divine Revelation, by which the soul is made wise unto eternal life. It is a fearful sin to despise the claims of God the Father, and God the Son. But it is a transcendent sin to resist and beat back, after it has been given, that mysterious, that holy, that immediately Divine influence, by which alone the heart of stone can be made the heart of flesh. For, it indicates something more than the ordinary carelessness of a sinner. It evinces a determined obstinacy in sin,—nay, a Satanic opposition to God and goodness. It is of such a guilt as this, that the apostle John remarks: "There is a sin unto death; I do not say that one should pray for it."[3]

Again, it is exceedingly hazardous to resist Divine influences, because they depend wholly upon the good pleasure of God, and not at all upon any established and uniform law. We must not, for a moment, suppose that the operations of the Holy Spirit upon the human soul are like those of the forces of nature upon the molecules of matter. They are not uniform and unintermittent, like gravitation, and chemical affinity. We may avail ourselves of the powers of nature at any moment, because they are steadily operative by an established law. They are laboring incessantly, and we may enter into their labors at any instant we please. But it is not so with supernatural and gracious influences. God's awakening and renewing power does not operate with the uniformity of those blind natural laws which He has impressed upon the dull clod beneath our feet. God is not one of the forces of nature. He is a Person and a Sovereign. His special and highest action upon the human soul is not uniform. His Spirit, He expressly teaches us, does not always strive with man. It is a wind that bloweth when and where it listeth. For this reason, it is dangerous to the religious interests of the soul, in the highest degree, to go counter to any impulses of the Spirit, however slight, or to neglect any of His admonitions, however gentle. If God in mercy has once come in upon a thoughtless mind, and wakened it to eternal realities; if He has enlightened it to perceive the things that make for its peace; and that mind slights this merciful interference, and stifles down these inward teachings, then God withdraws, and whether He will ever return again to that soul depends upon His mere sovereign volition. He has bound himself by no promise to do so. He has established no uniform law of operation, in the case. It is true that He is very pitiful and of tender mercy, and waits and bears long with the sinner; and it is also true, that He is terribly severe and just, when He thinks it proper to be so, and says to those who have despised His Spirit: "Because I have called and ye refused, and have stretched out my hand, and no man regarded, I will laugh at your calamity, and mock when your fear cometh."

Let no one say: "God has promised to bestow the Holy Ghost to every one who asks: I will ask at some future time." To "ask" for the Holy Spirit implies some already existing desire that He would enter the mind and convince of sin, and convert to God. It implies some craving, some yearning, for Divine influences; and this implies some measure of such influence already bestowed. Man asks for the Holy Spirit, only as he is moved by the Holy Spirit. The Divine is ever prevenient to the human. Suppose now, that a man resists these influences when they are already at work within him, and says: "I will seek them at a more convenient season." Think you, that when that convenient season comes round,—when life is waning, and the world is receding, and the eternal gulf is yawning,—think you that that man who has already resisted grace can make his own heart to yearn for it, and his soul to crave it? Do men at such times find that sincere desires, and longings, and aspirations, come at their beck? Can a man say, with any prospect of success: "I will now quench out this seriousness which the Spirit of God has produced in my mind, and will bring it up again ten years hence. I will stifle this drawing of the Eternal Father of my soul which I now feel at the roots of my being, and it shall re-appear at a future day."

No! While it is true that any one who "asks," who really wants a spiritual blessing, will obtain it, it is equally true that a man may have no heart to ask,— may have no desire, no yearning, no aspiration at all, and be unable to produce one. In this case there is no promise. Whosoever thirsts, and only he who thirsts, can obtain the water of life. Cherish, therefore, the faintest influences and operations of the Comforter. If He enlightens your conscience so that it reproaches you for sin, seek to have the work go on. Never resist any such convictions, and never attempt to stifle them. If the Holy Spirit urges you to confession of sin before God, yield instantaneously to His urging, and pour out your soul before the All-

Merciful. And when He says, "Behold the Lamb of God," look where He points, and be at peace and at rest. The secret of all spiritual success is an immediate and uniform submission to the influences of the Holy Ghost.

*[**Note 1:** [Greek: Anto, kath anto, meth anton, monoeides.]—PLATO:*
Convivium, p. 247, Ed. Bipont.]
*[**Note 2:** Guyon: translated by Cowper. is expressed by VAUGHAN in*
Works III. 85.—A similar thought "The Eclipse."
"Thy anger I could kiss, and will;
But O Thy grief, Thy grief doth kill."]
*[**Note 3:** The sin against the Holy Ghost is unpardonable, not because there is a grade of guilt*
in it too scarlet to be washed white by Christ's blood of atonement but, because it implies a
total quenching of that operation of the third Person of the Trinity which is the only power
adequate to the extirpation of sin from the human soul. The sin against the Holy Ghost is
tantamount, therefore, to everlasting sin. And it is noteworthy, that in Mark iii. 29 the read-
ing [Greek: amartaemartos], instead of [Greek: kriseos], is supported by a majority of the
oldest manuscripts and versions, and is adopted by Lachmann, Tischendorf, and Tregelles.
"He that shall blaspheme against the Holy Ghost.... is in danger of eternal sin."]

IX - The Impotence of The Law

HEBREWS vii. 19.—*"For the law made nothing perfect, but the bringing in of a better hope did; by the which we draw nigh to God."*

It is the aim of the Epistle to the Hebrews, to teach the insufficiency of the Jewish Dispensation to save the human race from the wrath of God and the power of sin, and the all-sufficiency of the Gospel Dispensation to do this. Hence, the writer of this Epistle endeavors with special effort to make the Hebrews feel the weakness of their old and much esteemed religion, and to show them that the only benefit which God intended by its establishment was, to point men to the perfect and final religion of the Gospel. This he does, by examining the parts of the Old Economy. In the first place, the sacrifices under the Mosaic law were not designed to extinguish the sense of guilt,—"for it is not possible that the blood of bulls and goats should take away sin,"—but were intended merely to awaken the sense of guilt, and thereby to lead the Jew to look to that mercy of God which at a future day was to be exhibited in the sacrifice of his eternal Son. The Jewish priesthood, again, standing between the sinner and God, were not able to avert the Divine displeasure,—for as sinners they were themselves exposed to it. They could only typify, and direct the guilty to, the great High Priest, the Messiah, whom God's mercy would send in the fulness of time. Lastly, the moral law, proclaimed amidst the thunderings and lightnings of Sinai, had no power to secure obedience, but only a fearful power to produce the consciousness of disobedience, and of exposure to a death far more awful than that threatened against the man who should touch the burning mountain.

It was, thus, the design of God, by this legal and preparatory dispensation, to disclose to man his ruined and helpless condition, and his need of looking to Him for everything that pertains to redemption. And he did it, by so arranging the dispensation that the Jew might, as it were, make the trial and see if he could be his own Redeemer. He instituted a long and burdensome round of observances, by means of which the Jew might, if possible, extinguish the remorse of his conscience, and produce the peace of God in his soul. God seems by the sacrifices under the law, and the many and costly offerings which the Jew was commanded to bring into the temple of the Lord, to have virtually said to him: "Thou art guilty, and My wrath righteously abides within thy conscience,—yet, do what thou canst to free thyself from it; free thyself from it if thou canst; bring an offering and come before Me. But when thou hast found that thy conscience still remains perturbed and unpacified, and thy heart still continues corrupt and sinful, then look away from thy agency and thy offering, to My clemency and My offering,—trust not in these finite sacrifices of the lamb and the goat, but let them merely remind thee of the infinite sacrifice which in the fulness of time I will provide for the sin of the world,—and thy peace shall be as a river, and thy righteousness as the waves of the sea."

But the proud and legal spirit of the Jew blinded him, and he did not perceive the true meaning and intent of his national religion. He made it an end, instead of a mere means to an end. Hence, it became a mechanical round of observances, kept up by custom, and eventually lost the power, which it had in the earlier and better ages of the Jewish commonwealth, of awakening the feeling of guilt and the sense of the need of a Redeemer. Thus, in the days of our Saviour's appearance upon the earth, the chosen guardians of this religion, which was intended to make men humble, and feel their personal ill-desert and need of mercy, had become self-satisfied and self-righteous. A religion designed to prompt the utterance of the greatest of its prophets: "Woe is me! I am a man of unclean lips, and I dwell in the midst of a people of unclean lips," now prompted the utterance of the Pharisee: "I thank Thee that I am not as other men are."

The Jew, in the times of our Saviour and his Apostles, had thus entirely mistaken the nature and purpose of the Old dispensation, and hence was the most bitter opponent of the New. He rested in the formal and ceremonial sacrifice of bulls and goats, and therefore counted the blood of the Son of God an unholy thing. He thought to appear before Him in whose sight the heavens are not clean, clothed in his own righteousness, and hence despised the righteousness of Christ. In reality, he appealed to the justice of God, and therefore rejected the religion of mercy.

But, this spirit is not confined to the Jew. It pervades the human race. Man is naturally a legalist. He desires to be justified by his own character and his own works, and reluctates at the thought of being accepted upon the ground of another's merits. This Judaistic spirit is seen wherever there is none of the publican's feeling when he said, "God be merciful to me a sinner." All confidence in personal virtue, all appeals to civil integrity, all attendance upon the ordinances of the Christian religion without the exercise of the Christian's penitence and faith, is, in reality; an exhibition of that same legal unevangelic spirit which in its extreme form inflated the Pharisee, and led him to tithe mint anise and cummin. Man's so general rejection of the Son of God as suffering the just for the unjust, as the manifestation of the Divine clemency towards a criminal, is a sign either that he is insensible of his guilt, or else that being somewhat conscious of it he thinks to cancel it himself.

Still, think and act as men may, the method of God in the Gospel is the only method. Other foundation can no man lay than is laid. For it rests upon stubborn facts, and inexorable principles. God knows that however anxiously a transgressor may strive to pacify his conscience, and prepare it for the judgment-day, its deep remorse can be removed only by the blood of incarnate Deity; that however sedulously he may attempt to obey the law, he will utterly fail, unless he is inwardly renewed and strengthened by the Holy Ghost. He knows that mere bare law can make no sinner perfect again, but that only the bringing in of a "better hope" can,—a hope by the which we draw nigh to God.

The text leads us to inquire: Why cannot the moral law make fallen man perfect? Or, in other words: Why cannot the ten commandments save a sinner?

That we may answer this question, we must first understand what is meant by a perfect man. It is one in whom there is no defect or fault of any kind,—one, therefore, who has no perturbation in his conscience, and no sin in his heart. It is a man who is entirely at peace with himself, and with God, and whose affections are in perfect conformity with the Divine law.

But fallen man, man as we find him universally, is characterized by both a remorseful conscience and an evil heart. His conscience distresses him, not indeed uniformly and constantly but, in the great emergencies of his life,—in the hour of sickness, danger, death,—and his heart is selfish and corrupt continually. He lacks perfection, therefore, in two particulars; first, in respect to acquittal at the bar of justice, and secondly, in respect to inward purity. That, therefore, which proposes to make him perfect again, must quiet the sense of guilt upon valid grounds, and must produce a holy character. If the method fails in either of these two respects, it fails altogether in making a perfect man.

But how can the moral law, or the ceremonial law, or both united, produce within the human soul the cheerful, liberating, sense of acquittal, and reconciliation with God's justice? Why, the very function and office-work of law, in all its forms, is to condemn and terrify the transgressor; how then can it calm and soothe him? Or, is there anything in the performance of duty,—in the act of obeying law,—that is adapted to produce this result, by taking away guilt? Suppose that a murderer could and should perform a perfectly holy act, would it be any relief to his anguished conscience, if he should offer it as an oblation to Eternal Justice for the sin that is past? if he should plead it as an offset for having killed a man? When we ourselves review the past, and see that we have not kept the law up to the present point in our lives, is the gnawing of the worm to be stopped, by resolving to keep it, and actually keeping it from this point? Can such a use of the law as this is,—can the performance of good works, imaginary or real ones, imperfect or perfect ones,—discharge the office of an atonement, and so make us perfect in the forum of conscience, and fill us with a deep and lasting sense of reconciliation with the offended majesty and justice of God? Plainly not. For there is nothing compensatory, nothing cancelling, nothing of the nature of a satisfaction of justice, in the best obedience that was ever rendered to moral law, by saint, angel, or seraph. Because the creature owes the whole. He is obligated from the very first instant of his existence, onward and evermore, to love God supremely, and to obey him perfectly in every act and element of his being. Therefore, the perfectly obedient saint, angel, and seraph must each say: "I am an unprofitable servant, I have done only that which it was my duty to do; I can make no amends for past failures; I can do no work that is meritorious and atoning." Obedience to law, then, by a creature, and still less by a sinner, can never atone for the sins that are past; can never make the guilty perfect "in things pertaining to conscience." And if a man, in this indirect and roundabout manner, neglects the provisions of the gospel, neglects the oblation of Jesus Christ, and betakes himself to the discharge of his own duty as a substitute therefor, he only finds that the flame burns hotter, and the fang of the worm is sharper. If he looks to the moral law in any form, and by any method, that he may get quit of his remorse and his fears of judgment, the feeling of unreconciliation with justice, and the fearful looking-for of judgment is only made more vivid and deep. Whoever attempts the discharge of duties for the purpose of atoning for his sins takes a direct method of increasing the pains and perturbations which he seeks to remove. The more he thinks of law, and the more he endeavors to obey it for the purpose of purchasing the pardon of past transgression, the more wretched does he become. Look into the lacerated conscience of Martin Luther before he found the Cross, examine the anxiety and gloom of Chalmers before he saw the Lamb of God, for proof that this is so. These men, at first, were most earnest in their use of the law in order to re-instate themselves in right relations with God's justice. But the more they toiled in this direction, the less they succeeded. Burning with inward anguish, and with God's arrows sticking fast in him, shall the transgressor get relief from the attribute of Divine justice, and the qualities of law? Shall the ten commandments of Sinai, in any of their forms or uses, send a cooling and calming virtue through the hot conscience? With these kindling flashes in his guilt-stricken spirit, shall he run into the very identical fire that kindled them? Shall he try to quench them in that "Tophet which is ordained of old; which is made deep and large; the pile of which is fire and much wood, and the breath of the Lord like a stream of brimstone doth kindle it?" And yet such is, in reality, the attempt of every man who, upon being convicted in his conscience of guilt before God, endeavors to attain peace by resolutions to alter his course of conduct, and strenuous endeavors to obey the commands of God,—in short by relying upon the law in any form, as a means of reconciliation. Such is the suicidal effort of every man who substitutes the law for the gospel, and expects to produce within himself the everlasting peace of God, by anything short of the atonement of God.

Let us fix it, then, as a fact, that the feeling of culpability and unreconciliation can never be removed, so long as we do not look entirely away from our own character and works to the mere pure mercy of God in the blood of Christ. The transgressor can never atone for crime by anything that he can suffer, or anything that he can do. He can never establish a ground of justification, a reason why he should be forgiven, by his tears, or his prayers, or his acts. Neither the law, nor his attempts to obey the law, can re-instate him in his original relations to justice, and make him perfect again in respect to his conscience. The ten commandments can never silence his inward misgivings, and his moral fears; for they are given for the very purpose of producing misgivings, and causing fears. "The law worketh wrath." And if this truth and fact be clearly perceived, and boldly acknowledged to his own mind, it will cut him off from all these legal devices and attempts, and will shut him up to the Divine mercy and the Divine promise in Christ, where alone he is safe.

We have thus seen that one of the two things necessary in order that apostate man may become perfect again,—viz., the pacification of his conscience,—cannot be obtained in and by the law, in any of its forms or uses. Let us now examine the other thing necessary in order to human perfection, and see what the law can do towards it.

The other requisite, in order that fallen man may become perfect again, is a holy heart and will. Can the moral law originate this? That we may rightly answer the question, let us remember that a holy will is one that keeps the law of God spontaneously and that a perfect heart is one that sends forth holy affections and pure thoughts as naturally as the sinful heart sends forth unholy affections and impure thoughts. A holy will, like an evil will, is a wonderful and wonderfully fertile power. It does not consist in an ability to make a few or many separate resolutions of obedience to the divine law, but in being itself one great inclination and determination continually and mightily going forth. A holy will, therefore, is one that from its very nature and spontaneity seeks God, and the glory of God. It does not even need to make a specific resolution to obey; any more than an affectionate child needs to resolve to obey its father.

In like manner, a perfect and holy heart is a far more profound and capacious thing than men who have never seriously tried to obtain it deem it to foe. It does not consist in the possession of a few or many holy thoughts mixed with some sinful ones, or in having a few or many holy desires together with some corrupt ones. A perfect heart is one undivided agency, and does not produce, as the imperfectly sanctified heart of the Christian does, fruits of holiness and fruits of sin, holy thoughts and unholy thoughts. It is itself a root and centre of holiness, and nothing but goodness springs up from it. The angels of God are totally holy. Their wills are unceasingly going forth towards Him with ease and delight; their hearts are unintermittently gushing out emotions of love, and feelings of adoration, and thoughts of reverence, and therefore the song that they sing is unceasing, and the smoke of their incense ascendeth forever and ever.

Such is the holy will, and the perfect heart, which fallen man must obtain in order to be fit for heaven. To this complexion must he come at last. And now we ask: Can the law generate all this excellence within the human soul? In order to answer this question, we must consider the nature of law, and the manner of its operation. The law, as antithetic to the gospel, and as the word is employed in the text, is in its nature mandatory and minatory. It commands, and it threatens. This is the style of its operation. Can a perfect heart be originated in a sinner by these two methods? Does the stern behest, "Do this or die," secure his willing and joyful obedience? On the contrary, the very fact that the law of God comes up before him coupled thus with a threatening evinces that his aversion and hostility are most intense. As the Apostle says, "The law is not made for a righteous man; but for the lawless and disobedient, for the ungodly and for sinners." Were man, like the angels on high, sweetly obedient to the Divine will, there would be no arming of law with terror, no proclamation of ten commandments amidst thunderings and lightnings. He would be a law unto himself, as all the heavenly

77

host are,—the law working impulsively within him by its own exceeding lawfulness and beauty. The very fact that God, in the instance of man, is compelled to emphasize the penalty along with the statute,—to say, "Keep my commandments upon pain of eternal death,"—is proof conclusive that man is a rebel, and intensely so.

And now what is the effect of this combination of command and threatening upon the agent? Is he moulded by it? Does it congenially sway and incline him? On the contrary, is he not excited to opposition by it? When the commandment "comes," loaded down with menace and damnation, does not sin "revive," as the Apostle affirms?[1] Arrest the transgressor in the very act of disobedience, and ring in his ears the "Thou shalt not" of the decalogue, and does he find that the law has the power to alter his inclination, to overcome his carnal mind, and make him perfect in holiness? On the contrary, the more you ply him with the stern command, and the more you emphasize the awful threatening, the more do you make him conscious of inward sin, and awaken his depravity. "The law,"—as St. Paul affirms in a very remarkable text,—"is the strength of sin,[2]" instead of being its destruction. Nay, he had not even ([Greek: te]) known sin, but by the law: for he had not known lust, except the law had said, "Thou shalt not lust." The commandment stimulates instead of extirpating his hostility to the Divine government; and so long as the mere command, and the mere threat,—which, as the hymn tells us, is all the law can do,—are brought to bear, the depravity of the rebellious heart becomes more and more apparent, and more and more intensified.

There is no more touching poem in all literature than that one in which the pensive and moral Schiller portrays the struggle of an ingenuous youth who would find the source of moral purification in the moral law; who would seek the power that can transform him, in the mere imperatives of his conscience, and the mere struggling and spasms of his own will. He represents him as endeavoring earnestly and long to feel the force of obligation, and as toiling sedulously to school himself into virtue, by the bare power, by the dead lift, of duty. But the longer he tries, the more he loathes the restraints of law. Virtue, instead of growing lovely to him, becomes more and more severe, austere, and repellant. His life, as the Scripture phrases it, is "under law," and not under love. There is nothing spontaneous, nothing willing, nothing genial in his religion. He does not enjoy religion, but he endures religion. Conscience does not, in the least, renovate his will, but merely checks it, or goads it. He becomes wearied and worn, and conscious that after all his self-schooling he is the same creature at heart, in his disposition and affections, that he was at the commencement of the effort, he cries out, "O Virtue, take back thy crown, and let me sin."[3] The tired and disgusted soul would once more do a spontaneous thing.

Was, then, that which is good made death unto this youth, by a Divine arrangement? Is this the original and necessary relation which law sustains to the will and affections of an accountable creature? Must the pure and holy law of God, from the very nature of things, be a weariness and a curse? God forbid. But sin that it might appear sin, working death in the sinner by that which is good,—that sin by the commandment might become, might be seen to be, exceeding sinful. The law is like a chemical test. It eats into sin enough to show what sin is, and there stops. The lunar caustic bites into the dead flesh of the mortified limb; but there is no healing virtue in the lunar caustic. The moral law makes no inward alterations in a sinner. In its own distinctive and proper action upon the heart and will of an apostate being, it is fitted only to elicit and exasperate his existing enmity. It can, therefore, no more be a source of sanctification, than it can be of justification.

Of what use, then, is the law to a fallen man?—some one will ask. Why is the commandment enunciated in the Scriptures, and why is the Christian ministry perpetually preaching it to men dead in trespasses and sins? If the law can sub-due no man's obstinate will, and can renovate no man's corrupt heart,—if it can make nothing perfect in human character,—then, "wherefore serveth the law?" "It was added because of transgressions,"—says the Apostle in answer to this very question.[4] It is preached and forced home in order to detect sin, but not to remove it; to bring men to a consciousness of the evil of their hearts, but not to change their hearts. "For," continues the Apostle, "if there had been a law given which could have given life"—which could produce a transformation of charac-ter,—"then verily righteousness should have been by the law," It is not because the stern and threatening commandment can impart spiritual vitality to the sin-ner, but because it can produce within him the keen vivid sense of spiritual death, that it is enunciated in the word of God, and proclaimed from the Christian pulpit. The Divine law is waved like a flashing sword before the eyes of man, not because it can make him alive but, because it can slay him, that he may then be made alive, not by the law but by the Holy Ghost,—by the Breath that cometh from the four winds and breathes on the slain.

It is easy to see, by a moment's reflection, that, from the nature of the case, the moral law cannot be a source of spiritual life and sanctification to a soul that has lost these. For law primarily supposes life, supposes an obedient inclination, and therefore does not produce it. It is not the function of any law to impart that moral force, that right disposition of the heart, by which its command is to be obeyed. The State, for example, enacts a law against murder, but this mere en-actment does not, and cannot, produce a benevolent disposition in the citizens of the commonwealth, in case they are destitute of it. How often do we hear the remark, that it is impossible to legislate either morality or religion into the peo-ple. When the Supreme Governor first placed man under the obligations and sovereignty of law, He created him in His own image and likeness: endowing him with that holy heart and right inclination which obeys the law of God with ease and delight. God made man upright, and in this state he could and did keep the commands of God perfectly. If, therefore, by any subsequent action upon their part, mankind have gone out of the primary relationship in which they stood to law, and have by their apostasy lost all holy sympathy with it, and all affectionate disposition to obey it, it only remains for the law (not to change along with them, but) to continue immutably the same pure and righteous thing, and to say, "Obey perfectly, and thou shalt live; disobey in a single instance, and thou shalt die."

But the text teaches us, that although the law can make no sinful man perfect, either upon the side of justification, or of sanctification, "the bringing in of a bet-ter hope" can. This hope is the evangelic hope,—the yearning desire, and the humble trust,—to be forgiven through the atonement of the Lord Jesus Christ, and to be sanctified by the indwelling power of the Holy Ghost. A simple, but a most powerful thing! Does the law, in its abrupt and terrible operation in my conscience, start out the feeling of guiltiness until I throb with anguish, and moral fear? I hope, I trust, I ask, to be pardoned through the blood of the Eternal Son of God my Redeemer. I will answer all these accusations of law and conscience, by pleading what my Lord has done.

Again, does the law search me, and probe me, and elicit me, and reveal me, until I would shrink out of the sight of God and of myself? I hope, I trust, I ask, to be made pure as the angels, spotless as the seraphim, by the transforming grace of the Holy Spirit. This confidence in Christ's Person and Work is the anchor,—an anchor that was never yet wrenched from the clefts of the Rock of Ages, and never will be through the aeons of aeons. By this hope, which goes away from self, and goes away from the law, to Christ's oblation and the Holy Spirit's energy, we do indeed draw very nigh to God,—"heart to heart, spirit to spirit, life to life."

1. The unfolding of this text of Scripture shows, in the first place, the importance of having a distinct and discriminating conception of law, and especially of its proper function in reference to a sinful being. Very much is gained when we understand precisely what the moral law, as taught in the Scriptures, and written in our consciences, can do, and cannot do, towards our salvation. It can do nothing positively and efficiently. It cannot extinguish a particle of our guilt, and it cannot purge away a particle of our corruption. Its operation is wholly negative and preparatory. It is merely a schoolmaster to conduct us to Christ. And the more definitely this truth and fact is fixed in our minds, the more intelligently shall we proceed in our use of law and conscience.

2. In the second place, the unfolding of this text shows the importance of using the law faithfully and fearlessly within its own limits; and in accordance with its proper function. It is frequently asked what the sinner shall do in the work of salvation. The answer is nigh thee, in thy mouth, and in thy heart. Be continually applying the law of God to your personal character and conduct. Keep an active and a searching conscience within your sinful soul. Use the high, broad, and strict commandment of God as an instrumentality by which all ease, and all indifference, in sin shall be banished from the breast. Employ all this apparatus of torture, as perhaps it may seem to you in some sorrowful hours, and break up that moral drowze and lethargy which is ruining so many souls. And then cease this work, the instant you have experimentally found out that the law reaches a limit beyond which it cannot go,—that it forgives none of the sins which it detects, produces no change in the heart whose vileness it reveals, and makes no lost sinner perfect again. Having used the law legitimately, for purposes of illumination and conviction merely, leave it forever as a source of justification and sanctification, and seek these in Christ's atonement, and the Holy Spirit's gracious operation in the heart. Then sin shall not have dominion over you; for you shall not be under law, but under grace. After that faith is come, ye are no longer under a schoolmaster. For ye are then the children of God by faith in Christ Jesus.[5]

How simple are the terms of salvation! But then they presuppose this work of the law,—this guilt-smitten conscience, and this wearying sense of bondage to sin. It is easy for a thirsty soul to drink down the draught of cold water. Nothing is simpler, nothing is more grateful to the sensations. But suppose that the soul is satiated, and is not a thirsty one. Then, nothing is more forced and repelling than this same draught. So is it with the provisions of the gospel. Do we feel ourselves to be guilty beings; do we hunger, and do we thirst for the expiation of our sins? Then the blood of Christ is drink indeed, and his flesh is meat with emphasis. But are we at ease and self-contented? Then nothing is more distasteful than the terms of salvation. Christ is a root out of dry ground. And so long as we remain in this unfeeling and torpid state, salvation is an utter impossibility. The seed of the gospel cannot germinate and grow upon a rock.

[Note 1: Rom. vii. 9-12.] *[Note 2: 1 Cor. xv. 56.]* *[Note 3: SCHILLER: Der Kampf.]*
[Note 4: Galatians iii. 19.] *[Note 5: Galatians iii. 25, 26.]*

X - Self-Scrutiny in God's Presence

ISAIAH, i. 11.—"Come now, and let us reason together, saith the Lord; though your sins be as scarlet, they shall be as white as snow; though they be red like crimson, they shall be as wool."

These words were at first addressed to the Church of God. The prophet Isaiah begins his prophecy, by calling upon the heavens and the earth to witness the exceeding sinfulness of God's chosen people. "Hear, O heavens, and give ear O earth: for the Lord hath spoken; I have nourished and brought up children, and they have rebelled against me. The ox knoweth his owner, and the ass his master's crib: but Israel doth not know, my people doth not consider." Such ingratitude and sin as this, he naturally supposes would shock the very heavens and earth.

Then follows a most vehement and terrible rebuke. The elect people of God are called "Sodom," and "Gomorrah." "Hear the word of the Lord ye rulers of Sodom: give ear unto the law of our God ye people of Gomorrah. Why should ye be stricken, any more? ye will revolt more and more." This outflow of holy displeasure would prepare us to expect an everlasting reprobacy of the rebellious and unfaithful Church, but it is strangely followed by the most yearning and melting entreaty ever addressed by the Most High to the creatures of His footstool: "Come now, and let us reason together, though your sins be as scarlet, they shall be as white as snow; though they be red like crimson, they shall be as wool."

These words have, however, a wider application; and while the unfaithful children of God ought to ponder them long and well, it is of equal importance that "the aliens from the commonwealth of Israel" should reflect upon them, and see their general application to all transgressors, so long as they are under the Gospel dispensation. Let us, then, consider two of the plain lessons taught, in these words of the prophet, to every unpardoned man.

I. The text represents God as saying to the transgressor of his law, "Come and let us reason together." The first lesson to be learned, consequently, is the duty of examining our moral character and conduct, along with God.

When a responsible being has made a wrong use of his powers, nothing is more reasonable than that he should call himself to account for this abuse. Nothing, certainly, is more necessary. There can be no amendment for the future, until the past has been cared for. But that this examination may be both thorough and profitable, it must be made in company with the Searcher of hearts.

For there are always two beings who are concerned with sin; the being who commits it, and the Being against whom it is committed. We sin, indeed, against ourselves; against our own conscience, and against our own best interest. But we sin in a yet higher, and more terrible sense, against Another than ourselves, compared with whose majesty all of our faculties and interests, both in time and eternity, are altogether nothing and vanity. It is not enough, therefore, to refer our sin to the law written on the heart, and there stop. We must ultimately pass beyond conscience itself, to God, and say, "Against Thee have I sinned." It is not the highest expression of the religious feeling, when we say, "How can I do this great wickedness, and sin against my conscience?" He alone has reached the summit of vision who looks beyond all finite limits, however wide and distant, beyond all finite faculties however noble and elevated, and says, "How can I do this great wickedness, and sin against God?"

Whenever, therefore, an examination is made into the nature of moral evil as it exists in the individual heart, both parties concerned should share in the examination. The soul, as it looks within, should invite the scrutiny of God also, and as fast as it makes discoveries of its transgression and corruption should realize that the Holy One sees also. Such a joint examination as this produces a very keen and clear sense of the evil and guilt of sin. Conscience indeed makes cowards of us all, but when the eye of God is felt to be upon us, it smites us to the ground. "When Thou with rebukes,"—says the Psalmist,—"dost correct man for his iniquity, Thou makest his beauty to consume away like a moth." One great reason why the feeling which the moralist has towards sin is so tame and languid, when compared with the holy abhorrence of the regenerate mind, lies in the fact that he has not contemplated human depravity in company with a sin-hating Jehovah. At the very utmost, he has been shut up merely with a moral sense which he has insulated from its dread ground and support,—the personal character and holy emotions of God. What wonder is it, then, that this finite faculty should lose much of its temper and severity, and though still condemning sin (for it must do this, if it does anything), fails to do it with that spiritual energy which characterizes the conscience when God is felt to be co-present and co-operating. So it is, in other provinces. We feel the guilt of an evil action more sharply, when we know that a fellow-man saw us commit it, than when we know that no one but ourselves is cognizant of the deed. The flush of shame often rises into our face, upon learning accidentally that a fellow-being was looking at us, when we did the wrong action without any blush. How much more criminal, then, do we feel, when distinctly aware that the pure and holy God knows our transgression. How much clearer is our perception of the nature of moral evil, when we investigate it along with Him whose eyes are a flame of fire.

It is, consequently, a very solemn moment, when the human spirit and the Eternal Mind are reasoning together about the inward sinfulness. When the soul is shut up along with the Holy One of Israel, there are great searchings of heart.

Man is honest and anxious at such a time. His usual thoughtlessness and torpidity upon the subject of religion leaves him, and he becomes a serious and deeply-interested creature. Would that the multitudes who listen so languidly to the statements of the pulpit, upon these themes of sin and guilt, might be closeted with the Everlasting Judge, in silence and in solemn reflection. You who have for years been told of sin, but are, perhaps, still as indifferent regarding it as if there were no stain, upon the conscience,—would that you might enter into an examination of yourself, alone with your Maker. Then would you become as serious, and as anxious, as you will be in that moment when you shall be informed that the last hour of your life upon earth has come.

Another effect of this "reasoning together" with God, respecting our character and conduct, is to render our views discriminating. The action of the mind is not only intense, it is also intelligent. Strange as it may sound, it is yet a fact, that a review of our past lives conducted under the eye of God, and with a recognition of His presence and oversight, serves to deliver the mind from confusion and panic, and to fill it with a calm and rational fear. This is of great value. For, when a man begins to be excited upon the subject of religion,—it may be for the first time, in his unreflecting and heedless life,—he is oftentimes terribly excited. He is now brought suddenly into the midst of the most solemn things. That sin of his, the enormity of which he had never seen before, now reveals itself in a most frightful form, and he feels as the murderer does who wakes in the morning and begins to realize that he has killed a man. That holy Being, of whose holiness he had no proper conception, now rises dim and awful before his half-opened inward eye, and he trembles like the pagan before the unknown God whom he ignorantly worships. That eternity, which he had heard spoken of with total indifference, now flashes penal flames in his face. Taken and held in this state of mind, the transgressor is confusedly as well as terribly awakened, and he needs first of all to have this experience clarified, and know precisely for what he is trembling, and why. This panic and consternation must depart, and a calm intelligent anxiety must take its place. But this cannot be, unless the mind turns towards God, and invites His searching scrutiny, and His aid in the search after sin. So long as we shrink away from our Judge, and in upon ourselves, in these hours of conviction,—so long as we deal only with the workings of our own minds, and do not look up and "reason together" with God,—we take the most direct method of producing a blind, an obscure, and a selfish agony. We work ourselves, more and more, into a mere phrenzy of excitement. Some of the most wretched and fanatical experience in the history of the Church is traceable to a solitary self-brooding, in which, after the sense of sin had been awakened, the soul did not discuss the matter with God.

For the character and attributes of God, when clearly seen, repress all fright, and produce that peculiar species of fear which is tranquil because it is deep. Though the soul, in such an hour, is conscious that God is a fearful object of sight for a transgressor, yet it continues to gaze at Him with an eager straining eye. And in so doing, the superficial tremor and panic of its first awakening to the subject of religion passes off, and gives place to an intenser moral feeling, the calmness of which is like the stillness of fascination. Nothing has a finer effect upon a company of awakened minds, than to cause the being and attributes of

God, in all their majesty and purity, to rise like an orb within their horizon; and the individual can do nothing more proper, or more salutary, when once his sin begins to disquiet him, and the inward perturbation commences, than to collect and steady himself, in an act of reflection upon that very Being who abhors sin. Let no man, in the hour of conviction and moral fear, attempt to run away from the Divine holiness. On the contrary, let him rush forward and throw himself down prostrate before that Dread Presence, and plead the merits of the Son of God, before it. He that finds his life shall lose it; but he that loses his life shall find it. Except a corn of wheat fall into the ground and die, it remains a single unproductive corn of wheat; but if it die, it germinates and brings forth much fruit. He who does not avoid a contact between the sin of his soul and the holiness of his God, but on the contrary seeks to have these two things come together, that each may be understood in its own intrinsic nature and quality, takes the only safe course. He finds that, as he knows God more distinctly, he knows himself more distinctly; and though as yet he can see nothing but displeasure in that holy countenance, he is possessed of a well-defined experience. He knows that he is wrong, and his Maker is right; that he is wicked, and that God is holy. He perceives these two fundamental facts with a simplicity, and a certainty, that admits of no debate. The confusion and obscurity of his mind, and particularly the queryings whether these things are so, whether God is so very holy and man is so very sinful, begin to disappear, like a fog when disparted and scattered by sunrise. Objects are seen in their true proportions and meanings; right and wrong, the carnal mind and the spiritual mind, heaven and hell,—all the great contraries that pertain to the subject of religion,—are distinctly understood, and thus the first step is taken towards a better state of things in the soul.

Let no man, then, fear to invite the scrutiny of God, in connection with his own scrutiny of himself. He who deals only with the sense of duty, and the operations of his own mind, will find that these themselves become more dim and indistinct, so long as the process of examination is not conducted in this joint manner; so long as the mind refuses to accept the Divine proposition, "Come now, and let us reason together." He, on the other hand, who endeavors to obtain a clear view of the Being against whom he has sinned, and to feel the full power of His holy eye as well as of His holy law, will find that his sensations and experiences are gaining a wonderful distinctness and intensity that will speedily bring the entire matter to an issue.

II. For then, by the blessing of God, he learns the second lesson taught in the text: viz., that there is forgiveness with God. Though, in this process of joint examination, your sins be found to be as scarlet, they shall be as white as snow; though they be discovered to be red like crimson, they shall be as wool.

If there were no forgiveness of sins, if mercy were not a manifested attribute of God, all self-examination, and especially all this conjoint divine scrutiny, would be a pure torment and a pure gratuity. It is wretchedness to know that we are guilty sinners, but it is the endless torment to know that there is no forgiveness, either here or hereafter. Convince a man that he will never be pardoned, and you shut him up with the spirits in prison. Compel him to examine himself under the eye of his God, while at the same time he has no hope of mercy,—and there would be nothing unjust in this,—and you distress him with the keenest and most living torment of which a rational spirit is capable. Well and natural was it, that the earliest creed of the Christian Church emphasized the doctrine of the Divine Pity; and in all ages the Apostolic Symbol has called upon the guilt-stricken human soul to cry, "I believe in the forgiveness of sins."

We have the amplest assurance in the whole written Revelation of God, but nowhere else, that "there is forgiveness with Him, that He may be feared." "Whoso confesseth and forsaketh his sins shall find mercy;" and only with such an assurance as this from His own lips, could we summon courage to look into our character and conduct, and invite God to do the same. But the text is an exceedingly explicit assertion of this great truth. The very same Being who invites us to reason with Him, and canvass the subject of our criminality, in the very same breath, if we may so speak, assures us that He will forgive all that is found in this examination. And upon such terms, cannot the criminal well afford to examine into his crime? He has a promise beforehand, that if he will but scrutinize and confess his sin it shall be forgiven. God would have been simply and strictly just, had He said to him: "Go down into the depths of thy transgressing spirit, see how wicked thou hast been and still art, and know that in my righteous severity I will never pardon thee, world without end." But instead of this, He says: "Go down into the depths of thy heart, see the transgression and the corruption all along the line of the examination, confess it into my ear, and I will make the scarlet and crimson guilt white in the blood of my own Son." These declarations of Holy Writ, which are a direct verbal statement from the lips of God, and which specify distinctly what He will do and will not do in the matter of sin, teach us that however deeply our souls shall be found to be stained, the Divine pity outruns and exceeds the crime. "For as the heavens are high above the earth, so great is his mercy towards them that fear him. He that spared not his own Son, but delivered him up for us all, how shall he not with him also freely give us all things?" Here upon earth, there is no wickedness that surpasses the pardoning love of God in Christ. The words which Shakspeare puts into the mouth of the remorseful, but impenitent, Danish king are strictly true:

"What if this cursed hand
Were thicker than itself with brother's blood?
Is there not rain enough in the sweet heavens
To wash it white as snow? Whereto serves mercy,
But to confront the visage of offence?" [1]

Anywhere this side of the other world, and at any moment this side of the grave, a sinner, if penitent (but penitence is not always at his control), may obtain forgiveness for all his sins, through Christ's blood of atonement. He must not hope for mercy in the future world, if he neglects it here. There are no acts of pardon passed in the day of judgment. The utterance of Christ in that day is not the utterance, "Thy sins are forgiven thee," but, "Come ye blessed," or "Depart ye cursed." So long, and only so long, as there is life there is hope, and however great may be the conscious criminality of a man while he is under the economy of Redemption, and before he is summoned to render up his last account, let him not despair but hope in Divine grace.

85

Now, he who has seriously "reasoned together" with God, respecting his own character, is far better prepared to find God in the forgiveness of sins, than he is who has merely brooded over his own unhappiness, without any reference to the qualities and claims of his Judge. It has been a plain and personal matter throughout, and having now come to a clear and settled conviction that he is a guilty sinner, he turns directly to the great and good Being who stands immediately before him, and prays to be forgiven, and is forgiven. One reason why the soul so often gropes days and months without finding a sin-pardoning God lies in the fact, that its thoughts and feelings respecting religious subjects, and particularly respecting the state of the heart, have been too vague and indistinct. They have not had an immediate and close reference to that one single Being who is most directly concerned, and who alone can minister to a mind diseased. The soul is wretched, and there may be some sense of sin, but there is no one to go to,—no one to address with an appealing cry. "Oh that I knew where I might find him," is its language. "Oh that I might come even to his seat. Behold I go forward, but he is not there; and backward, but I cannot perceive him." But this groping would cease were there a clear view of God. There might not be peace and a sense of reconciliation immediately; but there would be a distinct conception of the one thing needful in order to salvation. This would banish all other subjects and objects. The eye would be fixed upon the single fact of sin, and the simple fact that none but God can forgive it. The whole inward experience would thus be narrowed down to a focus. Simplicity and intensity would be introduced into the mental state, instead of the previous confusion and vagueness. Soliloquy would end, and prayer, importunate, agonizing prayer, would begin. That morbid and useless self-brooding would cease, and those strong cryings and wrestlings till day-break would commence, and the kingdom of heaven would suffer this violence, and the violent would take it by force. "When I kept silence; my bones waxed old, through my roaring all the day long. For day and night thy hand was heavy upon me; my moisture was turned into the drought of summer. I acknowledged my sin unto thee, and mine iniquity I no longer hid. I said, I will confess my transgressions unto the Lord; and thou forgavest the iniquity of my sin. For this,"—because this is Thy method of salvation,—"shall every one that is godly pray unto thee, in a time when thou mayest be found." (Ps. xxxii. 3-6.)

Self-examination, then, when joined with a distinct recognition of the Divine character, and a conscious sense of God's scrutiny, paradoxical as it may appear, is the surest means of producing a firm conviction in a guilty mind that God is merciful, and is the swiftest way of finding Him to be so. Opposed as the Divine nature is to sin, abhorrent as iniquity is to the pure mind of God, it is nevertheless a fact, that that sinner who goes directly into this Dread Presence with all his sins upon his head, in order to know them, to be condemned and crushed by them, and to confess them, is the one who soonest returns with peace and hope in his soul. For, he discovers that God is as cordial and sincere in His offer to forgive, as He is in His threat to punish; and having, to his sorrow, felt the reality and power of the Divine anger, he now to his joy feels the equal reality and power of the Divine love.

And this is the one great lesson which every man must learn, or perish forever. The truthfulness of God, in every respect, and in all relations,—His strict fidelity to His word, both under the law and under the gospel,—is a quality of which every one must have a vivid knowledge and certainty, in order to salvation. Men perish through unbelief. He that doubteth is damned. To illustrate. Men pass through this life doubting and denying God's abhorrence of sin, and His determination to punish it forever and ever. Under the narcotic and stupefying influence of this doubt and denial, they remain in sin, and at death go over into the immediate presence of God, only to discover that all His statements respecting His determination upon this subject are true,—awfully and hopelessly true. They then spend an eternity, in bewailing their infatuation in dreaming, while here upon earth, that the great and holy God did not mean what he said.

Unbelief, again, tends to death in the other direction, though it is far less liable to result in it. The convicted and guilt-smitten man sometimes doubts the truthfulness of the Divine promise in Christ. He spends days of darkness and nights of woe, because he is unbelieving in regard to God's compassion, and readiness to forgive a penitent; and when, at length, the light of the Divine countenance breaks upon him, he wonders that he was so foolish and slow of heart to believe all that God himself had said concerning the "multitude" of his tender mercies. Christian and Hopeful lay long and needlessly in the dungeon of Doubting Castle, until the former remembered that the key to all the locks was in his bosom, and had been all the while. They needed only to take God at his word. The anxious and fearful soul must believe the Eternal Judge implicitly, when he says: "I will justify thee through the blood of Christ." God is truthful under the gospel, and under the law; in His promise of mercy, and in His threatening of eternal woe. And "if we believe not, yet He abideth faithful; He cannot deny Himself." He hath promised, and He hath threatened; and, though heaven and earth pass away, one jot or one tittle of that promise shall not fail in the case of those who confidingly trust it, nor shall one iota or scintilla of the threatening fail in the instance of those who have recklessly and rashly disbelieved it.

In respect, then, to both sides of the revelation of the Divine character,—in respect to the threatening and the promise,—men need to have a clear perception, and an unwavering belief. He that doubteth in either direction is damned. He who does not believe that God is truthful, when He declares that He will "punish iniquity, transgression and sin," and that those upon the left hand shall "go away into everlasting punishment," will persist in sin until he passes the line of probation and be lost. And he who does not believe that God is truthful, when He declares that He will forgive scarlet and crimson sins through the blood of Christ, will be overcome by despair and be also lost. But he who believes both Divine statements with equal certainty, and perceives both facts with distinct vision, will be saved.

From these two lessons of the text, we deduce the following practical directions:

1. First: In all states of religious anxiety, we should betake ourselves instantly and directly to God. There is no other refuge for the human soul but God in Christ, and if this fails us, we must renounce all hope here and hereafter.

"If this fail,
The pillared firmament is rottenness,

And earth's base built on stubble." [2]

We are, therefore, from the nature of the case, shut up to this course. Suppose the religious anxiety arise from a sense of sin, and the fear of retribution. God is the only Being that can forgive sins. To whom, then, can such an one go but unto Him? Suppose the religious anxiety arises from a sense of the perishing nature of earthly objects, and the soul feels as if all the foundation and fabric of its hope and comfort were rocking into irretrievable ruin. God is the only Being who can help in this crisis. In either or in any case,—be it the anxiety of the unforgiven, or of the child of God,—whatever be the species of mental sorrow, the human soul is by its very circumstances driven to its Maker, or else driven to destruction.

What more reasonable course, therefore, than to conform to the necessities of our condition. The principal part of wisdom is to take things as they are, and act accordingly. Are we, then, sinners, and in fear for the final result of our life? Though it may seem to us like running into fire, we must nevertheless betake ourselves first and immediately to that Being who hates and punishes sin. Though we see nothing but condemnation and displeasure in those holy eyes, we must nevertheless approach them just and simply as we are. We must say with king David in a similar case, when he had incurred the displeasure of God: "I am in a great strait; [yet] let me fall into the hand of the Lord, for very great are his mercies" (1 Chron. xx. 13). We must suffer the intolerable brightness to blind and blast us in our guiltiness, and let there be an actual contact between the sin of our soul and the holiness of our God. If we thus proceed, in accordance with the facts of our case and our position, we shall meet with a great and joyful surprise. Flinging ourselves helpless, and despairing of all other help,—rashly, as it will seem to us, flinging ourselves off from the position where we now are, and upon which we must inevitably perish, we shall find ourselves, to our surprise and unspeakable joy, caught in everlasting, paternal arms. He who loses his life,—he who dares to lose his life,—shall find it.

2. Secondly: In all our religious anxiety, we should make a full and plain statement of everything to God. God loves to hear the details of our sin, and our woe. The soul that pours itself out as water will find that it is not like water spilt upon the ground, which cannot be gathered up again. Even when the story is one of shame and remorse, we find it to be mental relief, patiently and without any reservation or palliation, to expose the whole not only to our own eye but to that of our Judge. For, to this very thing have we been invited. This is precisely the "reasoning together" which God proposes to us. God has not offered clemency to a sinful world, with the expectation or desire that there be on the part of those to whom it is offered, such a stinted and meagre confession, such a glozing over and diminution of sin, as to make that clemency appear a very small matter. He well knows the depth and the immensity of the sin which He proposes to pardon, and has made provision accordingly. In the phrase of Luther, it is no painted sinner who is to be forgiven, and it is no painted Saviour who is offered. The transgression is deep and real, and the atonement is deep and real. The crime cannot be exaggerated, neither can the expiation. He, therefore, who makes the plainest and most child-like statement of himself to God, acts most in accordance with the mind, and will, and gospel of God. If man only be hearty, full, and unreserved in confession, he will find God to be hearty, full, and unreserved in absolution.

Man is not straitened upon the side of the Divine mercy. The obstacle in the way of his salvation is in himself; and the particular, fatal obstacle consists in the fact that he does not feel that he needs mercy. God in Christ stands ready to pardon, but man the sinner stands up before Him like the besotted criminal in our courts of law, with no feeling upon the subject. The Judge assures him that He has a boundless grace and clemency to bestow, but the stolid hardened man is not even aware that he has committed a dreadful crime, and needs grace and clemency. There is food in infinite abundance, but no hunger upon the part of man. The water of life is flowing by in torrents, but men have no thirst. In this state of things, nothing can be done, but to pass a sentence of condemnation. God cannot forgive a being who does not even know that he needs to be forgiven. Knowledge then, self-knowledge, is the great requisite; and the want of it is the cause of perdition. This "reasoning together" with God, respecting our past and present character and conduct, is the first step to be taken by any one who would make preparation for eternity. As soon as we come to a right understanding of our lost and guilty condition, we shall cry: "Be merciful to me a sinner; create within me a clean heart, O God." Without such an understanding,—such an intelligent perception of our sin and guilt,—we never shall, and we never can.

[**Note 1:** SHAKSPEARE: Hamlet, Act iii. Sc. 4.]
[**Note 2:** MILTON: Comus, 597-599.]

XI - Sin Is Spiritual Slavery

John viii. 34.—*"Jesus answered them, Verily, verily I say unto you, whosoever committeth sin is the servant of sin."*

The word [Greek: doulos] which is translated "servant," in the text, literally signifies a slave; and the thought which our Lord actually conveyed to those who heard Him is, "Whosoever committeth sin is the slave of sin." The apostle Peter, in that second Epistle of his which is so full of terse and terrible description of the effects of unbridled sensuality upon the human will, expresses the same truth. Speaking of the influence of those corrupting and licentious men who have "eyes full of adultery, and that cannot cease from sin," he remarks that while they promise their dupes "liberty, they themselves are the servants [slaves] of corruption: for of whom a man is overcome, of the same is he brought in bondage."

Such passages as these, of which there are a great number in the Bible, direct attention to the fact that sin contains an element of servitude,—that in the very act of transgressing the law of God there is a reflex action of the human will upon itself, whereby it becomes less able than before to keep that law. Sin is the suicidal action of the human will. It destroys the power to do right, which is man's true freedom. The effect of vicious habit in diminishing a man's ability to resist temptation is proverbial. But what is habit but a constant repetition of wrong decisions, every single one of which reacts upon the faculty that put them forth, and renders it less strong and less energetic, to do the contrary. Has the old debauchee, just tottering into hell, as much power of active resistance against the sin which has now ruined him, as the youth has who is just beginning to run that awful career? Can any being do a wrong act, and be as sound in his will and as spiritually strong, after it, as he was before it? Did that abuse of free agency by Adam, whereby the sin of the race was originated, leave the agent as it found him,—uninjured and undebilitated in his voluntary power?

The truth and fact is, that sin in and by its own nature and operations, tends to destroy all virtuous force, all holy energy, in any moral being. The excess of will to sin is the same as the defect of will to holiness. The degree of intensity with which any man loves and inclines to evil is the measure of the amount of power to good which he has thereby lost. And if the intensity be total, then the loss is entire. Total depravity carries with it total impotence and helplessness. The more carefully we observe the workings of our own wills, the surer will be our conviction that they can ruin themselves. We shall indeed find that they cannot be forced, or ruined from the outside. But, if we watch the influence upon the will itself, of its own wrong decisions, its own yielding to temptations, we shall discover that the voluntary faculty may be ruined from within; may be made impotent to good by its own action; may surrender itself with such an intensity and entireness to appetite, passion, and self-love, that it becomes unable to reverse itself, and overcome its own wrong disposition and direction. And yet there is no compulsion, from first to last, in the process. The man follows himself. He pursues his own inclination. He has his own way and does as he pleases. He loves what he inclines to love, and hates what he inclines to hate. Neither God, nor the world, nor Satan himself, force him to do wrong. Sin is the most spontaneous of self-motion. But self-motion has consequences as much as any other motion. Because transgression is a self-determined act, it does not follow that it has no reaction and results, but leaves the will precisely as it found it. It is strictly true that man was not necessitated to apostatize; but it is equally true that if by his own self-decision he should apostatize, he could not then and afterwards be as he was before. He would lose a knowledge of God and divine things which he could never regain of himself. And he would lose a spiritual power which he could never again recover of himself. The bondage of which Christ speaks, when He says, "Whosoever committeth sin is the slave of sin," is an effect within the soul itself of an unforced act of self-will, and therefore is as truly guilt as any other result or product of self-will,—as spiritual blindness, or spiritual hardness, or any other of the qualities of sin. Whatever springs from will, we are responsible for. The drunkard's bondage and powerlessness issues from his own inclination and self-indulgence, and therefore the bondage and impotence is no excuse for his vice. Man's inability to love God supremely results from his intense self-will and self-love; and therefore his impotence is a part and element of his sin, and not an excuse for it.

"If weakness may excuse,
What murderer, what traitor, parricide,
Incestuous, sacrilegious, may not plead it?
All wickedness is weakness." [1]

The doctrine, then, which is taught in the text, is the truth that sin is spiritual slavery; and it is to the proof and illustration of this position that we invite attention.

The term "spiritual" is too often taken to mean unreal, fanciful, figurative. For man is earthly in his views as well as in his feelings, and therefore regards visible and material things as the emphatic realities. Hence he employs material objects as the ultimate standard, by which he measures the reality of all other things. The natural man has more consciousness of his body, than he has of his soul; more sense of this world, than of the other. Hence we find that the carnal man expresses his conception of spiritual things, by transferring to them, in a weak and secondary signification, words which he applies in a strong and vivid way only to material objects. He speaks of the "joy" of the spirit, but it is not such a reality for him as is the "joy" of the body. He speaks of the "pain" of the spirit, but it has not such a poignancy for him as that anguish which thrills through his muscles and nerves. He knows that the "death" of the body is a terrible event, but transfers the word "death" to the spirit with a vague and feeble meaning, not realizing that the second death is more awful than the first, and is accompanied with a spiritual distress compared with which, the sharpest agony of material dissolution would be a relief. He understands what is meant by the "life" of the body, but when he hears the "eternal life" of the spirit spoken of, or when he reads of it in the Bible, it is with the feeling that it cannot be so real and lifelike as that vital principle whose currents impart vigor and warmth to his bodily frame. And yet, the life of the spirit is more intensely real than the life of the body is; for it has power to overrule and absorb it. Spiritual life, when in full play, is bliss ineffable. It translates man into the third heavens, where the fleshly life is lost sight of entirely, and the being, like St. Paul, does not know whether he is in the body or out of the body.

The natural mind is deceived. Spirit has in it more of reality than matter has; because it is an immortal and indestructible essence, while matter is neither. Spiritual things are more real than visible things; because they are eternal, and eternity is more real than time. Statements respecting spiritual objects, therefore, are more solemnly true than any that relate to material things. Invisible and spiritual realities, therefore, are the standard by which all others should be tried; and human language when applied to them, instead of expressing too much, expresses too little. The imagery and phraseology by which the Scriptures describe the glory of God, the excellence of holiness, and the bliss of heaven, on the one side, and the sinfulness of sin with the woe of hell, on the other, come short of the sober and actual matter of fact.

We should, therefore, beware of the error to which in our unspirituality we are specially liable; and when we hear Christ assert that "whosoever committeth sin is the slave of sin," we should believe and know, that these words are not extravagant, and contain no subtrahend,—that they indicate a self-enslavement of the human will which is so real, so total, and so absolute, as to necessitate the renewing grace of God in order to deliverance from it.

This bondage to sin may be discovered by every man. It must be discovered, before one can cry, "Save me or I perish." It must be discovered, before one can feelingly assent to Christ's words, "Without me ye can do nothing." It must be discovered, before one can understand the Christian paradox, "When I am weak, then am I strong." To aid the mind, in coming to the conscious experience of the truth taught in the text, we remark:

I. Sin is spiritual slavery, if viewed in reference to man's sense of obligation to be perfectly holy.

The obligation to be holy, just, and good, as God is, rests upon every rational being. Every man knows, or may know, that he ought to be perfect as his Father in heaven is perfect, and that he is a debtor to this obligation until he has fully met it. Hence even the holiest of men are conscious of sin, because they are not completely up to the mark of this high calling of God. For, the sense of this obligation is an exceeding broad one,—like the law itself which it includes and enforces. The feeling of duty will not let us off, with the performance of only a part of our duty. Its utterance is: "Verily I say unto you, till heaven and earth pass, one jot or one tittle shall in no wise pass from the law till all be fulfilled." Law spreads itself over the whole surface and course of our lives, and insists imperatively that every part and particle of them be pure and holy.

Again, this sense of obligation to be perfect as God is perfect, is exceedingly deep. It is the most profound sense of which man is possessed, for it outlives all others. The feeling of duty to God's law remains in a man's mind either to bless him or to curse him, when all other feelings depart. In the hour of death, when all the varied passions and experiences which have engrossed the man his whole lifetime are dying out of the soul, and are disappearing, one after another, like signal-lights in the deepening darkness, this one particular feeling of what he owes to the Divine and the Eternal law remains behind, and grows more vivid, and painful, as all others grow dimmer and dimmer. And therefore it is, that in this solemn hour man forgets whether he has been happy or unhappy, successful or unsuccessful, in the world, and remembers only that he has been a sinner in it. And therefore it is, that a man's thoughts, when he is upon his death-bed, do not settle upon his worldly matters, but upon his sin. It is because the human conscience is the very core and centre of the human being, and its sense of obligation to be holy is deeper than all other senses and sensations, that we hear the dying man say what the living and prosperous man is not inclined to say: "I have been wicked; I have been a sinner in the earth."

Now it might seem, at first sight, that this broad, deep, and abiding sense of obligation would be sufficient to overcome man's love of sin, and bring him up to the discharge of duty,—would be powerful enough to subdue his self-will. Can it be that this strong and steady draft of conscience,—strong and steady as gravitation,—will ultimately prove ineffectual? Is not truth mighty, and must it not finally prevail, to the pulling down of the stronghold which Satan has in the human heart? So some men argue. So some men claim, in opposition to the doctrine of Divine influences and of regeneration by the Holy Ghost.

We are willing to appeal to actual experience, in order to settle the point. And we affirm in the outset, that exactly in proportion as a man hears the voice of conscience sounding its law within his breast, does he become aware, not of the strength but, of the bondage of his will, and that in proportion as this sense of obligation to be perfectly holy rises in his soul, all hope or expectation of ever becoming so by his own power sets in thick night.

In our careless unawakened state, which is our ordinary state, we sin on from day to day, just as we live on from day to day, without being distinctly aware of it. A healthy man does not go about, holding his fingers upon his wrist, and counting every pulse; and neither does a sinful man, as he walks these streets and transacts all this business, think of and sum up the multitude of his transgressions. And yet, that pulse all the while beats none the less; and yet, that will all the while transgresses none the less. So long as conscience is asleep, sin is pleasant. The sinful activity goes on without notice, we are happy in sin, and we do not feel that it is slavery of the will. Though the chains are actually about us, yet they do not gall us. In this condition, which is that of every unawakened sinner, we are not conscious of the "bondage of corruption." In the phrase of St. Paul, "we are alive without the law." We have no feeling sense of duty, and of course have no feeling sense of sin. And it is in this state of things, that arguments are framed to prove the mightiness of mere conscience, and the power of bare truth and moral obligation, over the perverse human heart and will.

But the Spirit of God awakens the conscience; that sense of obligation to be perfectly holy which has hitherto slept now starts up, and begins to form an estimate of what has been done in reference to it. The man hears the authoritative and startling law: "Thou shalt be perfect, as God is." And now, at this very instant and point, begins the consciousness of enslavement,—of being, in the expressive phrase of Scripture, "sold under sin." Now the commandment "comes," shows us first what we ought to be and then what we actually are, and we "die."[2] All moral strength dies out of us. The muscle has been cut by the sword of truth, and the limb drops helpless by the side. For, we find that the obligation is immense. It extends to all our outward acts; and having covered the whole of this great surface, it then strikes inward and reaches to every thought of the mind, and every emotion of the heart, and every motive of the will. We discover that we are under obligation at every conceivable point in our being and in our history, but that we have not met obligation at a single point. When we see that the law of God is broad and deep, and that sin is equally broad and deep within us; when we learn that we have never thought one single holy thought, nor felt one single holy feeling, nor done one single holy deed, because self-love is the root and principle of all our work, and we have never purposed or desired to please God by any one of our actions; when we find that everything has been required, and that absolutely nothing has been done, that we are bound to be perfectly holy this very instant, and as matter of fact are totally sinful, we know in a most affecting manner that "whosoever committeth sin is the slave of sin".

But suppose that after this disheartening and weakening discovery of the depth and extent of our sinfulness, we proceed to take the second step, and attempt to extirpate it. Suppose that after coming to a consciousness of all this obligation resting upon us, we endeavor to comply with it. This renders us still more painfully sensible of the truth of our Saviour's declaration. Even the regenerated man, who in this endeavor has the aid of God, is mournfully conscious that sin is the enslavement of the human will. Though he has been freed substantially, he feels that the fragments of the chains are upon him still. Though the love of God is the predominant principle within him, yet the lusts and propensities of the old nature continually start up like devils, and tug at the spirit, to drag it down to its old bondage. But that man who attempts to overcome sin, without first crying, "Create within me a clean heart, O God," feels still more deeply that sin is spiritual slavery. When he comes to know sin in reference to the obligation to be perfectly holy, it is with vividness and hopelessness. He sees distinctly that he ought to be a perfectly good being instantaneously. This point is clear. But instead of looking up to the hills whence cometh his help, he begins, in a cold legal and loveless temper, to draw upon his own resources. The first step is to regulate his external conduct by the Divine law. He tries to put a bridle upon his tongue, and to walk carefully before his fellow-men. He fails to do even this small outside thing, and is filled with discouragement and despondency.

But the sense of duty reaches beyond the external conduct, and the law of God pierces like the two-edged sword of an executioner, and discerns the thoughts and motives of the heart. Sin begins to be seen in its relation to the inner man, and he attempts again to reform and change the feelings and affections of his soul. He strives to wring the gall of bitterness out of his own heart, with his own hands. But he fails utterly. As he resolves, and breaks his resolutions; as he finds evil thoughts and feelings continually coming up from the deep places of his heart; he discovers his spiritual impotence,—his lack of control over what is deepest, most intimate, and most fundamental in his own character,—and cries out: "I am a slave, I am a slave to myself."

If then, you would know from immediate consciousness that "whosoever committeth sin is the slave of sin," simply view sin in the light of that obligation to be perfectly pure and holy which necessarily, and forever, rests upon a responsible being. If you would know that spiritual slavery is no extravagant and unmeaning phrase, but denotes a most real and helpless bondage, endeavor to get entirely rid of sin, and to be perfect as the spirits of just men made perfect.

II. Sin is spiritual slavery, if viewed in reference to the aspirations of the human soul.

Theology makes a distinction between common and special grace,—between those ordinary influences of the Divine Spirit which rouse the conscience, and awaken some transient aspirations after religion, and those extraordinary influences which actually renew the heart and will. In speaking, then, of the aspirations of the human soul, reference is had to all those serious impressions, and those painful anxieties concerning salvation, which require to be followed up by a yet mightier power from God, to prevent their being entirely suppressed again, as they are in a multitude of instances, by the strong love of sin and the world. For though man has fallen into a state of death in trespasses and sins, so that if cut off from every species of Divine influence, and left entirely to himself, he would never reach out after anything but the sin which he loves, yet through the common influences of the Spirit of Grace, and the ordinary workings of a rational nature not yet reprobated, he is at times the subject of internal stirrings and aspirations that indicate the greatness and glory of the heights whence he fell. Under the power of an awakened conscience, and feeling the emptiness of the world, and the aching void within him, man wishes for something better than he has, or than he is. The minds of the more thoughtful of the ancient pagans were the subjects of these impulses, and aspirations; and they confess their utter inability to realize them. They are expressed upon every page of Plato, and it is not surprising that some of the Christian Fathers should have deemed Platonism, as well as Judaism, to be a preparation for Christianity, by its bringing man to a sense of his need of redemption. And it would stimulate Christians in their efforts to give revealed religion to the heathen, did they ponder the fact which the journals of the missionary sometimes disclose, that the Divine Spirit is brooding with His common and preparatory influence over the chaos of Paganism, and that here and there the heathen mind faintly aspires to be freed from the bondage of corruption,—that dim stirrings, impulses, and wishes for deliverance, are awake in the dark heart of Paganism, but that owing to the strength and inveteracy of sin in that heart they will prove ineffectual to salvation, unless the gospel is preached, and the Holy Spirit is specially poured out in answer to the prayers of Christians.

Now, all these phenomena in the human soul go to show the rigid bondage of sin, and to prove that sin has an element of servitude in it. For when these impulses, wishes, and aspirations are awakened, and the man discovers that he is unable to realize them in actual character and conduct, he is wretchedly and thoroughly conscious that "whosoever committeth sin is the slave of sin." The immortal, heaven-descended spirit, feeling the kindling touch of truth and of the Holy Ghost, thrills under it, and essays to soar. But sin hangs heavy upon it, and it cannot lift itself from the earth. Never is man so sensible of his enslavement and his helplessness, as when he has a wish but has no will.[3]

Look, for illustration, at the aspirations of the drunkard to be delivered from the vice that easily besets him. In his sober moments, they come thick and fast, and during his sobriety, and while under the lashings of conscience, he wishes, nay, even longs, to be freed from drunkenness. It may be, that under the impulse of these aspirations he resolves never to drink again. It may be, that amid the buoyancy that naturally accompanies the springing of hope and longing in the human soul, he for a time seems to himself to be actually rising up from his "wallowing in the mire," and supposes that he shall soon regain his primitive condition of temperance. But the sin is strong; for the appetite that feeds it is in his blood. Temptation with its witching solicitation comes before the will,—the weak, self-enslaved will. He aspires to resist, but will not; the spirit would soar, but the flesh will creep; the spirit has the wish, but the flesh has the will; the man longs to be sober, but actually is and remains a drunkard. And never,—be it noticed,—never is he more thoroughly conscious of being a slave to himself, than when he thus ineffectually aspires and wishes to be delivered from himself.

What has been said of drunkenness, and the aspiration to be freed from it, applies with full force to all the sin and all the aspirations of the human soul. There is no independent and self-realizing power in a mere aspiration. No man overcomes even his vices, except as he is assisted by the common grace of God. The self-reliant man invariably relapses into his old habits. He who thinks he stands is sure to fall. But when, under the influence of God's common grace, a man aspires to be freed from the deepest of all sin, because it is the source of all particular acts of transgression,—when he attempts to overcome and extirpate the original and inveterate depravity of his heart,—he feels his bondage more thoroughly than ever. If it is wretchedness for the drunkard to aspire after freedom from only a single vice, and fail of reaching it, is it not the depth of woe, when a man comes to know "the plague of his heart," and his utter inability to cleanse and cure it? In this case, the bondage of self-will is found to be absolute.

At first sight, it might seem as if these wishes and aspirations of the human spirit, faint though they be, are proof that man is not totally depraved, and that his will is not helplessly enslaved. So some men argue. But they forget, that these aspirations and wishes are never realized. There is no evidence of power, except from its results. And where are the results? Who has ever realized these wishes and aspirations, in his heart and conduct? The truth is, that every unattained aspiration that ever swelled the human soul is proof positive, and loud, that the human soul is in bondage. These ineffectual stirrings and impulses, which disappear like the morning cloud and the early dew, are most affecting evidences that "whosoever committeth sin is the slave of sin." They prove that apostate man has sunk, in one respect, to a lower level than that of the irrational creation. For, high ideas and truths cannot raise him. Lofty impulses result in no alteration, or elevation. Even Divine influences leave him just where they find him, unless they are exerted in their highest grade of irresistible grace. A brute surrenders himself to his appetites and propensities, and lives the low life of nature, without being capable of aspirations for anything purer and nobler. But man does this very thing,—nay, immerses himself in flesh, and sense, and self, with an entireness and intensity of which the brute is incapable,—in the face of impulses and stirrings of mind that point him to the pure throne of God, and urge him to soar up to it! The brute is a creature of nature, because he knows no better, and can desire nothing better; but man is "as the beasts that perish," in spite of a better knowledge and a loftier aspiration!

If then, you would know that "whosoever committeth sin is the slave of sin," contemplate sin in reference to the aspirations of an apostate spirit originally made in the image of God, and which, because it is not eternally reprobated, is not entirely cut off from the common influences of the Spirit of God. Never will you feel the bondage of your will more profoundly, than when under these influences, and in your moments of seriousness and anxiety respecting your soul's salvation, you aspire and endeavor to overcome inward sin, and find that unless God grant you His special and renovating grace, your heart will be sinful through all eternity, in spite of the best impulses of your best hours. These upward impulses and aspirations cannot accompany the soul into the state of final hopelessness and despair, though Milton represents Satan as sometimes looking back with a sigh, and a mournful memory, upon what he had once been,[4]—yet if they should go with us there, they would make the ardor of the fire more fierce, and the gnaw of the worm more fell. For they would help to reveal the strength of our sin, and the intensity of our rebellion.

III. Sin is spiritual slavery, if viewed in reference to the fears of the human soul.

The sinful spirit of man fears the death of the body, and the Scriptures assert that by reason of this particular fear we are all our lifetime in bondage. Though we know that the bodily dissolution can have no effect upon the imperishable essence of an immortal being, yet we shrink back from it, as if the sentence, "Dust thou art, and unto dust thou shalt return," had been spoken of the spirit,—as if the worm were to "feed sweetly" upon the soul, and it were to be buried up in the dark house of the grave. Even the boldest of us is disturbed at the thought of bodily death, and we are always startled when the summons suddenly comes: "Set thy house in order, for thou must die."

Again, the spirit of man fears that "fearful something after death," that eternal judgment which must be passed upon all. We tremble at the prospect of giving an account of our own actions. We are afraid to reap the harvest, the seed of which we have sown with our own hands. The thought of going to a just judgment, and of receiving from the Judge of all the earth, who cannot possibly do injustice to any of His creatures, only that which is our desert, shocks us to the centre of our being! Man universally is afraid to be judged with a righteous judgment! Man universally is terrified by the equitable bar of God!

Again, the apostate spirit of man has an awful dread of eternity. Though this invisible realm is the proper home of the human soul, and it was made to dwell there forever, after the threescore and ten years of its residence in the body are over, yet it shrinks back from an entrance into this untried world, and clings with the desperate force of a drowning man to this "bank and shoal of time." There are moments in the life of a guilty man when the very idea of eternal existence exerts a preternatural power, and fills him with a dread that paralyzes him. Never is the human being stirred to so great depths, and roused to such intensity of action, as when it feels what the Scripture calls "the power of an endless life." All men are urged by some ruling passion which is strong. The love of wealth, or of pleasure, or of fame, drives the mind onward with great force, and excites it to mighty exertions to compass its end. But never is a man pervaded by such an irresistible and overwhelming influence as that which descends upon him in some season of religious gloom,—some hour of sickness, or danger, or death,—when the great eternity, with all its awful realities, and all its unknown terror, opens upon his quailing gaze. There are times in man's life, when he is the subject of movements within that impel him to deeds that seem almost superhuman; but that internal ferment and convulsion which is produced when all eternity pours itself through his being turns his soul up from the centre. Man will labor convulsively, night and day, for money; he will dry up the bloom and freshness of health, for earthly power and fame; he will actually wear his body out for sensual pleasure. But what is the intensity and paroxysm of this activity of mind and body, if compared with those inward struggles and throes when the overtaken and startled sinner sees the eternal world looming into view, and with strong crying and tears prays for only a little respite, and only a little preparation! "Millions for an inch of time,"—said the dying English Queen. "O Eternity! Eternity! how shall I grapple with the misery that I must meet with in eternity,"—says the man in the iron cage of Despair. This finite world has indeed great power to stir man, but the other world has an infinitely greater power. The clouds which float in the lower regions of the sky, and the winds that sweep them along, produce great ruin and destruction upon the earth, but it is only when the "windows of heaven are opened" that "the fountains of the great deep are broken up," and "all in whose nostrils is the breath of life die," and "every living substance is destroyed which is upon the face of the ground." When fear arises in the soul of man, in view of an eternal existence for which he is utterly unprepared, it is overwhelming. It partakes of the immensity of eternity, and holds the man with an omnipotent grasp.

If, now, we view sin in relation to these great fears of death, judgment, and eternity, we see that it is spiritual slavery, or the bondage of the will. We discover that our terror is no more able to deliver us from the "bondage of corruption," than our aspiration is. We found that in spite of the serious stirrings and impulses which sometimes rise within us, we still continue immersed in sense and sin; and we shall also find that in spite of the most solemn and awful fears of which a finite being is capable, we remain bondmen to ourselves, and our sin. The dread that goes down into hell can no more ransom us, than can the aspiration that goes up into heaven. Our fear of eternal woe can no more change the heart, than our wish for eternal happiness can. We have, at some periods, faintly wished that lusts and passions had no power over us; and perhaps we have been the subject of still higher aspirings. But we are the same beings, still. We are the same self-willed and self-enslaved sinners, yet. We have all our lifetime feared death, judgment, and eternity, and under the influence of this fear we have sometimes resolved and promised to become Christians. But we are the very same beings, still; we are the same self-willed and self-enslaved sinners yet.

Oh, never is the human spirit more deeply conscious of its bondage to its darling iniquity, than when these paralyzing fears shut down upon it, like night, with "a horror of great darkness." When under their influence, the man feels most thoroughly and wretchedly that his sin is his ruin, and yet his sinful determination continues on, because "whosoever committeth sin is the slave of sin," Has it never happened that, in "the visions of the night when deep sleep falleth upon men," a spirit passed before your face, like that which stood still before the Temanite; and there was silence, and a voice saying, "Man! Man! thou must die, thou must be judged, thou must inhabit eternity?" And when the spirit had departed, and while the tones of its solemn and startling cry were still rolling through your soul, did not a temptation to sin solicit you, and did you not drink in its iniquity like water? Have you not found out, by mournful experience, that the most anxious forebodings of the human spirit, the most alarming fears of the human soul, and the most solemn warnings that come forth from eternity, have no prevailing power over your sinful nature, but that immediately after experiencing them, and while your whole being is still quivering under their agonizing touch, you fall, you rush, into sin? Have you not discovered that even that most dreadful of all fears,—the fear of the holy wrath of almighty God,—is not strong enough to save you from yourself? Do you know that your love of sin has the power to stifle and overcome the mightiest of your fears, when you are strongly tempted to self-indulgence? Have you no evidence, in your own experience, of the truth of the poet's words:

"The Sensual and the Dark rebel in vain, Slaves by their own compulsion."

If, then, you would know that "whosoever committeth sin is the slave of sin," contemplate sin in relation to the fears which of necessity rest upon a spirit capable, as yours is, of knowing that it must leave the body, that it must receive a final sentence at the bar of judgment, and that eternity is its last and fixed dwelling-place. If you would know with sadness and with profit, that sin is the enslavement of the will that originates it, consider that all the distressing fears that have ever been in your soul, from the first, have not been able to set you free in the least from innate depravity: but, that in spite of them all your will has been steadily surrendering itself, more and more, to the evil principle of self-love and enmity to God. Call to mind the great fight of anguish and terror which you have sometimes waged with sin, and see how sin has always been victorious. Remember that you have often dreaded death,—but you are unjust still. Remember that you have often trembled at the thought of eternal judgment,—but you are unregenerate still. Remember that you have often started back, when the holy and retributive eternity dawned like the day of doom upon you,—but you are impenitent still. If you view your own personal sin in reference to your own personal fears, are you not a slave to it? Will or can your fears, mighty as they sometimes are, deliver you from the bondage of corruption, and lift you above that which you love with all your heart, and strength, and might?

It is perfectly plain, then, that "whosoever committeth sin is the slave of sin," whether we have regard to the feeling of obligation to be perfectly holy which is in the human conscience; or to the ineffectual aspirations which sometimes arise in the human spirit; or to the dreadful fears which often fall upon it. Sin must have brought the human will into a real and absolute bondage, if the deep and solemn sense of indebtedness to moral law; if the "thoughts that wander through eternity;" if the aspirations that soar to the heaven of heavens, and the fears that descend to the very bottom of hell,—if all these combined forces and influences cannot free it from its power.

It was remarked in the beginning of this discourse, that the bondage of sin is the result of the reflex action of the human will upon itself. It is not a slavery imposed from without, but from within. The bondage of sin is only a particular aspect of sin itself. The element of servitude, like the element of blindness, or hardness, or rebelliousness, is part and particle of that moral evil which deserves the wrath and curse of God. It, therefore, no more excuses or palliates, than does any other self-originated quality in sin. Spiritual bondage, like spiritual enmity to God, or spiritual ignorance of Him, or spiritual apathy towards Him, is guilt and crime.

And in closing, we desire to repeat and emphasize this truth. Whoever will enter upon that process of self-wrestling and self-conflict which has been described, will come to a profound sense of the truth which our Lord taught in the words of the text. All such will find and feel that they are in slavery, and that their slavery is their condemnation. For the anxious, weary, and heavy-laden sinner, the problem is not mysterious, because it finds its solution in the depths of his own self-consciousness. He needs no one to clear it up for him, and he has neither doubts nor cavils respecting it.

But, an objection always assails that mind which has not the key of an inward moral struggle to unlock the problem for it. When Christ asserts that "whosoever committeth sin is the slave of sin," the easy and indifferent mind is swift to draw the inference that this bondage is its misfortune, and that the poor slave does not deserve to be punished, but to be set free. He says as St. Paul did in another connection: "Nay verily, but let them come themselves, and fetch us out." But this slavery is a self-enslavement. The feet of this man have not been thrust into the stocks by another. This logician must refer everything to its own proper author, and its own proper cause. Let this spiritual bondage, therefore, be charged upon the self that originated it. Let it be referred to that self-will in which it is wrapped up, and of which it is a constituent element. It is a universally received maxim, that the agent is responsible for the consequences of a voluntary act, as well as for the act itself. If, therefore, the human will has inflicted a suicidal blow upon itself, and one of the consequences of its own determination is a total enslavement of itself to its own determination, then this enslaving result of the act, as well the act itself, must all go in to constitute and swell the sum-total of human guilt. The miserable drunkard, therefore, cannot be absolved from the drunkard's condemnation, upon the plea that by a long series of voluntary acts he has, in the end, so enslaved himself that no power but God's grace can save him. The marble-hearted fiend in hell, the absolutely lost spirit in despair, cannot relieve his torturing sense of guilt, by the reflection that he has at length so hardened his own heart that he cannot repent. The unforced will of a moral being must be held responsible for both its direct, and its reflex action; for both its sin, and its bondage in sin.

The denial of guilt, then, is not the way out. He who takes this road "kicks against the goads." And he will find their stabs thickening, the farther he travels, and the nearer he draws to the face and eyes of God. But there is a way out. It is the way of self-knowledge and confession. This is the point upon which all the antecedents of salvation hinge. He who has come to know, with a clear discrimination, that he is in a guilty bondage to his own inclination and lust, has taken the very first step towards freedom. For, the Redeemer, the Almighty Deliverer, is near the captive, so soon as the captive feels his bondage and confesses it. The mighty God walking upon the waves of this sinful, troubled life, stretches out His arm, the very instant any sinking soul cries, "Lord save me." And unless that appeal and confession of helplessness is made, He, the Merciful and the Compassionate, will let the soul go down before His own eyes to the unfathomed abyss. If the sinking Peter had not uttered that cry, the mighty hand of Christ would not have been stretched forth. All the difficulties disappear, so soon as a man understands the truth of the Divine affirmation: "O Israel thou hast destroyed thyself,"—it is a real destruction, and it is thy own work,—"but in ME is thy help."

*[**Note 1:** MILTON: Samson Agonistes, 832-834.—One key to the solution of the problem, how there can be bondage in the very seat of freedom,—how man can be responsible for sin, yet helpless in it,—is to be found in this fact of a reflex action of the will upon itself, or, a reaction of self-action. Philosophical speculation upon the nature of the human will has not, hitherto, taken this fact sufficiently into account. The following extracts corroborate the view presented above. "My will the enemy held, and thence had made a chain for me, and bound me. For, of a perverse will comes lust; and a lust yielded to becomes custom; and custom not resisted becomes necessity. By which links, as it were, joined together as in a chain, a hard bondage held me enthralled." AUGUSTINE: Confessions, VIII. v. 10. "Every degree of inclination contrary to duty, which is and must be sinful, implies and involves an equal degree of difficulty and inability to obey. For, indeed, such inclination of the heart to disobey, and the difficulty or inability to obey, are precisely one and the same. This kind of difficulty or inability, therefore, always is great according to the strength and fixedness of the inclination to disobey; and it becomes total and absolute [inability], when the heart is totally corrupt and wholly opposed to obedience.... No man can act contrary to his present inclination or choice. But who ever imagined that this rendered his inclination and choice innocent and blameless, however wrong and unreasonable it might be." SAMUEL HOPKINS: Works, I. 233-*

235. "Moral inability" is the being "unable to be willing." EDWARDS: Freedom of the Will, Part I, sect. iv. "Propensities,"—says a writer very different from those above quoted,—"that are easily surmounted lead us unresistingly on; we yield to temptations so trivial that we despise their danger. And so we fall into perilous situations from which we might easily have preserved ourselves, but from which we now find it impossible to extricate ourselves without efforts so superhuman as to terrify us, and we finally fall into the abyss, saying to the Almighty, 'Why hast Thou made me so weak?' But notwithstanding our vain pretext, He addresses our conscience, saying, 'I have made thee too weak to rise from the pit, because I made thee strong enough not to fall therein." ROUSSEAU: Confessions, Book II.]
*[**Note 2:** Romans vii. 9-11.]*
*[**Note 3:** Some of the Schoolmen distinguished carefully between the two things, and denominated the former, velleitas, and the latter, voluntas.]*
*[**Note 4:** MILTON: Paradise Lost, IV. 23-25; 35-61.]*

XII - The Original and The Actual Relation of Man to Law

ROMANS vii. 10.—*"The commandment which, was ordained to life, I found to be unto death."*

The reader of St. Paul's Epistles is struck with the seemingly disparaging manner in which he speaks of the moral law. In one place, he tells his reader that "the law entered that the offence might abound;" in another, that "the law worketh wrath;" in another, that "sin shall not have dominion" over the believer because he is "not under the law;" in another, that Christians "are become dead to the law;" in another, that "they are delivered from the law;" and in another, that "the strength of sin is the law." This phraseology sounds strangely, respecting that great commandment upon which the whole moral government of God is founded. We are in the habit of supposing that nothing that springs from the Divine law, or is in any way connected with it, can be evil or the occasion of evil. If the law of holiness is the strength of sin; if it worketh wrath; if good men are to be delivered from it; what then shall be said of the law of sin? Why is it, that St. Paul in a certain class of his representations appears to be inimical to the ten commandments, and to warn Christians against them? "Is the law sin?" is a question that very naturally arises, while reading some of his statements; and it is a question which he himself asks, because he is aware that it will be likely to start in the mind of some of his readers. And it is a question to which he replies: "God forbid. Nay I had not known sin, but by the law."

The difficulty is only seeming, and not real. These apparently disparaging representations of the moral law are perfectly reconcilable with that profound reverence for its authority which St. Paul felt and exhibited, and with that solemn and cogent preaching of the law for which he was so distinguished. The text explains and resolves the difficulty. "The commandment which was ordained to life, I found to be unto death." The moral law, in its own nature, and by the Divine ordination, is suited to produce holiness and happiness in the soul of any and every man. It was ordained to life. So far as the purpose of God, and the original nature and character of man, are concerned, the ten commandments are perfectly adapted to fill the soul with peace and purity. In the unfallen creature, they work no wrath, neither are they the strength of sin. If everything in man had remained as it was created, there would have been no need of urging him to "become dead to the law," to be "delivered from the law," and not be "under the law." Had man kept his original righteousness, it could never be said of him that "the strength of sin is the law." On the contrary, there was such a mutual agreement between the unfallen nature of man and the holy law of God, that the latter was the very joy and strength of the former. The commandment was ordained to life, and it was the life and peace of holy Adam.

The original relation between man's nature and the moral law was precisely like that between material nature and the material laws. There has been no apostasy in the system of matter, and all things remain there as they were in the beginning of creation. The law of gravitation, this very instant, rules as peacefully and supremely in every atom of matter, as it did on the morning of creation. Should material nature be "delivered" from the law of gravitation, chaos would come again. No portion of this fair and beautiful natural world needs to become "dead" to the laws of nature. Such phraseology as this is inapplicable to the relation that exists between the world of matter, and the system of material laws, because, in this material sphere, there has been no revolution, no rebellion, no great catastrophe analogous to the fall of Adam. The law here was ordained to life, and the ordinance still stands. And it shall stand until, by the will of the Creator, these elements shall melt with fervent heat, and these heavens shall pass away with a great noise; until a new system of nature, and a new legislation for it, are introduced.

But the case is different with man. He is not standing where he was, when created. He is out of his original relations to the law and government of God, and therefore that which was ordained to him for life, he now finds to be unto death. The food which in its own nature is suited to minister to the health and strength of the well man, becomes poison and death itself to the sick man.

With this brief notice of the fact, that the law of God was ordained to life, and that therefore this disparaging phraseology of St. Paul does not refer to the intrinsic nature of law, which he expressly informs us "is holy just and good," nor to the original relation which man sustained to it before he became a sinner, let us now proceed to consider some particulars in which the commandment is found to be unto death, to every sinful man.

The law of God shows itself in the human soul, in the form of a sense of duty. Every man, as he walks these streets, and engages in the business or pleasures of life, hears occasionally the words: "Thou shalt; them shalt not." Every man, as he passes along in this earthly pilgrimage, finds himself saying to himself: "I ought, I ought not." This is the voice of law sounding in the conscience; and every man may know, whenever he hears these words, that he is listening to the same authority that cut the ten commandments into the stones of Sinai, and sounded that awful trumpet, and will one day come in power and great glory to judge the quick and dead. Law, we say, expresses itself for man, while here upon earth, through the sense of duty. "A sense of duty pursues us ever," said Webster, in that impressive allusion to the workings of conscience, in the trial of the Salem murderers. This is the accusing and condemning sensation, in and by which the written statute of God becomes a living energy, and a startling voice in the soul. Cut into the rock of Sinai, it is a dead letter; written and printed in our Bibles, it is still a dead letter; but wrought in this manner into the fabric of our own constitution, waylaying us in our hours of weakness, and irresolution, and secrecy, and speaking to our inward being in tones that are as startling as any that could be addressed to the physical ear,—undergoing this transmutation, and becoming a continual consciousness of duty and obligation, the law of God is more than a letter. It is a possessing spirit, and according as we obey or disobey, it is a guardian angel, or a tormenting fiend. We have disobeyed, and therefore the sense of duty is a tormenting sensation; the commandment which was ordained to life, is found to be unto death.

I. In the first place, to go into the analysis, the sense of duty is a sorrow and a pain to sinful man, because it places him under a continual restraint.

No creature can be happy, so long as he feels himself under limitations. To be checked, reined in, and thwarted in any way, renders a man uneasy and discontented. The universal and instinctive desire for freedom,—freedom from restraint,—is a proof of this. Every creature wishes to follow out his inclination, and in proportion as he is hindered in so doing, and is compelled to work counter to it, he is restless and dissatisfied.

Now the sense of duty exerts just this influence, upon sinful man. It opposes his wishes; it thwarts his inclination; it imposes a restraint upon his spontaneous desires and appetites. It continually hedges up his way, and seeks to stop him in the path of his choice and his pleasure. If his inclination were only in harmony with his duty; if his desires and affections were one with the law of God; there would be no restraint from the law. In this case, the sense of duty would be a joy and not a sorrow, because, in doing his duty, he would be doing what he liked. There are only two ways, whereby contentment can be introduced into the human soul. If the Divine law could be altered so that it should agree with man's sinful inclination, he could be happy in sin. The commandment having become like his own heart, there would, of course, be no conflict between the two, and he might sin on forever and lap himself in Elysium. And undoubtedly there are thousands of luxurious and guilty men, who, if they could, like the Eastern Semiramis, would make lust and law alike in their decree;[1] would transmute the law of holiness into a law of sin; would put evil for good, and good for evil, bitter for sweet and sweet for bitter; in order to be eternally happy in the sin that they love. They would bring duty and inclination into harmony, by a method that would annihilate duty, would annihilate the eternal distinction between right and wrong, would annihilate God himself. But this method, of course, is impossible. There can be no transmutation of law, though there can be of a creature's character and inclination. Heaven and earth shall pass away, but the commandment of God can never pass away. The only other mode, therefore, by which duty and inclination can be brought into agreement, and the continual sense of restraint which renders man so wretched be removed, is to change the inclination. The instant the desires and affections of our hearts are transformed, so that they accord with the Divine law, the conflict between our will and our conscience is at an end. When I come to love the law of holiness and delight in it, to obey it is simply to follow out my inclination. And this, we have seen, is to be happy.

But such is not the state of things, in the unrenewed soul. Duty and inclination are in conflict. Man's desires appetites and tendencies are in one direction, and his conscience is in the other. The sense of duty holds a whip over him. He yields to his sinful inclination, finds a momentary pleasure in so doing, and then feels the stings of the scorpion-lash. We see this operation in a very plain and striking manner, if we select an instance where the appetite is very strong, and the voice of conscience is very loud. Take, for example, that particular sin which most easily besets an individual. Every man has such a sin, and knows what it is, Let him call to mind the innumerable instances in which that particular temptation has assailed him, and he will be startled to discover how many thousands of times the sense of duty has put a restraint upon him. Though not in every single instance, yet in hundreds and hundreds of cases, the law of God has uttered the, "Thou shalt not," and endeavored to prevent the consummation of that sin. And what a wearisome experience is this. A continual forth-putting of an unlawful desire, and an almost incessant check upon it, from a law which is hated but which is feared. For such is the attitude of the natural heart toward the commandment. "The carnal mind is enmity against the law of God." The two are contrary to one another; so that when the heart goes out in its inclination, it is immediately hindered and opposed by the law. Sometimes the collision between them is terrible, and the soul becomes; an arena of tumultuous passions. The heart and will are intensely determined to do wrong, while the conscience is unyielding and uncompromising, and utters its denunciations, and thunders its warnings. And what a dreadful destiny awaits that soul, in whom this conflict and collision between the dictates of conscience, and the desires of the heart, is to be eternal! for whom, through all eternity, the holy law of God, which was ordained to life peace and joy, shall be found to be unto death and woe immeasurable!

II. In the second place, the sense of duty is a pain and sorrow to a sinful man, because it demands a perpetual effort from him.

No creature likes to tug, and to lift. Service must be easy, in order to be happy. If you lay upon the shoulders of a laborer a burden that strains his muscles almost to the point of rupture, you put him in physical pain. His physical structure was not intended to be subjected to such a stretch. His Creator designed that the burden should be proportioned to the power, in such a manner that work should be play. In the garden of Eden, physical labor was physical pleasure, because the powers were in healthy action, and the work assigned to them was not a burden. Before the fall, man was simply to dress and keep a garden; but after the fall, he was to dig up thorns and thistles, and eat his bread in the sweat of his face. This is a curse,—the curse of being compelled to toil, and lift, and put the muscle to such a tension that it aches. This is not the original and happy condition of the body, in which man was created. Look at the toiling millions of the human family, who like the poor ant "for one small grain, labor, and tug, and strive;" see them bending double, under the heavy weary load which they must carry until relieved by death; and tell me if this is the physical elysium, the earthly paradise, in which unfallen man was originally placed, and for which he was originally designed. No, the curse of labor, of perpetual effort, has fallen upon the body, as the curse of death has fallen upon the soul; and the uneasiness and unrest of the groaning and struggling body is a convincing proof of it. The whole physical nature of man groaneth and travaileth in pain together until now, waiting for the adoption, that is the redemption of the body from this penal necessity of perpetual strain and effort.

The same fact meets us when we pass from the physical to the moral nature of man, and becomes much more sad and impressive. By creation, it was a pleasure and a pastime for man to keep the law of God, to do spiritual work. As created, he was not compelled to summon his energies, and strain his will, and make a convulsive resolution to obey the commands of his Maker. Obedience was joy. Holy Adam knew nothing of effort in the path of duty. It was a smooth and broad pathway, fringed with flowers, and leading into the meadows of asphodel. It did not become the "straight and narrow" way, until sin had made obedience a toil, the sense of duty a restraint, and human life a race and a fight. By apostasy, the obligation to keep the Divine law perfectly, became repulsive. It was no longer easy for man to do right; and it has never been easy or spontaneous to him since. Hence, the attempt to follow the dictates of conscience always costs an unregenerate man an effort. He is compelled to make a resolution; and a resolution is the sign and signal of a difficult and unwelcome service. Take your own experience for an illustration. Did you ever, except as you were sweetly inclined and drawn by the renewing grace of God, attempt to discharge a duty, without discovering that you were averse to it, and that you must gather up your energies for the work, as the leaper strains upon the tendon of Achilles to make the mortal leap. And if you had not become weary, and given over the effort; if you had entered upon that sad but salutary passage in the religious experience which is delineated in the seventh chapter of Romans; if you had continued to struggle and strive to do your duty, until you grew faint and weak, and powerless, and cried out for a higher and mightier power to succor you; you would have known, as you do not yet, what a deadly opposition there is between the carnal mind and the law of God, and what a spasmodic effort it costs an unrenewed man even to attempt to discharge the innumerable obligations that rest upon him. Mankind would know more of this species of toil and labor, and of the cleaving curse involved in it, if they were under the same physical necessity in regard to it, that they lie under in respect to manual labor. A man must dig up the thorns and thistles, he must earn his bread in the sweat of his face, or he must die. Physical wants, hunger and thirst, set men to work physically, and keep them at it; and thus they well understand what it is to have a weary body, aching muscles, and a tired physical nature. But they are not under the same species of necessity, in respect to the wants and the work of the soul. A man may neglect these, and yet live a long and luxurious life upon the earth. He is not driven by the very force of circumstances, to labor with his heart and will, as he is to labor with his hands. And hence he knows little or nothing of a weary and heavy-laden soul; nothing of an aching heart and a tired will. He well knows how much strain and effort it costs to cut down forests, open roads, and reduce the wilderness to a fertile field; but he does not know how much toil and effort are involved, in the attempt to convert the human soul into the garden of the Lord.

Now in this demand for a perpetual effort which is made upon the natural man, by the sense of duty, we see that the law which was ordained to life is found to be unto death. The commandment, instead of being a pleasant friend and companion to the human soul, as it was in the beginning, has become a strict rigorous task-master. It lays out an uncongenial work for sinful man to do, and threatens him with punishment and woe if he does not do it. And yet the law is not a tyrant. It is holy, just, and good. This work which it lays out is righteous work, and ought to be done. The wicked disinclination and aversion of the sinner have compelled the law to assume this unwelcome and threatening attitude. That which is good was not made death to man by God's agency, and by a Divine arrangement, but by man's transgression.[2] Sin produces this misery in the human soul, through an instrument that is innocent, and in its own nature benevolent and kind. Apostasy, the rebellion and corruption of the human heart, has converted the law of God into an exacting task-master and an avenging magistrate. For the law says to every man what St. Paul says of the magistrate: "Rulers are not a terror to good works, but to the evil. Wilt thou, then, not be afraid of the power? Do that which is good, and thou shalt have praise of the same. For he is the minister of God to thee for good: but if thou do that which is evil, be afraid." If man were only conformed to the law; if the inclination of his heart were only in harmony with his sense of duty; the ten commandments would not be accompanied with any thunders or lightnings, and the discharge of duty would be as easy, spontaneous, and as much without effort, as the practice of sin now is.

Thus have we considered two particulars in which the Divine law, originally intended to render man happy, and intrinsically adapted to do so, now renders him miserable. The commandment which was ordained to life, he now finds to be unto death, because it places him under a continual restraint, and drives him to a perpetual effort. These two particulars, we need not say, are not all the modes in which sin has converted the moral law from a joy to a sorrow. We have not discussed the great subject of guilt and penalty. This violated law charges home the past disobedience and threatens an everlasting damnation, and thus fills the sinful soul with fears and forebodings. In this way, also, the law becomes a terrible organ and instrument of misery, and is found to be unto death. But the limits of this discourse compel us to stop the discussion here, and to deduce some practical lessons which are suggested by it.

1. In the first place, we are taught by the subject, as thus considered, that the mere sense of duty is not Christianity. If this is all that a man is possessed of, he is not prepared for the day of judgment, and the future life. For the sense of duty, alone and by itself, causes misery in a soul that has not performed its duty. The law worketh wrath, in a creature who has not obeyed the law. The man that doeth these things shall indeed live by them; but he who has not done them must die by them.

There have been, and still are, great mistakes made at this point. Men have supposed that an active conscience, and a lofty susceptibility towards right and wrong, will fit them to appear before God, and have, therefore, rejected Christ the Propitiation. They have substituted ethics for the gospel; natural religion for revealed. "I know," says Immanuel Kant, "of but two beautiful things; the starry heavens above my head, and the sense of duty within my heart."[3] But, is the sense of duty beautiful to apostate man? to a being who is not conformed to it? Does the holy law of God overarch him like the firmament, "tinged with a blue of heavenly dye, and starred with sparkling gold?" Nay, nay. If there be any beauty in the condemning law of God, for man the transgressor, it is the beauty of the lightnings. There is a splendor in them, but there is a terror also. Not until He who is the end of the law for righteousness has clothed me with His panoply, and shielded me from their glittering shafts in the clefts of the Rock, do I dare to look at them, as they leap from crag to crag, and shine from the east even unto the west.

We do not deny that the consciousness of responsibility is a lofty one, and are by no means insensible to the grand and swelling sentiments concerning the moral law, and human duty, to which this noble thinker gives utterance.[4] But we are certain that if the sense of duty had pressed upon him to the degree that it did upon St. Paul; had the commandment "come" to him with the convicting energy that it did to St. Augustine, and to Pascal; he too would have discovered that the law which was ordained to life is found to be unto death. So long as man stands at a distance from the moral law, he can admire its glory and its beauty; but when it comes close to him; when it comes home to him; when it becomes a discerner of the thoughts and intents of the heart; then its glory is swallowed up in its terror, and its beauty is lost in its truth. Then he who was alive without the law becomes slain by the law. Then this ethical admiration of the decalogue is exchanged for an evangelical trust in Jesus Christ.

2. And this leads us to remark, in the second place, that this subject shows the meaning of Christ's work of Redemption. The law for an alienated and corrupt soul is a burden. It cannot be otherwise; for it imposes a perpetual restraint, urges up to an unwelcome duty, and charges home a fearful guilt. Christ is well named the Redeemer, because He frees the sinful soul from all this. He delivers it from the penalty, by assuming it all upon Himself, and making complete satisfaction to the broken law. He delivers it from the perpetual restraint and the irksome effort, by so renewing and changing the heart that it becomes a delight to keep the law. We observed, in the first part of the discourse, that if man could only bring the inclination of his heart into agreement with his sense of duty, he would be happy in obeying, and the consciousness of restraint and of hateful effort would disappear. This is precisely what Christ accomplishes by His Spirit. He brings the human heart into harmony with the Divine law, as it was in the beginning, and thus rescues it from its bondage and its toil. Obedience becomes a pleasure, and the service of God, the highest Christian liberty. Oh, would that by the act of faith, you might experience this liberating effect of the redemption that is in Christ Jesus. So long as you are out of Christ, you are under a burden that will every day grow heavier, and may prove to be fixed and unremovable as the mountains. That is a fearful punishment which the poet Dante represents as being inflicted upon those who were guilty of pride. The poor wretches are compelled to support enormous masses of stone which bend them over to the ground, and, in his own stern phrase, "crumple up their knees into their breasts." Thus they stand, stooping over, every muscle trembling, the heavy stone weighing them down, and yet they are not permitted to fall, and rest themselves upon the earth.[5] In this crouching posture, they must carry the weary heavy load without relief, and with a distress so great that, in the poet's own language,

"it seemed As he, who showed most patience in his look, Wailing exclaimed: I can endure no more." [6]

Such is the posture of man unredeemed. There is a burden on him, under which he stoops and crouches. It is a burden compounded of guilt and corruption. It is lifted off by Christ, and by Christ only. The soul itself can never expiate its guilt; can never cleanse its pollution. We urge you, once more, to the act of faith in the Redeemer of the world. We beseech you, once more, to make "the redemption that is in Christ Jesus" your own. The instant you plead the merit of Christ's oblation, in simple confidence in its atoning efficacy, that instant the heavy burden is lifted off by an Almighty hand, and your curved, stooping, trembling, aching form once more stands erect, and you walk abroad in the liberty wherewith Christ makes the human creature free.

[Note 1:
        "She in vice
Of luxury was so shameless, that she made
Liking to be lawful by promulged decree,
To clear the blame she had herself incurr'd."
DANTE: *Inferno, v. 56.]*

[Note 2: Romans vii. 13, 14.]

[Note 3: KANT: *Kritik der Praktischen Vernunft (Beschlusz).—De Stael's rendering, which is so well known, and which I have employed, is less guarded than the original.]*

[Note 4: *Compare the fine apostrophe to Duty. PRAKTISCHE VERNUNFT, p. 214, (Ed. Rosenkranz.)]*

[Note 5: *"Let their eyes be darkened, that they may not see, and bow down their back alway." Rom. xi. 10.]*

[Note 6: DANTE: *Purgatory x. 126-128.]*

XIII - The Sin of Omission

Matthew xix. 20.—*"The young man saith unto him, All these things have I kept from my youth up: what lack I yet?"*

The narrative from which the text is taken is familiar to all readers of the Bible. A wealthy young man, of unblemished morals and amiable disposition, came to our Lord, to inquire His opinion respecting his own good estate. He asked what good thing he should do, in order to inherit eternal life. The fact that he applied to Christ at all, shows that he was not entirely at rest in his own mind. He could truly say that he had kept the ten commandments from his youth up, in an outward manner; and yet he was ill at ease. He was afraid that when the earthly life was over, he might not be able to endure the judgment of God, and might fail to enter into that happy paradise of which the Old Testament Scriptures so often speak, and of which he had so often read, in them. This young man, though a moralist, was not a self-satisfied or a self-conceited one. For, had he been like the Pharisee a thoroughly blinded and self-righteous person, like him he never would have approached Jesus of Nazareth, to obtain His opinion respecting his own religious character and prospects. Like him, he would have scorned to ask our Lord's judgment upon any matters of religion. Like the Pharisees, he would have said, "We see,"[1] and the state of his heart and his future prospects would have given him no anxiety. But he was not a conceited and presumptuous Pharisee. He was a serious and thoughtful person, though not a pious and holy one. For, he did not love God more than he loved his worldly possessions. He had not obeyed that first and great command, upon which hang all the law and the prophets, conformity to which, alone, constitutes righteousness: "Thou shalt love the Lord thy God with all thy heart, and all thy soul, and all thy mind, and all thy strength." He was not right at heart, and was therefore unprepared for death and judgment. This he seems to have had some dim apprehension of. For why, if he had felt that his external morality was a solid rock for his feet to stand upon, why should he have betaken himself to Jesus of Nazareth, to ask: "What lack I yet?"

It was not what he had done, but what he had left undone, that wakened fears and forebodings in this young ruler's mind. The outward observance of the ten commandments was right and well in its own way and place; but the failure to obey, from the heart, the first and great command was the condemnation that rested upon him. He probably knew this, in some measure. He was not confidently certain of eternal life; and therefore he came to the Great Teacher, hoping to elicit from Him an answer that would quiet his conscience, and allow him to repose upon his morality while he continued to love this world supremely. The Great Teacher pierced him with an arrow. He said to him, "If them wilt be perfect, go and sell that thou hast, and give to the poor, and thou shalt have treasure in heaven: and come and follow me." This direction showed him what he lacked.

This incident leads us to consider the condemnation that rests upon every man, for his failure in duty; the guilt that cleaves to him, on account of what he has not done. The Westminster Catechism defines sin to be "any want of conformity unto, or any transgression of, the law of God." Not to be conformed, in the heart, to the law and will of God, is as truly sin, as positively to steal, or positively to commit murder. Failure to come up to the line of rectitude is as punishable, as to step over that line. God requires of His creature that he stand squarely upon the line of righteousness; if therefore he is off that line, because he has not come up to it, he is as guilty as when he transgresses, or passes across it, upon the other side. This is the reason that the sin of omission is as punishable as the sin of commission. In either case alike, the man is off the line of rectitude. Hence, in the final day, man will be condemned for what he lacks, for what he comes short of, in moral character. Want of conformity to the Divine law as really conflicts with the Divine law, as an overt transgression does, because it carries man off and away from it. One of the Greek words for sin [Greek: (amurtanein)] signifies, to miss the mark. When the archer shoots at the target, he as really fails to strike it, if his arrow falls short of it, as when he shoots over and beyond it. If he strains upon the bow with such a feeble force, that the arrow drops upon the ground long before it comes up to the mark, his shot is as total a failure, as when he strains upon the bow-string with all his force, but owing to an ill-directed aim sends his weapon into the air. One of the New Testament terms for sin contains this figure and illustration, in its etymology. Sin is a want of conformity unto, a failure to come clear up to, the line and mark prescribed by God, as well a violent and forcible breaking over and beyond the line and the mark. The lack of holy love, the lack of holy fear, the lack of filial trust and confidence in God,—the negative absence of these and other qualities in the heart is as truly sin and guilt, as is the positive and open violation of a particular commandment, in the act of theft, or lying, or Sabbath-breaking.

We propose, then, to direct attention to that form and aspect of human depravity which consists in coming short of the aim and end presented to man by his Maker,—that form and aspect of sin which is presented in the young ruler's inquiry: "What lack I yet?"

It is a comprehensive answer to this question to say, that every natural man lacks sincere and filial love of God. This was the sin of the moral, but worldly, the amiable, but earthly-minded, young man. Endow him, in your fancy, with all the excellence you please, it still lies upon the face of the narrative, that he loved money more than he loved the Lord God Almighty. When the Son of God bade him go and sell his property, and give it to the poor, and then come and follow Him as a docile disciple like Peter and James and John, he went away sad in his mind; for he had great possessions. This was a reasonable requirement, though a very trying one. To command a young man of wealth and standing immediately to strip himself of all his property, to leave the circle in which he had been born and brought up, and to follow the Son of Man, who had not where to lay His head, up and down through Palestine, through good report and through evil report,— to put such a burden upon such a young man was to lay him under a very heavy load. Looking at it from a merely human and worldly point of view, it is not strange that the young ruler declined to take it upon his shoulders; though he felt sad in declining, because he had the misgiving that in declining he was sealing his doom. But, had he loved the Lord God with all his heart; had he been conformed unto the first and great command, in his heart and affections; had he not lacked a spiritual and filial affection towards his Maker; he would have obeyed.

For, the circumstances under which this command was given must be borne in mind. It issued directly from the lips of the Son of God Himself. It was not an ordinary call of Providence, in the ordinary manner in which God summons man to duty. There is reason to suppose that the young ruler knew and felt that Christ had authority to give such directions. We know not what were precisely his views of the person and office of Jesus of Nazareth; but the fact that he came to Him seeking instruction respecting the everlasting kingdom of God and the endless life of the soul, and the yet further fact that he went away in sadness because he did not find it in his heart to obey the instructions that he had received, prove that he was at least somewhat impressed with the Divine authority of our Lord. For, had he regarded Him as a mere ordinary mortal, knowing no more than any other man concerning the eternal kingdom of God, why should His words have distressed him? Had this young ruler taken the view of our Lord which was held by the Scribes and Pharisees, like them he would never have sought instruction from Him in a respectful and sincere manner; and, like them, he would have replied to the command to strip himself of all his property, leave the social circles to which he belonged, and follow the despised Nazarene, with the curling lip of scorn. He would not have gone away in sorrow, but in contempt. We must assume, therefore, that this young ruler felt that the person with whom he was conversing, and who had given him this extraordinary command, had authority to give it. We do not gather from the narrative that he doubted upon this point. Had he doubted, it would have relieved the sorrow with which his mind was disturbed. He might have justified his refusal to obey, by the consideration that this Jesus of Nazareth had no right to summon him, or any other man, to forsake the world and attach himself to His person and purposes, if any such consideration had entered his mind. No, the sorrow, the deep, deep sorrow and sadness, with which he went away to the beggarly elements of his houses and his lands, proves that he knew too well that this wonderful Being who was working miracles, and speaking words of wisdom that never man spake, had indeed authority and right to say to him, and to every other man, "Go and sell that thou hast, and give to the poor, and thou shalt have treasure in heaven: and come and follow me."

Though the command was indeed an extraordinary one, it was given in an extraordinary manner, by an extraordinary Being. That young ruler was not required to do any more than you and I would be obligated to do, in the same circumstances. It is indeed true, that in the ordinary providence of God, you and I are not summoned to sell all our possessions, and distribute them to the poor, and to go up and down the streets of this city, or up and down the high-ways and by-ways of the land, as missionaries of Christ. But if the call were extraordinary,—if the heavens should open above our heads, and a voice from the skies should command us in a manner not to be doubted or disputed to do this particular thing, we ought immediately to do it. And if the love of God were in our hearts; if we were inwardly "conformed unto" the Divine law; if there were nothing lacking in our religious character; we should obey with the same directness and alacrity with which Peter and Andrew, and James and John, left their nets and their fishing-boat, their earthly avocations, their fathers and their fathers' households, and followed Christ to the end of their days. In the present circumstances of the church and the world, Christians must follow the ordinary indications of Divine Providence; and though these do unquestionably call upon them to make far greater sacrifices for the cause of Christ than they now make, yet they do not call upon them to sell all that they have, and give it to the poor. But they ought to be ready and willing to do so, in case God by any remarkable and direct expression should indicate that this is His will and pleasure. Should our Lord, for illustration, descend again, and in His own person say to His people, as He did to the young ruler: "Sell all that ye have, and give to the poor, and go up and down the earth preaching the gospel," it would be the duty of every rich Christian to strip himself of all his riches, and of every poor Christian to make himself yet poorer, and of the whole Church to adopt the same course that was taken by the early Christians, who "had all things common, and sold their possessions and goods and parted them to all men, as every man had need." The direct and explicit command of the Lord Jesus Christ to do any particular thing must be obeyed at all hazards, and at all cost. Should He command any one of His disciples to lay down his life, or to undergo a severe discipline and experience in His service, He must be obeyed. This is what He means when He says, "If any man come to me, and hate not his father, and mother, and wife, and children, and brethren, and sisters, yea and his own life also, he cannot be my disciple. And whosoever doth not bear his cross, and come after me, cannot be my disciple" (Luke xiv. 26, 27).

The young ruler was subjected to this test. It was his privilege,—and it was a great privilege,—to see the Son of God face to face; to hear His words of wisdom and authority; to know without any doubt or ambiguity what particular thing God would have him do. And he refused to do it. He was moral; he was amiable; but he refused point-blank to obey the direct command of God addressed to him from the very lips of God. It was with him as it would be with us, if the sky should open over our heads, and the Son of God should descend, and with His own lips should command us to perform a particular service, and we should be disobedient to the heavenly vision, and should say to the Eternal Son of God: "We will not." Think you that there is nothing lacking in such a character as this? Is this religious perfection? Is such a heart as this "conformed unto" the law and will of God?

If, then, we look into the character of the young ruler, we perceive that there was in it no supreme affection for God. On the contrary, he loved himself with all his heart, and soul, and mind, and strength. Even his religious anxiety, which led him to our Lord for His opinion concerning his good estate, proved to be a merely selfish feeling. He desired immortal felicity beyond the tomb,—and the most irreligious man upon earth desires this,—but he did not possess such an affection for God as inclined, and enabled, him to obey His explicit command to make a sacrifice of his worldly possessions for His glory. And this lack of supreme love to God was sin. It was a deviation from the line of eternal rectitude and righteousness, as really and truly as murder, adultery, or theft, or any outward breach of any of those commandments which he affirmed he had kept from his youth up. This coming short of the Divine honor and glory was as much contrary to the Divine law, as any overt transgression of it could be.

For love is the fulfilling of the law. The whole law, according to Christ, is summed up and contained, in these words: "Thou shall love the Lord thy God with all thy heart, and thy neighbor as thyself." To be destitute of this heavenly affection is, therefore, to break the law at the very centre and in the very substance of it. Men tell us, like this young ruler, that they do not murder, lie, or steal,—that they observe all the commandments of the second table pertaining to man and their relations to man,—and ask, "What lack we yet?" Alexander Pope, in the most brilliant and polished poetry yet composed by human art, sums up the whole of human duty in the observance of the rules and requirements of civil morality, and affirms that "an honest man is the noblest work of God." But is this so? Has religion reached its last term, and ultimate limit, when man respects the rights of property? Is a person who keeps his hands off the goods and chattels of his fellow-creature really qualified for the heavenly state, by reason of this fact and virtue of honesty? Has he attained the chief end of man?[2] Even if we could suppose a perfect obedience of all the statutes of the second table, while those of the first table were disobeyed; even if one could fulfil all his obligations to his neighbor, while failing in all his obligations to his Maker; even if we should concede a perfect morality, without any religion; would it be true that this morality, or obedience of only one of the two tables that cover the whole field of human duty, is sufficient to prepare man for the everlasting future, and the immediate presence of God? Who has informed man that the first table of the law is of no consequence; and that if he only loves his neighbor as himself, he need not love his Maker supremely?

No! Affection in the heart towards the great and glorious God is the sum and substance of religion, and whoever is destitute of it is irreligious and sinful in the inmost spirit, and in the highest degree. His fault relates to the most excellent and worthy Being in the universe. He comes short of his duty, in reference to that Being who more than any other one is entitled to his love and his services. We say, and we say correctly, that if a man fails of fulfilling his obligations towards those who have most claims upon him, he is more culpable than when he fails of his duty towards those who have less claims upon him. If a son comes short of his duty towards an affectionate and self-sacrificing mother, we say it is a greater fault, than if he comes short of his duty to a fellow-citizen. The parent is nearer to him than the citizen, and he owes unto her a warmer affection of his heart, and a more active service of his life, than he owes to his fellow-citizen. What would be thought of that son who should excuse his neglect, or ill-treatment, of the mother that bore him, upon the ground that he had never cheated a fellow-man and had been scrupulous in all his mercantile transactions! This but feebly illustrates the relation which every man sustains to God, and the claim which God has upon every man. Our first duty and obligation relates to our Maker. Our fellow-creatures have claims upon us; the dear partners of our blood have claims upon us; our own personality, with its infinite destiny for weal or woe, has claims upon us. But no one of these; not all of them combined; have upon us that first claim, which God challenges for Himself. Social life,—the state or the nation to which we belong,—cannot say to us: "Thou shalt love me with all thy heart, and soul, and mind, and strength." The family, which is bone of our bone, and flesh of our flesh, cannot say to us: "Thou shalt love us, with all thy soul, mind, heart, and strength." Even our own deathless and priceless soul cannot say to us: "Thou shalt love me supremely, and before all other beings and things." But the infinite and adorable God, the Being that made us, and has redeemed us, can of right demand that we love and honor Him first of all, and chiefest of all.

There are two thoughts suggested by the subject which we have been considering, to which we now invite candid attention.

1. In the first place, this subject convicts every man of sin. Our Lord, by his searching reply to the young ruler's question, "What lack I yet?" sent him away very sorrowful; and what man, in any age and country, can apply the same test to himself, without finding the same unwillingness to sell all that he has and give to the poor,—the same indisposition to obey any and every command of God that crosses his natural inclinations? Every natural man, as he subjects his character to such a trial as that to which the young ruler was subjected, will discover as he did that he lacks supreme love of God, and like him, if he has any moral earnestness; if he feels at all the obligation of duty; will go away very sorrowful, because he perceives very plainly the conflict between his will and his conscience. How many a person, in the generations that have already gone to the judgment-seat of Christ, and in the generation that is now on the way thither, has been at times brought face to face with the great and first command, "Thou shall love the Lord thy God with all thy heart," and by some particular requirement has been made

113

conscious of his utter opposition to that great law. Some special duty was urged upon him, by the providence, or the word, or the Spirit of God, that could not be performed unless his will were subjected to God's will, and unless his love for himself and the world were subordinated to his love of his Maker. If a young man, perhaps he was commanded to consecrate his talents and education to a life of philanthropy and service of God in the gospel, instead of a life devoted to secular and pecuniary aims. God said to him, by His providence, and by conscience, "Go teach my gospel to the perishing; go preach my word, to the dying and the lost." But he loved worldly ease pleasure and reputation more than he loved God; and he refused, and went away sorrowful, because this poor world looked very bright and alluring, and the path of self-denial and duty looked very forbidding. Or, if he was a man in middle life, perhaps he was commanded to abate his interest in plans for the accumulation of wealth, to contract his enterprises, to give attention to the concerns of his soul and the souls of his children, to make his own peace with God, and to consecrate the remainder of his life to Christ and to human welfare; and when this plain and reasonable course of conduct was dictated to him, he found his whole heart rising up against the proposition. Our Lord, alluding to the fact that there was nothing in common between His spirit, and the spirit of Satan, said to His disciples, "The prince of this world cometh, and hath nothing in me" (John xiv. 30). So, when the command to love God supremely comes to this man of the world, in any particular form, "it hath nothing in him." This first and great law finds no ready and genial response within his heart, but on the contrary a recoil within his soul as if some great monster had started up in his pathway. He says, in his mind, to the proposition: "Anything but that;" and, with the young ruler, he goes away sorrowful, because he knows that refusal is perdition.

Is there not a wonderful power to convict of sin, in this test? If you try yourself, as the young man did, by the command, "Thou shalt not kill," "Thou shalt not steal," "Thou shalt not commit adultery," you may succeed, perhaps, in quieting your conscience, to some extent, and in possessing yourself of the opinion of your fitness for the kingdom of God. But ask yourself the question, "Do I love God supremely, and am I ready and willing to do any and every particular thing that He shall command me to do, even if it is plucking out a right eye, or cutting off a right hand, or selling all my goods to give to the poor?" try yourself by this test, and see if you lack anything in your moral character. When this thorough and proper touch-stone of character is applied, there is not found upon earth a just man that doeth good and sinneth not. Every human creature, by this test is concluded under sin. Every man is found, lacking in what he ought to possess, when the words of the commandment are sounded in his ear: "Thou shalt love the Lord thy God with all thy heart, and all thy soul, and all thy mind, and all thy strength." This sum and substance of the Divine law, upon which hang all the other laws, convinces every man of sin. For there is no escaping its force. Love of God is a distinct and definite feeling, and every person knows whether he ever experienced it. Every man knows whether it is, or is not, an affection of his heart; and he knows that if it be wanting, the foundation of religion is wanting in his soul, and the sum and substance of sin is there.

2. And this leads to the second and concluding thought suggested, by the subject, namely, that except a man be born again, he cannot see the kingdom of God. If there be any truth in the discussion through which we have passed, it is plain and incontrovertible, that to be destitute of holy love to God is a departure and deviation from the moral law. It is a coming short of the great requirement that rests upon every accountable creature of God, and this is as truly sin and guilt as any violent and open passing over and beyond the line of rectitude. The sin of omission is as deep and damning as the sin of commission. "Forgive,"—said the dying archbishop Usher,—"forgive all my sins, especially my sins of omission."

But, how is this lack to be supplied? How is this great hiatus in human character to be filled up? How shall the fountain of holy and filial affection towards God be made to gush up into everlasting life, within your now unloving and hostile heart? There is no answer to this question of questions, but in the Person and Work of the Holy Ghost. If God shall shed abroad His love in your heart, by the Holy Ghost which is given unto you, you will know the blessedness of a new affection; and will be able to say with Peter, "Thou knowest all things; thou knowest that I love thee." You are shut up to this method, and this influence. To generate within yourself this new spiritual emotion which you have never yet felt, is utterly impossible. Yet you must get it, or religion, is impossible, and immortal life is impossible. Would that you might feel your straits, and your helplessness. Would that you might perceive your total lack of supreme love of God, as the young ruler perceived his; and would that, unlike him, instead, of going away from the Son of God, you would go to Him, crying, "Lord create within me a clean heart, and renew within me a right spirit." Then the problem would be solved, and having peace with God through the blood of Christ, the love of God would be shed abroad in your hearts, through the Holy Ghost given unto you.

*[**Note 1:** John ix. 41.]*
*[**Note 2:** Even if we should widen the meaning of the word "honest," in the above-mentioned dictum of Pope, and make it include the Latin "honestum," the same objection would lie against dictum. Honor and high-mindedness towards man is not love and reverence towards God. The spirit of chivalry is not the spirit of Christianity.]*

XIV - The Sinfulness of Original Sin

MATTHEW xix. 20.—*"The young man saith unto him, All these things have I kept from my youth up: what lack I yet?"*

In the preceding discourse from these words, we discussed that form and aspect of sin which consists in "coming short" of the Divine Law; or, as the Westminster Creed states it, in a "want of conformity" unto it. The deep and fundamental sin of the young ruler, we found, lay in what he lacked. When our Lord tested him, he proved to be utterly destitute of love to God. His soul was a complete vacuum, in reference to that great holy affection which fills the hearts of all the good beings before the throne of God, and without which no creature can stand, or will wish to stand, in the Divine presence. The young ruler, though outwardly moral and amiable, when searched in the inward parts was found wanting in the sum and substance of religion. He did not love God; and he did love himself and his possessions.

What man has omitted to do, what man is destitute of,—this is a species of sin which he does not sufficiently consider, and which is weighing him down to perdition. The unregenerate person when pressed to repent of his sins, and believe on the Lord Jesus Christ, often beats back the kind effort, by a question like that which Pilate put to the infuriated Jews: "Why, what evil have I done?" It is the subject of his actual and overt transgressions that comes first into his thoughts, and, like the young ruler, he tells his spiritual friend and adviser that he has kept all the commandments from his youth up. The conviction of sin would be more common if the natural man would consider his failures; if he would look into his heart and perceive what he is destitute of, and into his conduct and see what he has left undone.

In pursuing this subject, we propose to show, still further, the guiltiness of every man, from the fact that he lacks the original righteousness that once belonged to him. We shall endeavor to prove that every child of Adam is under condemnation, or, in the words of Christ, that "the wrath of God abides upon him" (John iii. 36), because he is not possessed of that pure and perfect character which, his Maker gave him in the beginning. Man is culpable for not continuing to stand upon the high and sinless position, in which he was originally placed. When the young ruler's question is put to the natural man, and the inquiry is made as to his defects and deficiency, it is invariably discovered that he lacks the image of God in which he was created. And for a rational being to be destitute of the image of God is sin, guilt, and condemnation, because every rational being has once received this image.

God has the right to demand from every one of his responsible creatures, all that the creature might be, had he retained possession of the endowments which he received at creation, and had he employed them with fidelity. The perfect gifts and capacities originally bestowed upon man, and not the mutilated and damaged powers subsequently arising from a destructive act of self-will, furnish the proper rule of measurement, in estimating human merit or demerit. The faculties of intelligence and will as unfallen, and not as fallen, determine the amount of holiness and of service that may be demanded, upon principles of strict justice, from every individual. All that man "comes short" of this is so much sin, guilt, and condemnation.

When the great Sovereign and Judge looks down from His throne of righteousness and equity, upon any one of the children of men, He considers what that creature was by creation, and compares his present character and conduct with the character with which he was originally endowed, and the conduct that would naturally have flowed therefrom. God made man holy and perfect. God created man in his own image (Gen. i. 26), "endued with knowledge, righteousness, and true holiness, having the law of God written in his heart, and power to fulfil it." This is the statement of the Creed which we accept as a fair and accurate digest of the teachings of Revelation, respecting the primitive character of man, and his original righteousness. And all evangelical creeds, however they may differ from each other in their definitions of original righteousness, and their

116

estimate of the perfections and powers granted to man by creation, do yet agree that he stood higher when he came from the hand of God than he now stands; that man's actual character and conduct do not come up to man's created power and capacities. Solemn and condemning as it is, it is yet a fact, that inasmuch as every man was originally made in the holy image of God, he ought, this very instant to be perfectly holy. He ought to be standing upon a position that is as high above his actual position, as the heavens are high above the earth. He ought to be possessed of a moral perfection without spot or wrinkle, or any such thing. He ought to be as he was, when created in righteousness and true holiness. He ought to be dwelling high up on those lofty and glorious heights where he was stationed by the benevolent hand of his Maker, instead of wallowing in those low depths where he has fallen by an act of apostasy and rebellion. Nothing short of this satisfies the obligations that are resting upon him. An imperfect holiness, such as the Christian is possessed of while here upon earth, does not come up to the righteous requirement of the moral law; and certainly that kind of moral character which belongs to the natural man is still farther off from the sum-total that is demanded.

Let us press this truth, that we may feel its convicting and condemning energy. When our Maker speaks to us upon the subject of His claims and our obligations, He tells us that when we came forth from nonentity into existence, from His hand, we were well endowed, and well furnished. He tells us distinctly, that He did not create us the depraved and sinful beings that we now are. He tells us that these earthly affections, this carnal mind, this enmity towards the Divine law, this disinclination towards religion and spiritual concerns, this absorbing love of the world and this supreme love of self,—that these were not implanted or infused into the soul by our wise, holy, and good Creator. This is not His work. This is no part of the furniture with which mankind were set up for an everlasting existence. "God saw everything that he had made, and behold it was very good." (Gen. i. 31). We acknowledge the mystery that overhangs the union and connection of all men with the first man. We know that this corruption of man's nature, and this sinfulness of his heart, does indeed, appear at the very beginning of his individual life. He is conceived in sin, and shapen in iniquity (Ps. li. 5). This selfish disposition, and this alienation of the heart from God, is native depravity, is inborn corruption. This we know both from Revelation, and observation. But we also know, from the same infallible Revelation, that though man is born a sinner from the sinful Adam, he was created a saint in the holy Adam. By origin he is holy, and by descent he is sinful; because there has intervened, between his creation and his birth, that "offence of one man whereby all men were made sinners" (Rom. v. 18, 19). Though we cannot unravel the whole mystery of this subject, yet if we accept the revealed fact, and concede that God did originally make man in His own image, in righteousness and true holiness, and that man has since unmade himself, by the act of apostasy and rebellion,[1]—if we take this as the true and correct statement of the facts in the case, then we can see how and why it is, that God has claims upon His creature, man, that extend to what this creature originally was and was capable of becoming, and not merely to what he now is, and is able to perform.

When, therefore, the young ruler's question, "What lack I?" is asked and answered upon a broad scale, each and every man must say: "I lack original righteousness; I lack the holiness with which God created man; I lack that perfection of character which belonged to my rational and immortal nature coming fresh from the hand of God in the person of Adam; I lack all that I should now be possessed of, had that nature not apostatized from its Maker and its Sovereign." And when God forms His estimate of man's obligations; when He lays judgment to the line, and righteousness to the plummet; He goes back to the beginning, He goes back to creation, and demands from His rational and immortal creature that perfect service which, he was capable of rendering by creation, but which now he is unable to render because of subsequent apostasy. For, God cannot adjust His demands to the alterations which sinful man makes in himself. This would be to annihilate all demands and obligations. A sliding-scale would be introduced, by this method, that would reduce human duty by degrees to a minimum, where it would disappear. For, the more sinful a creature becomes, the less inclined, and consequently the less able does he become to obey the law of God. If, now, the Eternal Judge shapes His requisitions in accordance with the shifting character of His creature, and lowers His law down just as fast as the sinner enslaves himself to lust and sin, it is plain that sooner or later all moral obligation will run out; and whenever the creature becomes totally enslaved to self and flesh, there will no longer be any claims resting upon him. But this cannot be so. "For the kingdom of heaven,"—says our Lord,—"is as a man travelling into a far country, who called his own servants and delivered unto them his goods. And unto one he gave five talents, and to another two, and to another one; and straightway took his journey." When the settlement was made. Each and every one of the parties was righteously summoned to account for all that had originally been intrusted to him, and to show a faithful improvement of the same. If any one of the servants had been found to have "lacked" a part, or the whole, of the original treasure, because he had culpably lost it, think you that the fact that it was now gone from his possession, and was past recovery, would have been accepted as a valid excuse from the original obligations imposed upon him? In like manner, the fact, that man cannot reinstate himself in his original condition of holiness and blessedness, from which he has fallen by apostasy, will not suffice to justify him before God for being in a helpless state of sin and misery, or to give him any claims upon God for deliverance from it. God can and does pity him, in his ruined and lost estate, and if the creature will cast himself upon His mercy, acknowledging the righteousness of the entire claims of God upon him for a sinless perfection and a perfect service, he will meet and find mercy. But if he takes the ground that he does not owe such an immense debt as this, and that God has no right to demand from him, in his apostate and helpless condition, the same perfection of character and obedience which holy Adam possessed and rendered, and which the unfallen angels possess and render, God will leave him to the workings of conscience, and the operations of stark unmitigated law and justice. "The kingdom of heaven,"—says our Lord,—"is likened unto a certain king which would take account of his servants. And when he had begun to reckon, one was brought unto him which owed him ten thousand talents; but forasmuch as he had not to pay, his lord commanded him to be sold, and his wife, and children, and all that he had, and payment to be made. The servant therefore fell down, and worshipped him, saying, Lord, have patience with me, and I will pay thee all. Then the lord of that servant was moved with compassion, and loosed him, and forgave him the debt" (Matt, xviii. 28-27). But suppose that that servant had disputed the claim, and had put in an appeal to justice instead of an appeal to mercy, upon the ground that inasmuch as he had lost his property and had nothing to pay with, therefore he was not obligated to pay, think you that the king would have conceded the equity of the claim? On the contrary, he would have entered into no argument in so plain a case, but would have "delivered him to the tormentors, till he should pay all that was due unto him." So likewise shall the heavenly Father do also unto you, and to every man, who attempts to diminish the original claim of God to a perfect obedience and service, by pleading the fall of man, the corruption of human nature, the strength of sinful inclination and affections, and the power of earthly temptation. All these are man's work, and not that of the Creator. This helplessness and bondage grows directly out of the nature of sin. "Whosoever committeth sin is the slave of sin. Know ye not, that to whom ye yield yourselves slaves to obey, his slaves ye are to whom ye obey; whether of sin unto death, or of obedience unto righteousness?" (John viii. 34; Rom. vi. 16).

In view of the subject as thus discussed, we invite attention to some practical conclusions that flow directly out of it. For, though we have been speaking upon one of the most difficult themes in Christian theology, namely man's creation in holiness and his loss of holiness by the apostasy in Adam, yet we have at the same time been speaking of one of the most humbling, and practically profitable, doctrines in the whole circle of revealed truth. We never shall arrive at any profound sense of sin, unless we know and feel our guilt and corruption by nature; and we shall never arrive at any profound sense of our guilt and corruption by nature, unless we know and understand the original righteousness and innocence in which we were first created. We can measure the great depth of the abyss into which, we have fallen, only by looking up to those great heights in the garden of Eden, upon which our nature once stood beautiful and glorious, the very image and likeness of our Creator.

1. We remark then, in the first place, that it is the duty of every man to humble himself on account of his lack of original righteousness, and to repent of it as sin before God.

One of the articles of the Presbyterian Confession of Faith reads thus: Every sin, both original and actual, being a transgression of the righteous law of God, and contrary thereunto, doth, in its own nature, bring guilt upon the sinner, whereby he is "bound over to the wrath of God, and curse of the law, and so made subject to death, with all miseries spiritual, temporal, and eternal."[2] The Creed which we accept summons us to repent of original as well as actual sin; and it defines original sin to be "the want of original righteousness, together with the corruption of the whole nature." The want of original righteousness, then, is a ground of condemnation, and therefore a reason for shame, and godly sorrow. It is something which man once had, ought still to have, but now lacks; and therefore is ill-deserving, for the very same reason that the young ruler's lack of supreme love to God was ill-deserving.

If we acknowledge the validity of the distinction between a sin of omission and a sin of commission, and concede that each alike is culpable,[3] we shall find no difficulty with this demand of the Creed. Why should not you and I mourn over the total want of the image of God in our hearts, as much as over any other form and species of sin? This image of God consists in holy reverence. When we look into our hearts, and find no holy reverence there, ought we not to be filled with shame and sorrow? This image of God consists in filial and supreme affection for God, such as the young ruler lacked; and when we look into our hearts, and find not a particle of supreme love to God in them, ought we not to repent of this original, this deep-seated, this innate depravity? This image of God, again, which was lost in our apostasy, consisted in humble constant trust in God; and when we search our souls, and perceive that there is nothing of this spirit in them, but on the contrary a strong and overmastering disposition to trust in ourselves, and to distrust our Maker, ought not this discovery to waken in us the very same feeling that Isaiah gave expression to, when he said that the whole head is sick, and the whole heart is faint; the very same feeling that David gave expression to, when he cried: "Behold I was shapen in iniquity, and in sin did my mother conceive me?"

This is to repent of original sin, and there is no mystery or absurdity about it. It is to turn the eye inward, and see what is lacking in our heart and affections; and not merely what of outward and actual transgressions we have committed. Those whose idea of moral excellence is like that of the young ruler; those who suppose holiness to consist merely in the outward observance of the commandments of the second table; those who do not look into the depths of their nature, and contrast the total corruption that is there, with the perfect and positive righteousness that ought to be there, and that was there by creation,—all such will find the call of the Creed to repent of original sin as well as of actual, a perplexity and an impossibility. But every man who knows that the substance of piety consists in positive and holy affections,—in holy reverence, love and trust,—and who discovers that these are wanting in him by nature, though belonging to him by creation, will mourn in deep contrition and self-abasement over that act of apostasy by which this great change in human character, this great lack was brought about. 2. In the second place, it follows from the subject we have discussed, that every man must, by some method, recover his original righteousness, or be ruined forever. "Without holiness no man shall see the Lord." No rational creature is fit to appear in the presence of his Maker, unless he is as pure and perfect as he was originally made. Holy Adam was prepared by his creation in the image of God, to hold blessed communion with God, and if he and his posterity had never lost this image, they would forever be in fellowship with their Creator and Sovereign. Holiness, and holiness alone, enables the creature to stand with angelic tranquillity, in the presence of Him before whom the heavens and the earth flee away. The loss of original righteousness, therefore, was the loss of the wedding garment; it was the loss of the only robe in which the creature could appear at the banquet of God. Suppose that one of the posterity of sinful Adam, destitute of holy love reverence and faith, lacking positive and perfect righteousness, should be introduced into the seventh heavens, and there behold the infinite Jehovah. Would he not feel, with a misery and a shame that could not

120

be expressed, that he was naked? that he was utterly unfit to appear in such a Presence? No wonder that our first parents, after their apostasy, felt that they were unclothed. They were indeed stripped of their character, and had not a rag of righteousness to cover them. No wonder that they hid themselves from the intolerable purity and brightness of the Most High. Previously, they had felt no such emotion. They were "not ashamed," we are told. And the reason lay in the fact that, before their apostasy, they were precisely as they were made. They were endowed with the image of God; and their original righteousness and perfect holiness qualified them to stand before their Maker, and to hold blessed intercourse with Him. But the instant they lost their created endowment of holiness, they were conscious that they lacked that indispensable something wherewith to appear before God.

And precisely so is it, with their posterity. Whatever a man's theory of the future life may be, he must be insane, if he supposes that he is fit to appear before God, and to enter the society of heaven, if destitute of holiness, and wanting the Divine image. When the spirit of man returns to God who gave it, it must return as good as it came from His hands, or it will be banished from the Divine presence. Every human soul, when it goes back to its Maker, must carry with it a righteousness, to say the very least, equal to that in which it was originally created, or it will be cast out as an unprofitable and wicked servant. All the talents entrusted must be returned; and returned with usury. A modern philosopher and poet represents the suicide as justifying the taking of his own life, upon the ground that he was not asked in the beginning, whether he wanted life. He had no choice whether he would come into existence or not; existence was forced upon him; and therefore he had a right to put an end to it, if he so pleased. To this, the reply is made, that he ought to return his powers and faculties to the Creator in as good condition as he received them; that he had no right to mutilate and spoil them by abuse, and then fling the miserable relics of what was originally a noble creation, in the face of the Creator. In answer to the suicide's proposition to give back his spirit to God who gave it, the poet represents God as saying to him:

"Is't returned as 'twas sent? Is't no worse for the wear?
Think first what you are! Call to mind what you were!
I gave you innocence, I gave you hope,
Gave health, and genius, and an ample scope.
Return you me guilt, lethargy, despair?
Make out the invent'ry; inspect, compare!
Then die,—if die you dare!" [4]

Yes, this is true and solemn reasoning. You and I, and every man, must by some method, or other, go back to God as good as we came forth from Him. We must regain our original righteousness; we must be reinstated in our primal relation to God, and our created condition; or there is nothing in store for us, but the blackness of darkness. We certainly cannot stand in the judgment clothed with original sin, instead of original righteousness; full of carnal and selfish affections, instead of pure and heavenly affections. This great lack, this great vacuum, in our character, must by some method be filled up with solid, and everlasting excellencies, or the same finger that wrote, in letters of fire, upon the wall of the Babylonian monarch, the awful legend: "Thou art weighed in the balance, and art found wanting," will write it in letters of fire upon our own rational spirit.

There is but one method, by which man's original righteousness and innocency can be regained; and this method you well know. The blood of Jesus Christ sprinkled by the Holy Ghost, upon your guilty conscience, reinstates you in innocency. When that is applied, there is no more guilt upon you, than there was upon Adam the instant he came from the creative hand. "There is no condemnation to them that are in Christ Jesus." Who is he that condemneth, when it is Christ that died, and God that justifies? And when the same Holy Spirit enters your soul with renewing power, and carries forward His work of sanctification to its final completion, your original righteousness returns again, and you are again clothed in that spotless robe with which your nature was invested, on that sixth day of creation, when the Lord God said, "Let us make man in our image, and after our likeness." Ponder these truths, and what is yet more imperative, act upon them. Remember that you must, by some method, become a perfect creature, in order to become a blessed creature in heaven. Without holiness you cannot see the Lord. You must recover the character which you have lost, and the peace with God in which you were created. Your spirit, when it returns to God, must by some method be made equal to what it was when it came forth from Him. And there is no method, but the method of redemption by the blood and righteousness of Christ. Men are running to and fro after other methods. The memories of a golden age, a better humanity than they now know of, haunt them; and they sigh for the elysium that is gone. One sends you to letters, and culture, for your redemption. Another tells you that morality, or philosophy, will lift you again to those paradisaical heights that tower high above your straining vision. But miserable comforters are they all. No golden age returns; no peace with God or self is the result of such instrumentality. The conscience is still perturbed, the forebodings still overhang the soul like a black cloud, and the heart is as throbbing and restless as ever. With resoluteness, then, turn away from these inadequate, these feeble methods, and adopt the method of God Almighty. Turn away with contempt from human culture, and finite forces, as the instrumentality for the redemption of the soul which is precious, and which ceaseth forever if it is unredeemed. Go with confidence, and courage, and a rational faith, to God Almighty, to God the Redeemer. He hath power. He is no feeble and finite creature. He waves a mighty weapon, and sweats great drops of blood; travelling in the greatness of His strength. Hear His words of calm confidence and power: "Come unto me, all ye that labor and are heavy-laden, and I will give you rest."

[**Note 1:** *The Augustinian doctrine, that the entire human species was created on the sixth day, existed as a nature (not as individuals) in the first human pair, acted in and fell with them in the first transgression, and us thus fallen and vitiated by an act of self-will has been procreated or individualized, permits the theologian, to say that all men are equally concerned in the origin of sin, and to charge the guilt of its origin upon all alike.*]
[**Note 2:** *CONFESSION OF FAITH. VI. vi.*]
[**Note 3:** *One of the points of difference between the Protestant and the Papist, when the dogmatic position of each was taken, related to the guilt of original sin,—the former affirm-*

XV - The Approbation of Goodness is Not the Love of It

ROMANS ii. 21—23.— *"Thou therefore which, teachest another, teachest Thou not thyself? thou that preachest a man should not steal, dost thou steal? thou that sayest a man should not commit adultery, dost thou commit adultery? thou that abhorrest idols, dost thou commit sacrilege? thou that makest thy boast of the law, through, breaking the law dishonorest thou God?"*

The apostle Paul is a very keen and cogent reasoner. Like a powerful logician who is confident that he has the truth upon his side, and like a pureminded man who has no sinister ends to gain, he often takes his stand upon the same ground with his opponent, adopts his positions, and condemns him out of his own mouth. In the passage from which the text is taken, he brings the Jew in guilty before God, by employing the Jew's own claims and statements. "Behold thou art called a Jew, and restest in the law, and makest thy boast of God, and knowest his will, and approvest the things that are more excellent, and art confident that thou thyself art a guide of the blind, a light of them which are in darkness, an instructor of the foolish. Thou therefore which teachest another, teachest thou not thyself? thou that preachest that a man should not steal, dost thou steal? thou that makest thy boast of the law, through breaking the law dishonorest thou God?" As if he had said: "You claim to be one of God's chosen people, to possess a true knowledge of Him and His law; why do you not act up to this knowledge? why do you not by your character and conduct prove the claim to be a valid one?"

The apostle had already employed this same species of argument against the Gentile world. In the first chapter of this Epistle to the Romans, St. Paul demonstrates that the pagan world is justly condemned by God, because, they too, like the Jew, knew more than they practised. He affirms that the Greek and Roman world, like the Jewish people, "when they knew God, glorified him not as God, neither were thankful;" that as "they did not like to retain God in their knowledge, God gave them over to a reprobate mind;" and that "knowing the judgment of God, that they which commit such things" as he had just enumerated in that awful catalogue of pagan vices "are worthy of death, not only do the same, but have pleasure in them that do them." The apostle does not for an instant concede, that the Gentile can put in the plea that he was so entirely ignorant of the character and law of God, that he ought to be excused from the obligation to love and obey Him. He expressly affirms that where there is absolutely no law, and no knowledge of law, there can be no transgression; and yet affirms that in the day of judgment every mouth must be stopped, and the whole world must plead guilty before God. It is indeed true, that he teaches that there is a difference in the degrees of knowledge which the Jew and the Gentile respectively possess. The light of revealed religion, in respect to man's duty and obligations, is far

123

clearer than the light of nature, and increases the responsibilities of those who enjoy it, and the condemnation of those who abuse it; but the light of nature is clear and true as far as it goes, and is enough to condemn every soul outside of the pale of Revelation. For, in the day of judgment, there will not be a single human creature who can look his Judge in the eye, and say: "I acted up to every particle of moral light that I enjoyed; I never thought a thought, felt a feeling, or did a deed, for which my conscience reproached me."

It follows from this, that the language of the apostle, in the text, may be applied to every man. The argument that has force for the Jew has force for the Gentile. "Thou that teachest another, teachest thou not thyself? thou that preachest that a man should not steal, dost thou steal?" You who know the character and claims of God, and are able to state them to another, why do you not revere and obey them in your own person? You who approve of the law of God as pure and perfect, why do you not conform your own heart and conduct to it? You who perceive the excellence of piety in another, you who praise and admire moral excellence in your fellow-man, why do you not seek after it, and toil after it in your own heart? In paying this tribute of approbation to the character of a God whom you do not yourself love and serve, and to a piety in your neighbor which you do not yourself possess and cultivate, are you not writing down your own condemnation? How can you stand before the judgment-seat of God, after having in this manner confessed through your whole life upon earth that God is good, and His law is perfect, and yet through that whole life have gone counter to your own confession, neither loving that God, nor obeying that law? "To him that knoweth to do good and doeth it not, to him it is sin." (James iv. 17.)

The text then, together with the chains of reasoning that are connected with it, leads us to consider the fact, that a man may admire and praise moral excellence without possessing or practising it himself; that the approbation of goodness is not the same as the love of it.[1]

I. This is proved, in the first place, from the testimony of both God and man. The assertions and reasonings of the apostle Paul have already been alluded to, and there are many other passages of Scripture which plainly imply that men may admire and approve of a virtue which they do not practise. Indeed, the language of our Lord respecting the Scribes and Pharisees, may be applied to disobedient mankind at large: "Whatsoever they bid you observe, that observe and do; but do ye not after their works: for they say, and do not." (Matt, xxiii. 3.) The testimony of man is equally explicit. That is a very remarkable witness which the poet Ovid bears to this truth. "I see the right,"—he says,—"and approve of it, but I follow and practise the wrong." This is the testimony of a profligate man of pleasure, in whom the light of nature had been greatly dimmed in the darkness of sin and lust. But he had not succeeded in annihilating his conscience, and hence, in a sober hour, he left upon record his own damnation. He expressly informed the whole cultivated classical world, who were to read his polished numbers, that he that had taught others had not taught himself; that he who had said that a man should not commit adultery had himself committed adultery; that an educated Roman who never saw the volume of inspiration, and never heard of either Moses or Christ, nevertheless approved of and praised a virtue that he never put in practice. And whoever will turn to the pages of Horace, a kindred spirit to Ovid both in respect to a most exquisite taste and a most refined earthliness, will frequently find the same confession breaking out. Nay, open the volumes of Rousseau, and even of Voltaire, and read their panegyrics of virtue, their eulogies of goodness. What are these, but testimonies that they, too, saw the right and did the wrong. It is true, that the eulogy is merely sentimentalism, and is very different from the sincere and noble tribute which a good man renders to goodness. Still, it is valid testimony to the truth that the mere approbation of goodness is not the love of it. It is true, that these panegyrics of virtue, when read in the light of Rousseau's sensuality and Voltaire's malignity, wear a dead and livid hue, like objects seen in the illumination from phosphorus or rotten wood; yet, nevertheless, they are visible and readable, and testify as distinctly as if they issued from elevated and noble natures, that the teachings of man's conscience are not obeyed by man's heart,—that a man may praise and admire virtue, while he loves and practises vice.

II. A second proof that the approbation of goodness is not the love of it is found in the fact, that it is impossible not to approve of goodness, while it is possible not to love it. The structure of man's conscience is such, that he can commend only the right; but the nature of his will is such, that he may be conformed to the right or the wrong. The conscience can give only one judgment; but the heart and will are capable of two kinds of affection, and two courses of action. Every rational creature is shut up, by his moral sense, to but one moral conviction. He must approve the right and condemn the wrong. He cannot approve the wrong and condemn the right; any more than he can perceive that two and two make five. The human conscience is a rigid and stationary faculty. Its voice may be stifled or drowned, for a time; but it can never be made to titter two discordant voices. It is for this reason, that the approbation of goodness is necessary and universal. Wicked men and wicked angels must testify that benevolence is right, and malevolence is wrong; though they hate the former, and love the latter.

But it is not so with the human will. This is not a rigid and stationary faculty. It is capable of turning this way, and that way. It was created holy, and it turned from holiness to sin, in Adam's apostasy. And now, under the operation of the Divine Spirit, it turns back again, it converts from sin to holiness. The will of man is thus capable of two courses of action, while his conscience is capable of only one judgment; and hence he can see and approve the right, yet love and practise the wrong. If a man's conscience changed along with his heart and his will, so that when he began to love and practise sin, he at the same time began to approve of sin, the case would be different. If, when Adam apostatised from God, his conscience at that moment began to take sides with his sin, instead of condemning it, then, indeed, neither Ovid, nor Horace, nor Rousseau, nor any other one of Adam's posterity, would have been able to say: "I see the right and approve of it, while I follow the wrong." But it was not so. After apostasy, the conscience of Adam passed the same judgment upon sin that it did before. Adam heard its terrible voice speaking in concert with the voice of God, and hid himself. He never succeeded in bringing his conscience over to the side of his heart and will, and neither has any one of his posterity. It is impossible to do this. Satan himself, after millenniums of sin, still finds that his conscience, that the accusing and condemning law written on the heart, is too strong for him to alter, too rigid for him to bend. The utmost that either he, or any creature, can do, is to drown its verdict for a time in other sounds, only to hear the thunder-tones again, waxing longer and louder like the trumpet of Sinai.

Having thus briefly shown that the approbation of goodness is not the love of it, we proceed to draw some conclusions from the truth.

1. In the first place, it follows from this subject, that the mere workings of conscience are no proof of holiness. When, after the commission of a wrong act, the soul of a man is filled with self-reproach, he must not take it for granted that this is the stirring of a better nature within him, and is indicative of some remains of original righteousness. This reaction of conscience against his disobedience of law is as necessary, and unavoidable, as the action of his eyelids under the blaze of noon, and is worthy neither of praise nor blame, so far as he is concerned. It does not imply any love for holiness, or any hatred of sin. Nay, it may exist without any sorrow for sin, as in the instance of the hardened transgressor who writhes under its awful power, but never sheds a penitential tear, or sends up a sigh for mercy. The distinction between the human conscience, and the human heart, is as wide as between the human intellect, and the human heart.[2] We never think of confounding the functions and operations of the understanding with those of the heart. We know that an idea or a conception, is totally different from an emotion, or a feeling. How often do we remark, that a man may have an intellectual perception, without any correspondent experience or feeling in his heart. How continually does the preacher urge his hearers to bring their hearts into harmony with their understandings, so that their intellectual orthodoxy may become their practical piety.

Now, all this is true of the distinction between the conscience and the heart. The conscience is an intellectual faculty, and by that better elder philosophy which comprehended all the powers of the soul under the two general divisions of understanding and will, would be placed in the domain of the understanding. Conscience is a light, as we so often call it. It is not a life; it is not a source of life. No man's heart and will can be renewed or changed by his conscience. Conscience is simply a law. Conscience is merely legislative; it is never executive. It simply says to the heart and will: "Do thus, feel thus," but it gives no assistance, and imparts no inclination to obey its own command.

Those, therefore, commit a grave error both in philosophy and religion, who confound the conscience with the heart, and suppose that because there is in every man self-reproach and remorse after the commission of sin, therefore there is the germ of holiness within him. Holiness is love, the positive affection of the heart. It is a matter of the heart and the will. But this remorse is purely an affair of the conscience, and the heart has no connection with it. Nay, it appears in its most intense form, in those beings whose feelings emotions and determinations are in utmost opposition to God and goodness. The purest remorse in the universe is to be found in those wretched beings whose emotional and active powers, whose heart and will, are in the most bitter hostility to truth and righteousness. How, then, can the mere reproaches and remorse of conscience be regarded as evidence of piety?

2. But, we may go a step further than this, though in the same general direction, and remark, in the second place, that elevated moral sentiments are no certain proof of piety toward God and man. These, too, like remorse of conscience, spring out of the intellectual structure, and may exist without any affectionate love of God in the heart. There is a species of nobleness and beauty in moral excellence that makes an involuntary and unavoidable impression. When the Christian martyr seals his devotion to God and truth with his blood; when a meek and lowly disciple of Christ clothes his life of poverty, and self-denial, with a daily beauty greater than that of the lilies or of Solomon's array; when the poor widow with feeble and trembling steps comes up to the treasury of the Lord, and casts in all her living; when any pure and spiritual act is performed out of solemn and holy love of God and man, it is impossible not to be filled with sentiments of admiration, and oftentimes, with an enthusiastic glow of soul. We see this in the impression which the character of Christ universally makes. There are multitudes of men, to whom that wonderful sinless life shines aloft like a star. But they do not imitate it. They admire it, but they do not love it.[3] The spiritual purity and perfection of the Son of God rays out a beauty which really attracts their cultivated minds, and their refined taste; but when He says to them: "Take my yoke upon you, and learn of me, for I am meek and lowly of heart; take up thy cross daily and follow me;" they turn away sorrowful, like the rich young man in the Gospel,—sorrowful, because their sentiments like his are elevated, and they have a certain awe of eternal things, and know that religion is the highest concern; and sorrowful, because their hearts and wills are still earthly, there is no divine love in their souls, self is still their centre, and the self-renunciation that is required of them is repulsive. Religion is submission,—absolute submission to God,—and no amount of mere admiration of religion can be a substitute for it.

As a thoughtful observer looks abroad over society, he sees a very interesting class who are not far from the kingdom of God; who, nevertheless, are not within that kingdom, and who, therefore, if they remain where they are, are as certainly lost as if they were at an infinite distance from the kingdom. The homely proverb applies to them: "A miss is as good as a mile." They are those who suppose that elevated moral sentiments, an aesthetic pleasure in noble acts or noble truths, a glow and enthusiasm of the soul at the sight or the recital of examples of Christian virtue and Christian grace, a disgust at the gross and repulsive forms and aspects of sin,—that such merely intellectual and aesthetic experiences as these are piety itself. All these may be in the soul, without any godly sorrow over sin, any cordial trust in Christ's blood, any self-abasement before God, any daily conflict with indwelling corruption, any daily cross-bearing and toil for Christ's dear sake. These latter, constitute the essence of the Christian experience, and without them that whole range of elevated sentiments and amiable qualities, to which we have alluded, only ministers to the condemnation instead of the salvation of the soul. For, the question of the text comes home with solemn force, to all such persons. "Thou that makest thy boast of the law, through breaking of the law, dishonorest thou God?" If the beauty of virtue, and the grandeur of truth, and the sublimity of invisible things, have been able to make such an impression upon your intellects, and your tastes,—upon that part of your constitution which is fixed and stationary, which responds organically to such objects, and which is not the seat of moral character,—then why is there not a corresponding influence and impression made by them upon your heart? If you can admire and praise them, in this style, why do you not love them? Why is it, that when the character of Christ bows your intellect, it does not bend your will, and sway your affections? Must there not be an inveterate opposition and resistance in the heart? in the heart which can refuse submission to such high claims, when so distinctly seen? in the heart which can refuse to take the yoke, and learn of a Teacher who has already made such an impression upon the conscience and the understanding?

The human heart is, as the prophet affirms, desperately wicked, desperately selfish. And perhaps its self-love is never more plainly seen, than in such instances as those of that moral and cultivated young man mentioned in the Gospel, and that class in modern society who correspond to him. Nowhere is the difference between the approbation of goodness, and the love of it, more apparent. In these instances the approbation is of a high order. It is refined and sublimated by culture and taste. It is not stained by the temptations of low life, and gross sin. If there ever could be a case, in which the intellectual approbation of goodness would develop and pass over into the affectionate and hearty love of it, we should expect to find it here. But it is not found. The young man goes away,— sorrowful indeed,—but he goes away from the Redeemer of the world, never to return. The amiable, the educated, the refined, pass on from year to year, and, so far as the evangelic sorrow, and the evangelic faith are concerned, like the dying Beaufort depart to judgment making no sign. We hear their praises of Christian men, and Christian graces, and Christian actions; we enjoy the grand and swelling sentiments with which, perhaps, they enrich the common literature of the world; but we never hear them cry: "God be merciful to me a sinner; O Lamb of God, that takest away the sin of the world, grant me thy peace; Thou, O God, art the strength of my heart, and my portion forever."

3. In the third place, it follows from this subject, that in order to holiness in man there must be a change in his heart and will. If our analysis is correct, no possible modification of either his conscience, or his intellect, would produce holiness. Holiness is an affection of the heart, and an inclination of the will. It is the love and practice of goodness, and not the mere approbation and admiration of it. Now, suppose that the conscience should be stimulated to the utmost, and remorse should be produced until it filled the soul to overflowing, would there be in this any of that gentle and blessed affection for God and goodness, that heartfelt love of them, which is the essence of religion? Or, suppose that the intellect merely were impressed by the truth, and very clear perceptions of the Christian system and of the character and claims of its Author were imparted, would the result be any different? If the heart and will were unaffected; if the influences and impressions were limited merely to the conscience and the understanding; would not the seat of the difficulty still be untouched? The command is not: "Give me thy conscience," but, "Give me thy heart."

Hence, that regeneration of which our Lord speaks in his discourse with Nicodemus is not a radical change of the conscience, but of the will and affections. We have already seen that the conscience cannot undergo a radical change. It can never be made to approve what it once condemned, and to condemn what it once approved. It is the stationary legislative faculty, and is, of necessity, always upon the side of law and of God. Hence, the apostle Paul sought to commend the truth which he preached, to every man's conscience, knowing that every man's conscience was with him. The conscience, therefore, does not need to be converted, that is to say, made opposite to what it is. It is indeed greatly stimulated, and rendered vastly more energetic, by the regeneration of the heart; but this is not radically to alter it. This is to develop and educate the conscience; and when holiness is implanted in the will and affections, by the grace of the Spirit, we find that both the conscience and understanding are wonderfully unfolded and strengthened. But they undergo no revolution or conversion. The judgments of the conscience are the same after regeneration, that they were before; only more positive and emphatic. The convictions of the understanding continue, as before, to be upon the side of truth; only they are more clear and powerful.

The radical change, therefore, must be wrought in the heart and will. These are capable of revolutions and radical changes. They can apostatise in Adam, and be regenerated in Christ. They are not immovably fixed and settled, by their constitutional structure, in only one way. They have once turned from holiness to sin; and now they must be turned back again from sin to holiness. They must become exactly contrary to what they now are. The heart must love what it now hates, and must hate what it now loves. The will must incline to what it now disinclines, and disincline to what it now inclines. But this is a radical change, a total change, an entire revolution. If any man be in Christ Jesus, he is a new creature, in his will and affections, in his inclination and disposition. While, therefore, the conscience must continue to give the same old everlasting testimony as before, and never reverse its judgments in the least, the affections and will, the pliant, elastic, plastic part of man, the seat of vitality, of emotion, the seat of character, the fountain out of which proceed the evil thoughts or the good thoughts,—this executive, emotive, responsible part of man, must be reversed, converted, radically changed into its own contrary.

So long, therefore, as this change remains to be effected in an individual, there is and can be no holiness within him,—none of that holiness without which no man can see the Lord. There may be within him a very active and reproaching conscience; there may be intellectual orthodoxy and correctness in religious convictions; he may cherish elevated moral sentiments, and many attractive qualities springing out of a cultivated taste and a jealous self-respect may appear in his character; but unless he loves God and man out of a pure heart fervently, and unless his will is entirely and sweetly submissive to the Divine will, so that he can say: "Father not my will, but thine be done," he is still a natural man. He is still destitute of the spiritual mind, and to him it must be said, as it was to Nicodemus: "Except a man be born again, he cannot see the kingdom of God." The most important side of his being is still alienated from God. The heart with its affections; the will with its immense energies,—the entire active and emotive portions of his nature,—are still earthly, unsubmissive, selfish, and sinful.

4. In the fourth, and last place, we see from this subject the necessity of the operation of the Holy Spirit, in order to holiness in man.

There is no part of man's complex being which is less under his own control, than his own will, and his own affections. This he discovers, as soon as he attempts to convert them; as soon as he tries to produce a radical change in them. Let a man whose will, from centre to circumference, is set upon self and the world, attempt to reverse it, and set it with the same strength and energy upon God and heaven, and he will know that his will is too strong for him, and that he cannot overcome himself. Let a man whose affections cleave like those of Dives to earthly good, and find their sole enjoyment in earthly pleasures, attempt to change them into their own contraries, so that they shall cleave to God, and take a real delight in heavenly things,—let a carnal man try to revolutionize himself into a spiritual man,—and he will discover that the affections and feelings of his heart are beyond his control. And the reason of this is plain. The affections and will of a man show what he loves, and what he is inclined to. A sinful man cannot, therefore, overcome his sinful love and inclination, because he cannot make a beginning. The instant he attempts to love God, he finds his love of himself in the way. This new love for a new object, which he proposes to originate within himself, is prevented by an old love, which already has possession. This new inclination to heaven and Divine things is precluded by an old inclination, very strong and very set, to earth and earthly things. There is therefore no starting-point, in this affair of self-conversion. He proposes, and he tries, to think a holy thought, but there is a sinful thought already in the mind. He attempts to start out a Christian grace,—say the grace of humility,—but the feeling of pride already stands in the way, and, what is more, remains in the way. He tries to generate that supreme love of God, of which he has heard so much, but the supreme love of himself is ahead of him, and occupies the whole ground. In short, he is baffled at every point in this attempt radically to change his own heart and will, because at every point this heart and will are already committed and determined. Go down as low as he pleases, he finds sin,—love of sin, and inclination to sin. He never reaches a point where these cease; and therefore never reaches a point where he can begin a new love, and a new inclination. The late Mr. Webster was once engaged in a law case, in which he had to meet, upon the opposing side, the subtle and strong understanding of Jeremiah Mason. In one of his conferences with his associate counsel, a difficult point to be managed came to view. After some discussion, without satisfactory results, respecting the best method of handling the difficulty, one of his associates suggested that the point might after all, escape the notice of the opposing counsel. To this, Mr. Webster replied: "Not so; go down as deep as you will, you will find Jeremiah Mason below you." Precisely so in the case of which we are speaking. Go down as low as you please into your heart and will, you will find your self below you; you will find sin not only lying at the door, but lying in the way. If you move in the line of your feelings and affections, you will find earthly feelings and affections ever below you. If you move in the line of your choice and inclination, you will find a sinful choice and inclination ever below you. In chasing your sin through the avenues of your fallen and corrupt soul, you are chasing your horizon; in trying to get clear of it by your own isolated and independent strength, you are attempting (to use the illustration of Goethe, who however employed it for a false purpose) to jump off your own shadow.

This, then, is the reason why the heart and will of a sinful man are so entirely beyond his own control. They are preoccupied and predetermined, and therefore he cannot make a beginning in the direction of holiness. If he attempts to put forth a holy determination, he finds a sinful one already made and making,—and this determination is his determination, unforced, responsible and guilty. If he tries to start out a holy emotion, he finds a sinful emotion already beating and rankling,—and this emotion is his emotion, unforced, responsible, and guilty. There is no physical necessity resting upon him. Nothing but this love of sin and inclination to self stands in the way of a supreme love of God and holiness; but it stands in the way. Nothing but the sinful affection of the heart prevents a man from exercising a holy affection; but it prevents him effectually. An evil tree cannot bring forth good fruit; a sinful love and inclination cannot convert itself into a holy love and inclination; Satan cannot cast out Satan.

There is need therefore of a Divine operation to renew, to radically change, the heart and will. If they cannot renew themselves, they must be renewed; and there is no power that can reach them but that mysterious energy of the Holy Spirit which like the wind bloweth where it listeth, and we hear the sound thereof, but cannot tell whence it cometh or whither it goeth. The condition of the human heart is utterly hopeless, were it not for the promised influences of the Holy Ghost to regenerate it.

There are many reflections suggested by this subject; for it has a wide reach, and would carry us over vast theological spaces, should we attempt to exhaust it. We close with the single remark, that it should be man's first and great aim to obtain the new heart. Let him seek this first of all, and all things else will be added unto him. It matters not how active your conscience may be, how clear and accurate your intellectual convictions of truth may be, how elevated may be your moral sentiments and your admiration of virtue, if you are destitute of an evangelical experience. Of what value will all these be in the day of judgment, if you have never sorrowed for sin, never appropriated the atonement for sin, and never been inwardly sanctified? Our Lord says to every man: "Either make the tree good, and its fruit good; or else make the tree corrupt, and its fruit corrupt." The tree itself must be made good. The heart and will themselves must be renewed. These are the root and stock into which everything else is grafted; and so long as they remain in their apostate natural condition, the man is sinful and lost, do what else he may. It is indeed true, that such a change as this is beyond your power to accomplish. With man it is impossible; but with God it is a possibility, and a reality. It has actually been wrought in thousands of wills, as stubborn as yours; in millions of hearts, as worldly and selfish as yours. We commend you, therefore, to the Person and Work of the Holy Spirit. We remind you, that He is able to renovate and sweetly incline the obstinate will, to soften and spiritualize the flinty heart. He saith: "I will put a new spirit within you; and I will take the stony heart out of your flesh, and will give you an heart of flesh; that ye may walk in my statutes, and keep mine ordinances, and do them; and ye shall be my people, and I will be your God." Do not listen to these declarations and promises of God supinely; but arise and earnestly plead them. Take words upon your lips, and go before God. Say unto Him: "I am the clay, be thou the potter. Behold thou desirest truth in the inward parts, and in the hidden parts thou shalt make me to know wisdom. I will run in the way of thy commandments, when thou shalt enlarge my heart. Create within me a clean heart, O God, and renew within me a right spirit." Seek for the new heart. Ask for the new heart. Knock for the new heart. "For, if ye, being evil, know how to give good gifts unto your children, how much more shall your heavenly Father give the Holy Spirit to them that ask him."

And in giving the Holy Spirit, He gives the new heart, with all that is included in it, and all that issues from it.

[Note 1: See, upon this whole subject of conscience as distinguished from will, and of amiable instincts as distinguished from holiness, the profound and discriminating views of ED-WARDS: The Nature of Virtue, Chapters v. vi. vii.]
[Note 2: Compare, on this distinction, the AUTHOR'S' Discourses and Essays, p. 284 sq.]
[Note 3: The reader will recall the celebrated panegyric upon Christ by Rousseau.]

XVI - The Use of Fear in Religion

PROVERBS ix. 10.—*"The fear of the Lord is the beginning of wisdom." Luke xii. 4, 5.—"And I say unto you, my friends, Be not afraid of them that kill the body, and after that have no more that they can do. But I will forewarn you whom ye shall fear: Fear him, which after he hath killed hath power to cast into hell; yea, I say unto you, Fear him."*

The place which the feeling of fear ought to hold in the religious experience of mankind is variously assigned. Theories of religion are continually passing from one extreme to another, according as they magnify or disparage this emotion. Some theological schools are distinguished for their severity, and others for their sentimentalism. Some doctrinal systems fail to grasp the mercy of God with as much vigor and energy as they do the Divine justice, while others melt down everything that is scriptural and self-consistent, and flow along vaguely in an inundation of unprincipled emotions and sensibilities.

The same fact meets us in the experience of the individual. We either fear too much, or too little. Having obtained glimpses of the Divine compassion, how prone is the human heart to become indolent and self-indulgent, and to relax something of that earnest effort with which it had begun to pluck out the offending right eye. Or, having felt the power of the Divine anger; having obtained clear conceptions of the intense aversion of God towards moral evil; even the child of God sometimes lives under a cloud, because he does not dare to make a right use of this needed and salutary impression, and pass back to that confiding trust in the Divine pity which is his privilege and his birth-right, as one who has been sprinkled with atoning blood.

It is plain, from the texts of Scripture placed at the head of this discourse, that the feeling and principle of fear is a legitimate one.[1] In these words of God himself, we are taught that it is the font and origin of true wisdom, and are commanded to be inspired by it. The Old Testament enjoins it, and the New Testament repeats and emphasizes the injunction; so that the total and united testimony of Revelation forbids a religion that is destitute of fear.

The New Dispensation is sometimes set in opposition to the Old, and Christ is represented as teaching a less rigid morality than that of Moses and the prophets. But the mildness of Christ is not seen, certainly, in the ethical and preceptive part of His religion. The Sermon on the Mount is a more searching code of morals than the ten commandments. It cuts into human depravity with a more keen and terrible edge, than does the law proclaimed amidst thunderings and lightnings. Let us see if it does not. The Mosaic statute simply says to man: "Thou shalt not kill." But the re-enactment of this statute, by incarnate Deity, is accompanied with an explanation and an emphasis that precludes all misapprehension and narrow construction of the original law, and renders it a two-edged sword that pierces to the dividing asunder of soul and spirit. When the Hebrew legislator says to me: "Thou shalt not kill," it is possible for me, with my propensity to look upon the outward appearance, and to regard the external act alone, to deem myself innocent if I have never actually murdered a fellow-being. But when the Lord of glory tells me that "whosoever is angry with his brother" is in danger of the judgment, my mouth is stopped, and it is impossible for me to cherish a conviction of personal innocency, in respect to the sixth commandment. And the same is true of the seventh commandment, and the eighth commandment, and of all the statutes in the decalogue. He who reads, and ponders, the whole Sermon on the Mount, is painfully conscious that Christ has put a meaning into the Mosaic law that renders it a far more effective instrument of mental torture, for the guilty, than it is as it stands in the Old Testament. The lightnings are concentrated. The bolts are hurled with a yet more sure and deadly aim. The new meaning is a perfectly legitimate and logical deduction, and in this sense there is no difference between the Decalogue and the Sermon,—between the ethics of the Old and the ethics of the New Testament. But, so much more spiritual is the application, and so much more searching is the reach of the statute, in the last of the two forms of its statement, that it looks almost like a new proclamation of law.

Our Lord did not intend, or pretend, to teach a milder ethics, or an easier virtue, on the Mount of Beatitudes, than that which He had taught fifteen centuries before on Mt. Sinai. He indeed pronounces a blessing; and so did Moses, His servant, before Him. But in each instance, it is a blessing upon condition of obedience; which, in both instances, involves a curse upon disobedience. He who is meek shall be blest; but he who is not shall be condemned. He who is pure in heart, he who is poor in spirit, he who mourns over personal unworthiness, he who hungers and thirsts after a righteousness of which he is destitute, he who is merciful, he who is the peace-maker, he who endures persecution patiently, and he who loves his enemies,—he who is and does all this in a perfect manner, without a single slip or failure, is indeed blessed with the beatitude of God. But where is the man? What single individual in all the ages, and in all the generations since Adam, is entitled to the great blessing of these beatitudes, and not deserving of the dreadful curse which they involve? In applying such a high, ethereal test to human character, the Founder of Christianity is the severest and sternest preacher of law that has ever trod upon the planet. And he who stops with the merely ethical and preceptive part of Christianity, and rejects its forgiveness through atoning blood, and its regeneration by an indwelling Spirit,— he who does not unite the fifth chapter of Matthew, with the fifth chapter of Romans,—converts the Lamb of God into the Lion of the tribe of Judah. He makes use of everything in the Christian system that condemns man to everlasting destruction, but throws away the very and the only part of it that takes off the burden and the curse.

133

It is not, then, a correct idea of Christ that we have, when we look upon Him as unmixed complacency and unbalanced compassion. In all aspects, He was a complex personage. He was God, and He was man. As God, He could pronounce a blessing; and He could pronounce a curse, as none but God can, or dare. As man, He was perfect; and into His perfection of feeling and of character there entered those elements that fill a good being with peace, and an evil one with woe. The Son of God exhibits goodness and severity mingled and blended in perfect and majestic harmony; and that man lacks sympathy with Jesus Christ who cannot, while feeling the purest and most unselfish indignation towards the sinner's sin, at the same time give up his own individual life, if need be, for the sinner's soul. The two feelings are not only compatible in the same person, but necessarily belong to a perfect being. Our Lord breathed out a prayer for His murderers so fervent, and so full of pathos, that it will continue to soften and melt the flinty human heart, to the end of time; and He also poured out a denunciation of woes upon the Pharisees (Matt, xxiii.), every syllable of which is dense enough with the wrath of God, to sink the deserving objects of it "plumb down, ten thousand fathoms deep, to bottomless perdition in adamantine chains and penal fire." The utterances, "Father forgive them, for they know not what they do: Ye serpents, ye generation of vipers! how can ye escape the damnation of hell?" both fell from the same pure and gracious lips.

It is not surprising, therefore, that our Lord often appeals to the principle of fear. He makes use of it in all its various forms,—from that servile terror which is produced by the truth when the soul is just waked up from its drowze in sin, to that filial fear which Solomon affirms to be the beginning of wisdom.

The subject thus brought before our minds, by the inspired Word, has a wide application to all ages and conditions of human life, and all varieties of human character. We desire to direct attention to the use and value of religious fear, in the opening periods of human life. There are some special reasons why youth and early manhood should come under the influence of this powerful feeling. "I write unto you young men,"—says St. John,—"because ye are strong." We propose to urge upon the young, the duty of cultivating the fear of God's displeasure, because they are able to endure the emotion; because youth is the springtide and prime of human life, and capable of carrying burdens, and standing up under influences and impressions, that might crush a feebler period, or a more exhausted stage of the human soul.

I. In the first place, the emotion of fear ought to enter into the consciousness of the young, because youth is naturally light-hearted. "Childhood and youth," saith the Preacher, "are vanity." The opening period in human life is the happiest part of it, if we have respect merely to the condition and circumstances in which the human being is placed. He is free from all public cares, and responsibilities. He is encircled within the strong arms of parents, and protectors. Even if he tries, he cannot feel the pressure of those toils and anxieties which will come of themselves, when he has passed the line that separates youth from manhood. When he hears his elders discourse of the weight, and the weariness, of this working-day world, it is with incredulity and surprise. The world is bright before his eye, and he wonders that it should ever wear any other aspect. He cannot understand how the freshness, and vividness, and pomp of human life, should shift into its soberer and sterner forms; and he will not, until the...

"Shades of the prison-house begin to close
Upon the growing Boy." [2]

Now there is something, in this happy attitude of things, to fill the heart of youth with gayety and abandonment. His pulses beat strong and high. The currents of his soul flow like the mountain river. His mood is buoyant and jubilant, and he flings himself with zest, and a sense of vitality, into the joy and exhilaration all around him. But such a mood as this, unbalanced and untempered by a loftier one, is hazardous to the eternal interests of the soul. Perpetuate this gay festal abandonment of the mind; let the human being, through the whole of his earthly course, be filled with the sole single consciousness that this is the beautiful world; and will he, can he, live as a stranger and a pilgrim in it? Perpetuate that vigorous pulse, and that youthful blood which "runs tickling up and down the veins;" drive off, and preclude, all that care and responsibility which renders human life so earnest; and will the young immortal go through it, with that sacred fear and trembling with which he is commanded to work out his salvation?

Yet, this buoyancy and light-heartedness are legitimate feelings. They spring up, like wild-flowers, from the very nature of man. God intends that prismatic hues and auroral lights shall flood our morning sky. He must be filled with a sour and rancid misanthropy, who cannot bless the Creator that there is one part of man's sinful and cursed life which reminds of the time, and the state, when there was no sin and no curse. There is, then, to be no extermination of this legitimate experience. But there is to be its moderation and its regulation.

And this we get, by the introduction of the feeling and the principle of religious fear. The youth ought to seek an impression from things unseen and eternal. God, and His august attributes; Christ, and His awful Passion; heaven, with its sacred scenes and joys; hell, with its just woe and wail,—all these should come in, to modify, and temper, the jubilance that without them becomes the riot of the soul. For this, we apprehend, is the meaning of our Lord, when He says, "I will forewarn you whom ye shall fear: Fear him, which after he hath killed hath power to cast into hell; yea, I say unto you, Fear him." It is not so much any particular species of fear that we are shut up to, by these words, as it is the general habit and feeling. The fear of hell is indeed specified,—and this proves that such a fear is rational and proper in its own place,—but our Lord would not have us stop with this single and isolated form of the feeling. He recommends a solemn temper. He commands a being who stands continually upon the brink of eternity and immensity, to be aware of his position. He would have the great shadow of eternity thrown in upon time. He desires that every man should realize, in those very moments when the sun shines the brightest and the earth looks the fairest, that there is another world than this, for which man is not naturally prepared, and for which he must make a preparation. And what He enjoins upon mankind at large, He specially enjoins upon youth. They need to be sobered more than others. The ordinary cares of this life, which do so much towards moderating our desires and aspirations, have not yet pressed upon the ardent and expectant soul, and therefore it needs, more than others, to fear and to "stand in awe."

II. Secondly, youth is elastic, and readily recovers from undue depression. The skeptical Lucretius tells us that the divinities are the creatures of man's fears, and would make us believe that all religion has its ground in fright.[3] And do we not hear this theory repeated by the modern unbeliever? What means this appeal to a universal, and an unprincipled good-nature in the Supreme Being, and this rejection of everything in Christianity that awakens misgivings and forebodings within the sinful human soul? Why this opposition to the doctrine of an absolute, and therefore endless punishment, unless it be that it awakens a deep and permanent dread in the heart of guilty man?

Now, we are not of that number who believe that thoughtless and lethargic man has been greatly damaged by his moral fears. It is the lack of a bold and distinct impression from the solemn objects of another world, and the utter absence of fear, that is ruining man from generation to generation. If we were at liberty, and had the power, to induce into the thousands and millions of our race who are running the rounds of sin and vice, some one particular emotion that should be medicinal and salutary to the soul, we would select that very one which our Lord had in view when He said: "I will forewarn you whom ye shall fear: Fear him, which after he hath killed hath power to cast into hell; yea, I say unto you, Fear him." If we were at liberty, and had the power, we would instantaneously stop these human souls that are crowding our avenues, intent only upon pleasure and earth, and would fill them with the emotions of the day of doom; we would deluge them with the fear of God, that they might flee from their sins and the wrath to come.

But while we say this, we also concede that it is possible for the human soul to be injured, by the undue exercise of this emotion. The bruised reed may be broken, and the smoking flax may be quenched; and hence it is the very function and office-work of the Blessed Comforter, to prevent this. God's own children sometimes pass through a horror of great darkness, like that which enveloped Abraham; and the unregenerate mind is sometimes so overborne by its fears of death, judgment, and eternity, that the entire experience becomes for a time morbid and confused. Yet, even in this instance, the excess is better than the lack. We had better travel this road to heaven, than none at all. It is better to enter into the kingdom of God with one eye, than having two eyes to be cast into hell-fire. When the saints from the heavenly heights look back upon their severe religious experience here on earth,—upon their footprints stained with their own blood,—they count it a small matter that they entered into eternal joy through much tribulation. And if we could but for one instant take their position, we should form their estimate; we should not shrink, if God so pleased, from passing through that martyrdom and crucifixion which has been undergone by so many of those gentle spirits, broken spirits, holy spirits, upon whom the burden of mystery once lay like night, and the far heavier burden of guilt lay like hell.

There is less danger, however, that the feeling and principle of fear should exert an excessive influence upon youth. There is an elasticity, in the earlier periods of human life, that prevents long-continued depression. How rare it is to see a young person smitten with insanity. It is not until the pressure of anxiety has been long continued, and the impulsive spring of the soul has been destroyed, that reason is dethroned. The morning of our life may, therefore, be subjected to a subduing and repressing influence, with very great safety. It is well to bear the yoke in youth. The awe produced by a vivid impression from the eternal world may enter into the exuberant and gladsome experience of the young, with very little danger of actually extinguishing it, and rendering life permanently gloomy and unhappy.

III. Thirdly, youth is exposed to sudden temptations, and surprisals into sin. The general traits that have been mentioned as belonging to the early period in human life render it peculiarly liable to solicitations. The whole being of a healthful hilarious youth, who feels life in every limb, thrills to temptation, like the lyre to the plectrum. Body and soul are alive to all the enticements of the world of sense; and in certain critical moments, the entire sensorium, upon the approach of bold and powerful excitements, flutters and trembles like an electrometer in a thunder-storm. All passionate poetry breathes of youth and spring. Most of the catastrophes of the novel and the drama turn upon the violent action of some temptation, upon the highly excitable nature of youth. All literature testifies to the hazards that attend the morning of our existence; and daily experience and observation, certainly, corroborate the testimony. It becomes necessary, therefore, to guard the human soul against these liabilities which attend it in its forming period. And, next to a deep and all-absorbing love of God, there is nothing so well adapted to protect against sudden surprisals, as a profound and definite fear of God.

It is a great mistake, to suppose that apostate and corrupt beings like ourselves can pass through all the temptations of this life unscathed, while looking solely at the pleasant aspects of the Divine Being, and the winning forms of religious truth. We are not yet seraphs; and we cannot always trust to our affectionateness, to carry us through a violent attack of temptation. There are moments in the experience of the Christian himself, when he is compelled to call in the fear of God to his aid, and to steady his infirm and wavering virtue by the recollection that "the wages of sin is death." "By the fear of the Lord, men,"—and Christian men too,—"depart from evil." It will not always be so. When that which is perfect is come, perfect love shall cast out fear; but, until the disciple of Christ reaches heaven, his religious experience must be a somewhat complex one. A reasonable and well-defined apprehensiveness must mix with his affectionateness, and deter him from transgression, in those severe passages in his history when love is languid and fails to draw him. Says an old English divine: "The fear of God's judgments, or of the threatenings of God, is of much efficiency, when some present temptation presseth upon us. When conscience and the affections are divided; when conscience doth withdraw a man from sin, and when his carnal affections draw him forth to it; then should the fear of God come in. It is a holy design for a Christian, to counterbalance the pleasures of sin with the terrors of it, and thus to cure the poison of the viper by the flesh of the viper. Thus that admirable saint and martyr, Bishop Hooper, when he came to die, one endeavored to dehort him from death by this: O sir, consider that life is sweet and death is bitter; presently he replied, Life to come is more sweet, and death to come is more bitter, and so went to the stake and patiently endured the fire. Thus, as a Christian may sometimes outweigh the pleasures of sin by the consideration of the reward of God, so, sometimes, he may quench the pleasures of sin by the consideration of the terrors of God."[4]

But much more is all this true, in the instance of the hot-blooded youth. How shall he resist temptation, unless he has some fear of God before his eyes? There are moments in the experience of the young, when all power of resistance seems to be taken away, by the very witchery and blandishment of the object. He has no heart, and no nerve, to resist the beautiful siren. And it is precisely in these emergencies in his experience,—in these moments when this world comes up before him clothed in pomp and gold, and the other world is so entirely lost sight of, that it throws in upon him none of its solemn shadows and warnings,—it is precisely now, when he is just upon the point of yielding to the mighty yet fascinating pressure, that he needs to feel an impression, bold and startling, from the wrath of God. Nothing but the most active remedies will have any effect, in this tumult and uproar of the soul. When the whole system is at fever-heat, and the voice of reason and conscience is drowned in the clamors of sense and earth, nothing can startle and stop but the trumpet of Sinai.[5]

It is in these severe experiences, which are more common to youth than they are to manhood, that we see the great value of the feeling and principle of fear. It is, comparatively, in vain for a youth under the influence of strong temptations,—and particularly when the surprise is sprung upon him,—to ply himself with arguments drawn from the beauty of virtue, and the excellence of piety. They are too ethereal for him, in his present mood. Such arguments are for a calmer moment, and a more dispassionate hour. His blood is now boiling, and those higher motives which would influence the saint, and would have some influence with him, if he were not in this critical condition, have little power to deter him from sin. Let him therefore pass by the love of God, and betake himself to the anger of God, for safety. Let him say to himself, in this moment when the forces of Satan, in alliance with the propensities of his own nature, are making an onset,—when all other considerations are being swept away in the rush and whirlwind of his passions,—let him coolly bethink himself and say: "If I do this abominable thing which the soul of God hates, then God, the Holy and Immaculate, will burn my spotted soul in His pure eternal flame." For, there is great power, in what the Scriptures term "the terror of the Lord," to destroy the edge of temptation. "A wise man feareth and departeth from evil." Fear kills out the delight in sin. Damocles cannot eat the banquet with any pleasure, so long as the naked sword hangs by a single hair over his head. No one can find much enjoyment in transgression, if his conscience is feeling the action of God's holiness within it. And well would it be, if, in every instance in which a youth is tempted to fling himself into the current of sin that is flowing all around him, his moral sense might at that very moment be filled with some of that terror, and some of that horror, which breaks upon the damned in eternity. Well would it be, if the youth in the moment of violent temptation could lay upon the emotion or the lust that entices him, a distinct and red coal of hell-fire.[6] No injury would result from the most terrible fear of God, provided it could always fall upon the human soul in those moments of strong temptation, and of surprisals, when all other motives fail to influence, and the human will is carried headlong by the human passions. There may be a fear and a terror that does harm, but man need be under no concern lest he experience too much of this feeling, in his hours of weakness and irresolution, in his youthful days of temptation and of dalliance. Let him rather bless God that there is such an intense light, and such a pure fire, in the Divine Essence, and seek to have his whole vitiated and poisoned nature penetrated and purified by it. Have you never looked with a steadfast gaze into a grate of burning anthracite, and noticed the quiet intense glow of the heat, and how silently the fire throbs and pulsates through the fuel, burning up everything that is inflammable, and, making the whole mass as pure, and clean, and clear, as the element of fire itself? Such is the effect of a contact of God's wrath with man's sin; of the penetration of man's corruption by the wrath of the Lord.

IV. In the fourth place, the feeling and principle of fear ought to enter into the experience of both youth and manhood, because it relieves from all other fear. He who stands in awe of God can look down, from a very great height, upon all other perturbation. When we have seen Him from whose sight the heavens and the earth flee away, there is nothing, in either the heavens or the earth, that can produce a single ripple upon the surface of our souls. This is true, even of the unregenerate mind. The fear in this instance is a servile one,—it is not filial and affectionate,—and yet it serves to protect the subject of it from all other feelings of this species, because it is greater than all others, and like Aaron's serpent swallows up the rest. If we must be liable to fears,—and the transgressor always must be,—it is best that they should all be concentrated in one single overmastering sentiment. Unity is ever desirable; and even if the human soul were to be visited by none but the servile forms of fear, it would be better that this should be the "terror of the Lord." If, by having the fear of God before our eyes, we could thereby be delivered from the fear of man, and all those apprehensions which are connected with time and sense, would it not be wisdom to choose it? We should then know that there was but one quarter from which our peace could be assailed. This would lead us to look in that direction; and, here upon earth, sinful man cannot look at God long, without coming to terms and becoming reconciled with Him.

V. The fifth and last reason which we assign for cherishing the feeling and principle of fear applies to youth, to manhood, and to old age, alike: The fear of God conducts to the love of God. Our Lord does not command us to fear "Him, who after he hath killed hath power to cast into hell," because such a feeling as this is intrinsically desirable, and is an ultimate end in itself. It is, in itself, undesirable, and is only a means to an end. By it, our torpid souls are to be awakened from their torpor; our numbness and hardness of mind, in respect to spiritual objects, is to be removed. We are never for a moment, to suppose that the fear of perdition is set before us as a model and permanent form of experience to be toiled after,—a positive virtue and grace intended to be perpetuated through the whole future history of the soul. It is employed only as an antecedent to a higher and a happier emotion; and when the purpose for which it has been elicited has been answered, it then disappears. "Perfect love casteth out fear; for fear hath torment," (1 John iv. 18.[7])

But, at the same time, we desire to direct attention to the fact that he who has been exercised with this emotion, thoroughly and deeply, is conducted by it into the higher and happier form of religious experience. Religious fear and anxiety are the prelude to religious peace and joy. These are the discords that prepare for the concords. He, who in the Psalmist's phrase has known the power of the Divine anger, is visited with the manifestation of the Divine love. The method in the thirty-second psalm is the method of salvation. Day and night God's hand is heavy upon the soul; the fear and sense of the Divine displeasure is passing through the conscience, like electric currents. The moisture, the sweet dew of health and happiness, is turned into the drought of summer, by this preparatory process. Then the soul acknowledges its sin, and its iniquity it hides no longer. It confesses its transgressions unto the Lord,—it justifies and approves of this wrath which it has felt,—and He forgives the iniquity of its sin.

It is not a vain thing, therefore, to fear the Lord. The emotion of which we have been discoursing, painful though it be, is remunerative. There is something in the very experience of moral pain which brings us nigh to God. When, for instance, in the hour of temptation, I discern God's calm and holy eye bent upon me, and I wither beneath it, and resist the enticement because I fear to disobey, I am brought by this chapter in my experience into very close contact with my Maker. There has been a vivid and personal transaction between us. I have heard him say: "If thou doest that wicked thing thou shalt surely die; refrain from doing it, and I will love thee and bless thee." This is the secret of the great and swift reaction which often takes place, in the sinner's soul. He moodily and obstinately fights against the Divine displeasure. In this state of things, there is nothing but fear and torment. Suddenly he gives way, acknowledges that it is a good and a just anger, no longer seeks to beat it back from his guilty soul, but lets the billows roll over while he casts himself upon the Divine pity. In this act and instant,—which involves the destiny of the soul, and has millenniums in it,—when he recognizes the justice and trusts in the mercy of God, there is a great rebound, and through his tears he sees the depth, the amazing depth, of the Divine compassion. For, paradoxical as it appears, God's love is best seen in the light of God's displeasure. When the soul is penetrated by this latter feeling, and is thoroughly sensible of its own worthlessness,—when, man knows himself to be vile, and filthy, and fit only to be burned up by the Divine immaculateness,—then, to have the Great God take him to His heart, and pour out upon him the infinite wealth of His mercy and compassion, is overwhelming. Here, the Divine indignation becomes a foil to set off the Divine love. Read the sixteenth chapter of Ezekiel, with an eye "purged with euphrasy and rue," so that you can take in the full spiritual significance of the comparisons and metaphors, and your whole soul will dissolve in tears, as you perceive how the great and pure God, in every instance in which He saves an apostate spirit, is compelled to bow His heavens and come down into a loathsome sty of sensuality.[8] Would it be love of the highest order, in a seraph, to leave the pure cerulean and trail his white garments through the haunts of vice, to save the wretched inmates from themselves and their sins? O then what must be the degree of affection and compassion, when the infinite Deity, whose essence is light itself, and whose nature is the intensest contrary of all sin, tabernacles in the flesh upon the errand of redemption! And if the pure spirit of that seraph, while filled with an ineffable loathing, and the hottest moral indignation, at what he saw in character and conduct, were also yearning with an unspeakable desire after the deliverance of the vicious from their vice,—the moral wrath, thus setting in still stronger relief the moral compassion that holds it in check,—-what must be the relation between these two emotions in the Divine Being! Is not the one the measure of the other? And does not the soul that fears God in a submissive manner, and acknowledges the righteousness of the Divine displeasure with entire acquiescence and no sullen resistance, prepare the way, in this very act, for an equally intense manifestation of the Divine mercy and forgiveness?

The subject treated of in this discourse is one of the most important, and frequent, that is presented in the Scriptures. He who examines is startled to find that the phrase, "fear of the Lord," is woven into the whole web of Revelation from Genesis to the Apocalypse. The feeling and principle under discussion has a Biblical authority, and significance, that cannot be pondered too long, or too closely. It, therefore, has an interest for every human being, whatever may be his character, his condition, or his circumstances. All great religious awakenings begin in the dawning of the august and terrible aspects of the Deity upon the popular mind, and they reach their height and happy consummation, in that love and faith for which the antecedent fear has been the preparation. Well and blessed would it be for this irreverent and unfearing age, in which the advance in mechanical arts and vice is greater than that in letters and virtue, if the popular mind could be made reflective and solemn by this great emotion.

We would, therefore, pass by all other feelings, and endeavor to fix the eye upon the distinct and unambiguous fear of God, and would urge the young, especially, to seek for it as for hid treasures. The feeling is a painful one, because it is a preparatory one. There are other forms of religious emotion which are more attractive, and are necessary in their place; these you may be inclined to cultivate, at the expense of the one enjoined by our Lord in the text. But we solemnly and earnestly entreat you, not to suffer your inclination to divert your attention from your duty and your true interest. We tell you, with confidence, that next to the affectionate and filial love of God in your heart, there is no feeling or principle in the whole series that will be of such real solid service to you, as that one enjoined by our Lord upon "His disciples first of all." You will need its awing and repressing influence, in many a trying scene, in many a severe temptation. Be encouraged to cherish it, from the fact that it is a very effective, a very powerful emotion. He who has the fear of God before his eyes is actually and often kept from falling. It will prevail with your weak will, and your infirm purpose, when other motives fail. And if you could but stand where those do, who have passed through that fearful and dangerous passage through which you are now making a transit; if you could but know, as they do, of what untold value is everything that deters from the wrong and nerves to the right, in the critical moments of human life; you would know, as they do, the utmost importance of cherishing a solemn and serious dread of displeasing God. The more simple and unmixed this feeling is in your own experience, the more influential will it be. Fix it deeply in the mind, that the great God is holy. Recur to this fact continually. If the dread which it awakens casts a shadow over the gayety of youth, remember that you need this, and will not be injured by it. The doctrine commends itself to you, because you are young, and because you are strong. If it fills you with misgivings, at times, and threatens to destroy your peace of mind, let the emotion operate. Never stifle it, as you value your salvation. You had better be unhappy for a season, than yield to temptation and grievous snares which will drown you in perdition. Even if it hangs dark and low over the horizon of your life, and for a time invests this world with sadness, be resolute with yourself, and do not attempt to remove the feeling, except in the legitimate way of the gospel. Remember that every human soul out of Christ ought to fear, "for he that believeth not on the Son, the wrath of God abideth on him." And remember, also, that every one who believes in Christ ought not to fear; for "there is no condemnation to them that are in Christ Jesus, and he that believeth on the Son hath everlasting life."

And with this thought would we close. This fear of God may and should end in the perfect love that casteth out fear. This powerful and terrible emotion, which we have been considering, may and ought to prepare the soul to welcome the sweet and thrilling accents of Christ saying, "Come unto me all ye that are weary and heavy laden," with your fears of death, judgment, and eternity, "and I will give you rest." Faith in Christ lifts the soul above all fears, and eventually raises it to that serene world, that blessed state of being, where there is no more curse and no more foreboding.

> "Serene will be our days, and bright,
> And happy will our nature be,
> When love is an unerring light,
> And joy its own security."

[**Note 1:** *The moral and healthful influence of fear is implied in the celebrated passage in Aristotle's Poetics, whatever be the interpretation. He speaks of a cleansing [Greek: (katharsin)] of the mind, by means of the emotions of pity and terror [Greek: (phobos)] awakened by tragic poetry. Most certainly, there is no portion of Classical literature so purifying as the Greek Drama. And yet, the pleasurable emotions are rarely awakened by it. Righteousness and justice determine the movement of the plot, and conduct to the catastrophe; and the persons and forms that move across the stage are, not Venus and the Graces but,*
"ghostly Shapes To meet at noontide; Death the Skeleton And Time the Shadow."
All literature that tends upward contains the tragic element; and all literature that tends downward rejects it. Æschylus and Dante assume a world of retribution, and employ for the purposes of poetry the fear it awakens. Lucretius and Voltaire would disprove the existence of such a solemn world, and they make no use of such an emotion.]
[**Note 2:** WORDSWORTH: Intimations of Immortality.]
[**Note 3:** LUCRETIUS: De Rerum Natura, III. 989 sq.; V. 1160 sq.]
[**Note 4:** BATES: Discourse of the Fear of God.]
[**Note 5:** *"Praise be to Thee, glory to Thee, O Fountain of mercies: I was becoming more miserable and Thou becoming nearer, Thy right hand was continually ready to pluck me out of the mire, and to wash me thoroughly, and I knew it not; nor did anything call me back from a yet deeper gulf of carnal pleasures, but the fear of death, and of Thy judgment to come; which, amid all my changes, never departed from my breast."* AUGUSTINE: Confessions, vi. 16., (Shedd's Ed., p. 142.)]
[**Note 6:** *"Si te luxuria tentat, objice tibi memoriam mortis tuae, propone tibi futuruin judicium, reduc ad memoriam futura tormenta, propone tibi acterna supplicia; et etiaim propone aute oculos tuos perpetuosignes infernorum; propone tibi horribiles poenas gehennae. Memoria ardoris gehennae extinguat in te ardorem luxuriane."*
BERNARD: De Modo Bene Vivendi. Sermo lxvii.]
[**Note 7:** BAXTER (Narrative, Part I.) remarks "that fear, being an easier and irresistible passion, doth oft obscure that measure of love which is indeed within us; and that the soul of

a believer groweth up by degrees from the more troublesome and safe operation of fear, to the more high and excellent operations of complacential love."]

*[**Note 8:** "Thus saith the Lord God unto Jerusalem, thy birth and thy nativity is of the land of Canaan; thy father was an Amorite, and thy mother an Hittite. Thou wast cast out in the open field, to the loathing of thy person, in the day that thou wast born. And when I passed by thee and saw thee polluted in thy own blood, I said unto thee when, thou wast in thy blood, Live; yea I said unto thee when thou wast in thy blood, Live." Ezekiel xvi. 1, 5, 6.]*

XVII - The Present Life as Related to The Future

LUKE xvi. 25.— *"And Abraham said, Son remember that thou in thy lifetime received thy good things, and likewise Lazarus evil things; but now he is comforted, and thou art tormented."*

The parable of Dives and Lazarus is one of the most solemn passages in the whole Revelation of God. In it, our Lord gives very definite statements concerning the condition of those who have departed this life. It makes no practical difference, whether we assume that this was a real occurrence, or only an imaginary one,—whether there actually was such a particular rich man as Dives, and such a particular beggar as Lazarus, or whether the narrative was invented by Christ for the purpose of conveying the instruction which he desired to give. The instruction is given in either case; and it is the instruction with which we are concerned. Be it a parable, or be it a historical fact, our Lord here teaches, in a manner not to be disputed, that a man who seeks enjoyment in this life as his chief end shall suffer torments in the next life, and that he who endures suffering in this life for righteousness' sake shall dwell in paradise in the next,—that he who finds his life here shall lose his life hereafter, and that he who loses his life here shall find it here after.

For, we cannot for a moment suppose that such a Being as Jesus Christ merely intended to play upon the fears of men, in putting forth such a picture as this. He knew that this narrative would be read by thousands and millions of mankind; that they would take it from His lips as absolute truth; that they would inevitably infer from it, that the souls of men do verily live after death, that some of them are in bliss and some of them are in pain, and that the difference between them is due to the difference in the lives which they lead here upon earth. Now, if Christ was ignorant upon these subjects, He had no right to make such representations and to give such impressions, even through a merely imaginary narrative. And still less could He be justified in so doing, if, being perfectly informed upon the subject, He knew that there is no such place as that in which He puts the luxurious Dives, and no such impassable gulf as that of which He speaks. It will not do, here, to employ the Jesuitical maxim that the end justifies the means, and say, as some teachers have said, that the wholesome impression that will be made upon the vicious and the profligate justifies an appeal to their fears, by preaching the doctrine of endless retribution, although there is no such thing. This was a fatal error in the teachings of Clement of Alexandria, and Origen. "God threatens,"—said they,—"and punishes, but only to improve, never for purposes of retribution; and though, in public discourse, the fruitlessness of repentance after death be asserted, yet hereafter not only those who have not heard of Christ will receive forgiveness, but the severer punishment which befalls the obstinate unbelievers will, it may be hoped, not be the conclusion of their history."[1] But can we suppose that such a sincere, such a truthful and such a holy Being as the Son of God would stoop to any such artifice as this? that He who called Himself The Truth would employ a lie, either directly or indirectly, even to promote the spiritual welfare of men? He never spake for mere sensation. The fact, then, that in this solemn passage of Scripture we find the Redeemer calmly describing and minutely picturing the condition of two persons in the future world, distinctly specifying the points of difference between them, putting words into their mouths that indicate a sad and hopeless experience in one of them, and a glad and happy one in the other of them,—the fact that in this treatment of the awful theme our Lord, beyond all controversy, conveys the impression that these scenes and experiences are real and true,—is one of the strongest of all proofs that they are so.

The reader of Dante's Inferno is always struck with the sincerity and realism of that poem. Under the delineation of that luminous, and that intense understanding, hell has a topographic reality. We wind along down those nine circles as down a volcanic crater, black, jagged, precipitous, and impinging upon the senses at every step. The sighs and shrieks jar our own tympanum; and the convulsions of the lost excite tremors in our own nerves. No wonder that the children in the streets of Florence, as they saw the sad and earnest man pass along, his face lined with passion and his brow scarred with thought, pointed at him and said: "There goes the man who has been in hell." But how infinitely more solemn is the impression that is made by these thirteen short verses, of the sixteenth chapter of Luke's gospel, from the lips of such a Being as Jesus Christ! We have here the terse and pregnant teachings of one who, in the phrase of the early Creed, not only "descended into hell," but who "hath the keys of death and hell." We have here not the utterances of the most truthful, and the most earnest of all human poets,—a man who, we may believe, felt deeply the power of the Hebrew Bible, though living in a dark age, and a superstitious Church,—we have here the utterances of the Son of God, very God, of very God, and we may be certain that He intended to convey no impression that will not be made good in the world to come. And when every eye shall see Him, and all the sinful kindreds of the earth shall wail because of Him, there will not be any eye that can look into His and say: "Thy description, O Son of God, was overdrawn; the impression was greater than the reality." On the contrary, every human soul will say in the day of judgment: "We were forewarned; the statements were exact; even according to Thy fear, so is Thy wrath" (Ps. xc. 11).

But what is the lesson which we are to read by this clear and solemn light? What would our merciful Redeemer have us learn from this passage which He has caused to be recorded for our instruction? Let us listen with a candid and a feeling heart, because it comes to us not from an enemy of the human soul, not from a Being who delights to cast it into hell, but from a friend of the soul; because it comes to us from One who, in His own person and in His own flesh, suffered an anguish superior in dignity and equal in cancelling power to the pains of all the hells, in order that we, through repentance and faith, might be spared their infliction.

The lesson is this: The man who seeks enjoyment in this life, as his chief end, must suffer in the next life; and he who endures suffering in this life, for righteousness' sake, shall be happy in the next. "Son, remember that thou in thy lifetime receivedst thy good things, and likewise Lazarus evil things; but now he is comforted, and thou art tormented."

It is a fixed principle in the Divine administration, that the scales of justice shall in the end be made equal. If, therefore, sin enjoys in this world, it must sorrow in the next; and if righteousness sorrows in this world, it must enjoy in the next. The experience shall be reversed, in order to bring everything to a right position and adjustment. This is everywhere taught in the Bible. "Woe unto you that are rich! for ye have received your consolation. Woe unto you that are full! for ye shall hunger. Woe unto you that laugh now! for ye shall mourn and weep. Blessed are ye that hunger now; for ye shall be filled. Blessed are ye that weep now; for ye shall laugh" (Luke vi. 21, 24, 25). These are the explicit declarations of the Founder of Christianity, and they ought not to surprise us, coming as they do from Him who expressly declares that His kingdom is not of this world; that in this world His disciples must have tribulation, as He had; that through much tribulation they must enter into the kingdom of God; that whosoever doth not take up the cross daily, and follow Him, cannot be His disciple.

Let us notice some particulars, in which we see the operation of this principle. What are the "good things" which Dives receives here, for which he must be "tormented" hereafter? and what are the "evil things" which Lazarus receives in this world, for which he will be "comforted" in the world to come?

I. In the first place, the worldly man derives a more intense physical enjoyment from this world's goods, than does the child of God. He possesses more of them, and gives himself up to them with less self-restraint. The majority of those who have been most prospered by Divine Providence in the accumulation of wealth have been outside of the kingdom and the ark of God. Not many rich and not many noble are called. In the past history of mankind, the great possessions and the great incomes, as a general rule, have not been in the hands of humble and penitent men. In the great centres of trade and commerce,—in Venice, Amsterdam, Paris, London,—it is the world and not the people of God who have had the purse, and have borne what is put therein. Satan is described in Scripture, as the "prince of this world" (John xiv. 30); and his words addressed to the Son of God are true: "All this power and glory is delivered unto me, and to whomsoever I will, I give it." In the parable from which we are discoursing, the sinful man was the rich man, and the child of God was the beggar. And how often do we see, in every-day life, a faithful, prayerful, upright, and pure-minded man, toiling in poverty, and so far as earthly comforts are concerned enjoying little or nothing, while a selfish, pleasure-seeking, and profligate man is immersed in physical comforts and luxuries. The former is receiving evil things, and the latter is receiving good things, in this life.

Again, how often it happens that a fine physical constitution, health, strength, and vigor, are given to the worldling, and are denied to the child of God. The possession of worldly good is greatly enhanced in value, by a fine capability of enjoy-

145

ing it. When therefore we see wealth joined, with health, and luxury in all the surroundings and appointments combined with taste to appreciate them and a full flow of blood to enjoy them, or access to wide and influential circles, in politics and fashion, given to one who is well fitted by personal qualities to move in them,—when we see a happy adaptation existing between the man and his good fortune, as we call it,—we see not only the "good things," but the "good things" in their gayest and most attractive forms and colors. And how often is all this observed in the instance of the natural man; and how often is there little or none of this in the instance of the spiritual man. We by no means imply, that it is impossible for the possessor of this world's goods to love mercy, to do justly, and to walk humbly; and we are well aware that under the garb of poverty and toil there may beat a murmuring and rebellious heart. But we think that from generation to generation, in this imperfect and probationary world, it will be found to be a fact, that when merely earthly and physical good is allotted in large amounts by the providence of God; that when great incomes and ample means of luxury are given; in the majority of instances they are given to the enemies of God, and not to His dear children. So the Psalmist seems to have thought. "I was envious,"—he says,—"when I saw the prosperity of the wicked. For there are no bands in their death; but their strength is firm. They are not in trouble as other men; neither are they plagued like other men. Therefore pride compasseth them about as a chain; violence covereth them as a garment. Their eyes stand out with fatness; they have more than heart could wish. Behold these are the ungodly who prosper in the world; they increase in riches. Verily I have cleansed my heart in vain, and washed my hands in innocency. For all day long have I been plagued, and chastened every morning" (Ps. lxxiii). And it should be carefully noticed, that the Psalmist, even after further reflection, does not alter his statement respecting the relative positions of the godly and the ungodly in this world. He sees no reason to correct his estimate, upon this point. He lets it stand. So far as this merely physical existence is concerned, the wicked man has the advantage. It is only when the Psalmist looks beyond this life, that he sees the compensation, and the balancing again of the scales of eternal right and justice. "When I thought to know this,"—when I reflected upon this inequality, and apparent injustice, in the treatment of the friends and the enemies of God,—"it was too painful for me, until I went into the sanctuary of God,"—until I took my stand in the eternal world, and formed my estimate there,—"then understood I their end. Surely thou didst set them in slippery places: thou castedst them down to destruction. How are they brought into desolation as in a moment! They are utterly consumed with terrors." Dives passes from his fine linen and sumptuous fare, from his excessive physical enjoyment, to everlasting perdition.

II. In the second place, the worldly man derives more enjoyment from sin, and suffers less from it, in this life, than does the child of God. The really renewed man cannot enjoy sin. It is true that he does sin, owing to the strength of old habits, and the remainders of his corruption. But he does not really delight in it; and he says with St. Paul: "What I would, that do I not; but what I hate, that do I." His sin is a sorrow, a constant sorrow, to him. He feels its pressure and burden all his days, and cries: "O wretched man, who shall deliver me from the body of this death." If he falls into it, he cannot live in it; as a man may fall into water, but it is not his natural element.

Again, the good man not only takes no real delight in sin, but his reflections after transgression are very painful. He has a tender conscience. His senses have been trained and disciplined to discern good and evil. Hence, the sins that are committed by a child of God are mourned over with a very deep sorrow. The longer he lives, the more odious does sin become to him, and the more keen and bitter is his lamentation over it. Now this, in itself, is an "evil thing." Man was not made for sorrow, and sorrow is not his natural condition. This wearisome struggle with indwelling corruption, these reproaches of an impartial conscience, this sense of imperfection and of constant failure in the service of God,—all this renders the believer's life on earth a season of trial, and tribulation. The thought of its lasting forever would be painful to him; and if he should be told that it is the will of God, that he should continue to be vexed and foiled through all eternity, with the motions of sin in his members, and that his love and obedience would forever be imperfect, though he would be thankful that even this was granted him, and that he was not utterly cast off, yet he would wear a shaded brow, at the prospect of an imperfect, though a sincere and a struggling eternity.

But the ungodly are not so. The worldly man loves sin; loves pleasure; loves self. And the love is so strong, and accompanied with so much enjoyment and zest, that it is lust, and is so denominated in the Bible. And if you would only defend him from the wrath of God; if you would warrant him immunity in doing as he likes; if you could shelter him as in an inaccessible castle from the retributions of eternity; with what a delirium of pleasure would he plunge into the sin that he loves. Tell the avaricious man, that his avarice shall never have any evil consequences here or hereafter; and with what an energy would he apply himself to the acquisition of wealth. Tell the luxurious man, full of passion and full of blood, that his pleasures shall never bring down any evil upon him, that there is no power in the universe that can hurt him, and with what an abandonment would he surrender himself to his carnal elysium. Tell the ambitious man, fired with visions of fame and glory, that he may banish all fears of a final account, that he may make himself his own deity, and breathe in the incense of worshipers, without any rebuke from Him who says: "I am God, and my glory I will not give to another,"-assure the proud and ambitious man that his sin will never find him out, and with what a momentum will he follow out his inclination. For, in each of these instances there is a hankering and a lust. The sin is loved and revelled in, for its own deliciousness. The heart is worldly, and therefore finds its pleasure in its forbidden objects and aims. The instant you propose to check or thwart this inclination; the instant you try to detach this natural heart from its wealth, or its pleasure, or its earthly fame; you discover how closely it clings, and how strongly it loves, and how intensely it enjoys the forbidden object. Like the greedy insect in our gardens, it has fed until every fibre and tissue is colored with its food; and to remove it from the leaf is to tear and lacerate it.

Now it is for this reason, that the natural man receives "good things," or experiences pleasure, in this life, at a point where the spiritual man receives "evil things," or experiences pain. The child of God does not relish and enjoy sin in this style. Sin in the good man is a burden; but in the bad man it is a pleasure. It is all the pleasure he has. And when you propose to take it away from him, or when you ask him to give it up of his own accord, he looks at you and asks: "Will you take away the only solace I have? I have no joy in God. I take no enjoyment in divine things. Do you ask me to make myself wholly miserable?"

And not only does the natural man enjoy sin, but, in this life, he is much less troubled than is the spiritual man with reflections and self-reproaches on account of sin. This is another of the "good things" which Dives receives, for which he must be "tormented;" and this is another of the "evil things" which Lazarus receives, for which he must be "comforted." It cannot be denied, that in this world the child of God suffers more mental sorrow for sin, in a given period of time, than does the insensible man of the world. If we could look into the soul of a faithful disciple of Christ, we should discover that not a day passes, in which his conscience does not reproach him for sins of thought, word, or deed; in which he does not struggle with some bosom sin, until he is so weary that he cries out: "Oh that I had wings like a dove, so that I might fly away, and be at rest." Some of the most exemplary members of the Church go mourning from day to day, because their hearts are still so far from their God and Saviour, and their lives fall so far short of what they desire them to be.[2] Their experience is not a positively wretched one, like that of an unforgiven sinner when he is feeling the stings of conscience. They are forgiven. The expiating blood has soothed the ulcerated conscience, so that it no longer stings and burns. They have hope in God's mercy. Still, they are in grief and sorrow for sin; and their experience, in so far, is not a perfectly happy one, such as will ultimately be their portion in a better world. "If in this life only,"—says St. Paul,—"we have hope in Christ, we are of all men most miserable" (1 Cor. xv. 19).

But the stupid and impenitent man, a luxurious Dives, knows nothing of all this. His days glide by with no twinges of conscience. What does he know of the burden of sin? His conscience is dead asleep; perchance seared as with a hot iron. He does wrong without any remorse; he disobeys the express commands of God, without any misgivings or self-reproach. He is "alive, without the law,"-as St. Paul expresses it. His eyes stand out with fatness; and his heart, in the Psalmist's phrase, "is as fat as grease" (Ps. cxix. 70). There is no religious sensibility in him. His sin is a pleasure to him without any mixture of sorrow, because unattended by any remorse of conscience. He is receiving his "good things" in this life. His days pass by without any moral anxiety, and perchance as he looks upon some meek and earnest disciple of Christ who is battling with indwelling sin, and who, therefore, sometimes wears a grave countenance, he wonders that any one should walk so soberly, so gloomily, in such a cheery, such a happy, such a jolly world as this.

It is a startling fact, that those men in this world who have most reason to be distressed by sin are the least troubled by it; and those who have the least reason to be distressed are the most troubled by it. The child of God is the one who sorrows most; and the child of Satan is the one who sorrows least. Remember that we are speaking only of this life. The text reads: "Thou in thy lifetime receivedst thy good things, and likewise Lazarus evil things." And it is unquestionably so. The meek and lowly disciple of Christ, the one who is most entitled by his character and conduct to be untroubled by religious anxiety, is the very one who bows his head as a bulrush, and perhaps goes mourning all his days, fearing that he is not accepted, and that he shall be a cast-a-way; while the selfish and thoroughly irreligious man, who ought to be stung through and through by his own conscience, and feel the full energy of the law which he is continually breaking,—this man, who of all men ought to be anxious and distressed for sin, goes through a whole lifetime, perchance, without any convictions or any fears.

And now we ask, if this state of things ought to last forever? Is it right, is it just, that sin should enjoy in this style forever and forever, and that holiness should grieve and sorrow in this style forevermore? Would you have the Almighty pay a bounty upon unrighteousness, and place goodness under eternal pains and penalties? Ought not this state of things to be reversed? When Dives comes to the end of this lifetime; when he has run his round of earthly pleasure, faring sumptuously every day, clothed in purple and fine linen, without a thought of his duties and obligations, and without any anxiety and penitence for his sins,—when this worldly man has received all his "good things," and is satiated and hardened by them, ought he not then to be "tormented?" Ought this guilty carnal enjoyment to be perpetuated through all eternity, under the government of a righteous and just God? And, on the other hand, ought not the faithful disciple, who, perhaps, has possessed little or nothing of this world's goods, who has toiled hard, in poverty, in affliction, in temptation, in tribulation, and sometimes like Abraham in the horror of a great darkness, to keep his robes white, and his soul unspotted from the world,—when the poor and weary Lazarus comes to the end of this lifetime, ought not his trials and sorrows to cease? ought he not then to be "comforted" in the bosom of Abraham, in the paradise of God? There is that within us all, which answers, Yea, and Amen. Such a balancing of the scales is assented to, and demanded by the moral convictions. Hence, in the parable, Dives himself is represented as acquiescing in the eternal judgment. He does not complain of injustice. It is true, that at first he asks for a drop of water,—for some slight mitigation of his punishment. This is the instinctive request of any sufferer. But when his attention is directed to the right and the wrong of the case; when Abraham reminds him of the principles of justice by which his destiny has been decided; when he tells him that having taken his choice of pleasure in the world which he has left, he cannot now have pleasure in the world to which he has come; the wretched man makes no reply. There is nothing to be said. He feels that the procedure is just. He is then silent upon the subject of his own tortures, and only begs that his five brethren, whose lifetime is not yet run out, to whom there is still a space left for repentance, may be warned from his own lips not to do as he has done,—not to choose pleasure on earth as their chief good; not to take their "good things" in this life. Dives, the man in hell, is a witness to the justice of eternal punishment.

1. In view of this subject, as thus discussed, we remark in the first place, that no man can have his "good things," in other words, his chief pleasure, in both worlds. God and this world are in antagonism. "For all that is in the world, the lust of the flesh, the lust of the eyes, and the pride of life, is not of the Father, but is of the world. If any man love the world, the love of the Father is not in him" (1 John i. 15, 16). It is the height of folly, therefore, to suppose that a man can make earthly enjoyment his chief end while he is upon earth, and then pass to heaven when he dies. Just so far as he holds on upon the "good things" of this life, he relaxes his grasp upon the "good things" of the next. No man is capacious enough to hold both worlds in his embrace. He cannot serve God and Mammon. Look at this as a matter of fact. Do not take it as a theory of the preacher. It is as plain and certain that you cannot lay up your treasure in heaven while you are laying it up upon earth, as it is that your material bodies cannot occupy two portions of space at one and the same time. Dismiss, therefore, all expectations of being able to accomplish an impossibility. Put not your mind to sleep with the opiate, that in some inexplicable manner you will be able to live the life of a worldly man upon earth, and then the life of a spiritual man in heaven. There is no alchemy that can amalgamate substances that refuse to mix. No man has ever yet succeeded, no man ever will succeed, in securing both the pleasures of sin and the pleasures of holiness,—in living the life of Dives, and then going to the bosom of Abraham.

2. And this leads to the second remark, that every man must make his choice whether he will have his "good things" now, or hereafter. Every man is making his choice. Every man has already made it. The heart is now set either upon God, or upon the world. Search through the globe, and you cannot find a creature with double affections; a creature with two chief ends of living; a creature whose treasure is both upon earth and in heaven. All mankind are single-minded. They either mind earthly things, or heavenly things. They are inspired with one predominant purpose, which rules them, determines their character, and decides their destiny. And in all who have not been renewed by Divine grace, the purpose is a wrong one, a false and fatal one. It is the choice and the purpose of Dives, and not the choice and purpose of Lazarus.

3. Hence, we remark in the third place, that it is the duty and the wisdom of every man to let this world go, and seek his "good things" hereafter. Our Lord commands every man to sit down, like the steward in the parable, and make an estimate. He enjoins it upon every man to reckon up the advantages upon each side, and see for himself which is superior. He asks every man what it will profit him, "if he shall gain the whole world and lose his own soul; or, what he shall give in exchange for his soul." We urge you to make this estimate,—to compare the "good things" which Dives enjoyed, with the "torments" that followed them; and the "evil things" which Lazarus suffered, with the "comfort" that succeeded them. There can be no doubt upon which side the balance will fall. And we urge you to take the "evil things" now, and the "good things" hereafter. We entreat you to copy the example of Moses at the court of the Pharaohs, and in the midst of all regal luxury, who "chose rather to suffer affliction with the people of God, than enjoy the pleasures of sin for a season; esteeming the reproach of Christ, greater riches than the treasures in Egypt: for he had respect unto the recompense of reward." Take the narrow way. What though it be strait and narrow; you are not to walk in it forever. A few short years of fidelity will end the toilsome pilgrimage; and then you will come put into a "wealthy place." We might tell you of the joys of the Christian life that are mingled with its trials and sorrows even here upon earth. For, this race to which we invite you, and this fight to which we call you have their own peculiar, solemn, substantial joy. And even their sorrow is tinged with glory. In a higher, truer sense than Protesilaus in the poem says it of the pagan elysium, we may say even of the Christian race, and the Christian fight,

"Calm pleasures there abide—majestic pains." [3]

But we do not care, at this point, to influence you by a consideration of the amount of enjoyment, in this life, which you will derive from a close and humble walk with God. We prefer to put the case in its baldest form,—in the aspect in which we find it in our text. We will say nothing at all about the happiness of a Christian life, here in time. We will talk only of its tribulations. We will only say, as in the parable, that there are "evil things" to be endured here upon earth, in return for which we shall have "good things" in another life. There is to be a moderate and sober use of this world's goods; there is to be a searching sense of sin, and an humble confession of it before God; there is to be a cross-bearing every day, and a struggle with indwelling corruption. These will cost effort, watchfulness, and earnest prayer for Divine assistance. We do not invite you into the kingdom of God, without telling you frankly and plainly beforehand what must be done, and what must be suffered. But having told you this, we then tell you with the utmost confidence and assurance, that you will be infinitely repaid for your choice, if you take your "evil things" in this life, and choose your "good things" in a future. We know, and are certain, that this light affliction which endures but for a moment, in comparison with the infinite duration beyond the tomb, will work out a far more exceeding and eternal weight of glory. We entreat you to look no longer at the things which are seen, but at the things which are not seen; for the things that are seen are temporal, but the things that are not seen are eternal.

Learn a parable from a wounded soldier. His limb must be amputated, for mortification and gangrene have begun their work. He is told that the surgical operation, which will last a half hour, will yield him twenty or forty years of healthy and active life. The endurance of an "evil thing," for a few moments, will result in the possession of a "good thing," for many long days and years. He holds out the limb, and submits to the knife. He accepts the inevitable conditions under which he finds himself. He is resolute and stern, in order to secure a great good, in the future.

It is the practice of this same principle, though not in the use of the same kind of power, that we would urge upon you. Look up to God for grace and help, and deliberately forego a present advantage, for the sake of something infinitely more valuable hereafter. Do not, for the sake of the temporary enjoyment of Dives, lose the eternal happiness of Lazarus. Rather, take the place, and accept the "evil things," of the beggar. Look up to God for grace and strength to do it, and then live a life of contrition for sin, and faith in Christ's blood. Deny yourself, and take up the cross daily. Expect your happiness hereafter. Lay up your treasure above. Then, in the deciding day, it will be said of you, as it will be of all the true children of God: "These are they which came out of great tribulation, and have washed their robes, and made them white in the blood of the Lamb."

*[**Note 1:** SHEDD: History of Doctrine, II., 234 sq.]*
*[**Note 2:** The early religious experience of John Owen furnishes a striking illustration. "For a quarter of a year, he avoided almost all intercourse with men; could scarcely be induced to*

speak; and when he did say anything, it was in so disordered a manner as rendered him a wonder to many. Only those who have experienced the bitterness of a wounded spirit can form an idea of the distress he must have suffered. Compared with this anguish of soul, all the afflictions which befall a sinner [on earth] are trifles. One drop of that wrath which shall finally fill the cup of the ungodly, poured into the mind, is enough to poison all the comforts of life, and to spread mourning, lamentation, and woe over the countenance. Though the violence of Owen's convictions had subsided after the first severe conflict, they still continued to disturb his peace, and nearly five years elapsed from their commencement before he obtained solid comfort." ORME: Life of Owen, Chap. I.]
*[**Note 3**: WORDSWORTH: Laodamia.]*

XVIII - The Exercise of Mercy Optional with God

ROMANS ix. 15.—*"For He saith to Moses, I will have mercy on whom I will have mercy, and I will have compassion on whom I will have compassion."*

This is a part of the description which God himself gave to Moses, of His own nature and attributes. The Hebrew legislator had said to Jehovah: "I beseech thee show me thy glory." He desired a clear understanding of the character of that Great Being, under whose guidance he was commissioned to lead the people of Israel into the promised land. God said to him in reply: "I will make all my goodness pass before thee, and I will proclaim the name of the Lord before thee; and I will be gracious to whom I will be gracious, and will shew mercy on whom I will shew mercy."[1]

By this, God revealed to Moses, and through him to all mankind, the fact that He is a merciful being, and directs attention to one particular characteristic of mercy. While informing His servant, that He is gracious and clement towards a penitent transgressor, He at the same time teaches him that He is under no obligation, or necessity, to shew mercy. Grace is not a debt. "I will have mercy on whom I will have mercy, and I will have compassion on whom I will have compassion."

The apostle Paul quotes this declaration, to shut the mouth of him who would set up a claim to salvation; who is too proud to beg for it, and accept it as a free and unmerited favor from God. In so doing, he endorses the sentiment. The inspiration of his Epistle corroborates that of the Pentateuch, so that we have assurance made doubly sure, that this is the correct enunciation of the nature of mercy. Let us look into this hope-inspiring attribute of God, under the guidance of this text.

The great question that presses upon the human mind, from age to age, is the inquiry: Is God a merciful Being, and will He show mercy? Living as we do under the light of Revelation, we know little of the doubts and fears that spontaneously rise in the guilty human soul, when it is left solely to the light of nature to answer it. With the Bible in our hands, and hearing the good news of Redemption from our earliest years, it seems to be a matter of course that the Deity should pardon sin. Nay, a certain class of men in Christendom seem to have come to the opinion that it is more difficult to prove that God is just, than to prove that He is merciful.[2] But this is not the thought and feeling of man when outside of the pale of Revelation. Go into the ancient pagan world, examine the theologizing of the Greek and Roman mind, and you will discover that the fears of the justice far outnumbered the hopes of the mercy; that Plato and Plutarch and Cicero and Tacitus were far more certain that God would punish sin, than that He would, pardon it. This is the reason that there is no light, or joy, in any of the pagan religions. Except when religion was converted into the worship of Beauty, as in the instance of the later Greek, and all the solemn and truthful ideas of law and justice were eliminated from it, every one of the natural religions of the globe is filled with sombre and gloomy hues, and no others. The truest and best religions of the ancient world were always the sternest and saddest, because the unaided human mind is certain that God is just, but is not certain that He is merciful. When man is outside of Revelation, it is by no means a matter of course that God is clement, and that sin shall be forgiven. Great uncertainty overhangs the doctrine of the Divine mercy, from the position of natural religion, and it is only within the province of revealed truth that the uncertainty is removed. Apart from a distinct and direct promise from the lips of God Himself that He will forgive sin, no human creature can be sure that sin will ever be forgiven. Let us, therefore, look into the subject carefully, and see the reason why man, if left to himself and his spontaneous reflections, doubts whether there is mercy in the Holy One for a transgressor, and fears that there is none, and why a special revelation is consequently required, to dispel the doubt and the fear.

The reason lies in the fact, implied in the text, that the exercise of justice is necessary, while that of mercy is optional. "I will have mercy on whom I please to have mercy, and I will have compassion on whom I please to have compassion." It is a principle inlaid in the structure of the human soul, that the transgression of law must be visited with retribution. The pagan conscience, as well as the Christian, testifies that "the Soul that sinneth it shall die." There is no need of quoting from pagan philosophers to prove this. We should be compelled to cite page after page, should we enter upon the documentary evidence. Take such a tract, for example, as that of Plutarch, upon what he denominates "the slow vengeance of the Deity;" read the reasons which he assigns for the apparent delay, in this world, of the infliction of punishment upon transgressors; and you will perceive that the human mind, when left to its candid and unbiassed convictions, is certain that God is a holy Being and will visit iniquity with penalty. Throughout this entire treatise, composed by a man who probably never saw the Scriptures of either the New or the Old Dispensation, there runs a solemn and deep consciousness that the Deity is necessarily obliged, by the principles of justice, to mete out a retribution to the violator of law. Plutarch is engaged with the very same question that the apostle Peter takes up, in his second Epistle, when he answers the objection of the scoffer who asks: Where is the promise of God's coming in judgment? The apostle replies to it, by saying that for the Eternal Mind one day is as a thousand years, and a thousand years as one day, and that therefore "the Lord is not slack concerning His promise, as some men count slackness;" and Plutarch answers it in a different manner, but assumes and affirms with the same positiveness and certainty that the vengeance will ultimately come. No reader of this treatise can doubt for a moment, that its author believed in the future punishment of the wicked,—and in the future endless punishment of the incorrigibly wicked, because there is not the slightest hint or expectation of any exercise of mercy on the part of this Divinity whose vengeance, though slow, is sure and inevitable.[3] Some theorists tell us that the doctrine of endless punishment contradicts the instincts of the natural reason, and that it has no foundation in the constitution of the human soul. We invite them to read and ponder well, the speculations of one of the most thoughtful of pagans upon this subject, and tell us if they see any streaks or rays of light in it; if they see any inkling, any jot or tittle, of the doctrine of the Divine pity there. We challenge them to discover in this tract of Plutarch the slightest token, or sign, of the Divine mercy. The author believes in a hell for the wicked, and an elysium for the good; but those who go to hell go there upon principles of justice, and those who go to elysium go there upon the same principles. It is justice that must place men in Tartarus, and it is justice that must place them in Elysium. In paganism, men must earn their heaven. The idea of mercy,—of clemency towards a transgressor, of pity towards a criminal,—is entirely foreign to the thoughts of Plutarch, so far as they can be gathered from this tract. It is the clear and terrible doctrine of the pagan sage, that unless a man can make good his claim to eternal happiness upon the ground of law and justice,—unless he merits it by good works,—there is no hope for him in the other world.

The idea of a forgiving and tender mercy in the Supreme Being, exercised towards a creature whom justice would send to eternal retribution, nowhere appears in the best pagan ethics. And why should it? What evidence or proof has the human mind, apart from the revelations made to it in the Old and New Testaments, that God will ever forgive sin, or ever show mercy? In thinking upon the subject, our reason perceives, intuitively, that God must of necessity punish transgression; and it perceives with equal intuitiveness that there is no corresponding necessity that He should pardon it. We say with confidence and positiveness: "God must be just;" but we cannot say with any certainty or confidence at all: "God must be merciful." The Divine mercy is an attribute which is perfectly free and optional, in its exercises, and therefore we cannot tell beforehand whether it will or will not be shown to transgressors. We know nothing at all about it, until we hear some word from the lips of God Himself upon the point. When He opens the heavens, and speaks in a clear tone to the human race, saying, "I will forgive your iniquities," then, and not till then, do they know the fact. In reference to all those procedures which, like the punishment of transgression, are fixed and necessary, because they are founded in the eternal principles of law and justice, we can tell beforehand what the Divine method will be. We do not need any special revelation, to inform us that God is a just Being, and that His anger is kindled against wickedness, and that He will punish the transgressor. This class of truths, the Apostle informs us, are written in the human constitution, and we have already seen that they were known and dreaded in the pagan world. That which God must do, He certainly will do. He must be just, and therefore He certainly will punish sin, is the reasoning of the human mind, the-world over, and in every age.[4]

But, when we pass from the punishment of sin to the pardon of it, when we go over to the merciful side of the Divine Nature, we can come to no certain conclusions, if we are shut up to the workings of our own minds, or to the teachings of the world of nature about us. Picture to yourself a thoughtful pagan, like Solon the legislator of Athens, living in the heart of heathenism five centuries before Christ, and knowing nothing of the promise of mercy which broke faintly through the heavens immediately after the apostasy of the first human pair, and which found its full and victorious utterance in the streaming, blood of Calvary. Suppose that the accusing and condemning law written, upon his conscience had shown its work, and made him conscious of sin. Suppose that the question had risen within him, whether that Dread Being whom he "ignorantly worshipped," and against whom he had committed the offence, would forgive it; was there anything in his own soul, was there anything in the world around him or above him, that could give him an affirmative answer? The instant he put the question: Will God punish me for my transgression? the affirming voices were instantaneous and authoritative. "The soul that sinneth it shall die" was the verdict that came forth from the recesses of his moral nature, and was echoed and re-echoed in the suffering, pain, and physical death of a miserable and groaning world all around him. But when he put the other question to himself: Will the Deity pardon me for my transgression? there was no affirmative answer from any source of knowledge accessible to him. If he sought a reply from the depths of his own conscience, all that he could hear was the terrible utterance: "The soul that sinneth it shall die." The human conscience can no more promise, or certify, the forgiveness of sin, than the ten commandments can do so. When, therefore, this pagan, convicted of sin, seeks a comforting answer to his anxious inquiry respecting the Divine clemency towards a criminal, he is met only with retributive thunders and lightnings; he hears only that accusing and condemning law which is written on the heart, and experiences that fearful looking-for of judgment and fiery indignation which St. Paul describes, in the first chapter of Romans, as working in the mind of the universal pagan world.

But we need not go to Solon, and the pagan world, for evidence upon this subject. Why is it that a convicted man under the full light of the gospel, and with the unambiguous and explicit promise of God to forgive sins ringing in his ears,— why is it, that even under these favorable circumstances a guilt-smitten man finds it so difficult to believe that there is mercy for him, and to trust in it? Nay, why is it that he finds it impossible fully to believe that Jehovah is a sin-pardoning God, unless he is enabled so to do by the Holy Ghost? It is because he knows that God is under a necessity of punishing his sin, but is under no necessity of pardoning it. The very same judicial principles are operating in his mind that operate in that of a pagan Solon, or any other transgressor outside of the revelation of mercy. That which holds back the convicted sinner from casting himself upon the Divine pity is the perception that God must be just. This fact is certain, whether anything else is certain or not. And it is not until he perceives that God can be both just and the justifier of him that believeth in Jesus; it is not until he sees that, through the substituted sufferings of Christ, God can punish sin while at the same time He pardons it,—can punish it in the Substitute while He pardons it in the sinner,—it is not until he is enabled to apprehend the doctrine of vicarious atonement, that his doubts and fears respecting the possibility and reality of the Divine mercy are removed. The instant he discovers that the exercise of pardon is rendered entirely consistent with the justice of God, by the substituted death of the Son of God, he sees the Divine mercy, and that too in the high form of self-sacrifice, and trusts in it, and is at peace.

These considerations are sufficient to show, that according to the natural and spontaneous operations of the human intellect, justice stands in the way of the exercise of mercy, and that therefore, if man is not informed by Divine Revelation respecting this latter attribute, he can never acquire the certainty that God will forgive his sin. There are two very important and significant inferences from this truth, to which we now ask serious attention.

1. In the first place, those who deny the credibility, and Divine authority, of the Scriptures of the Old and New Testaments shut up the whole world to doubt and despair. For, unless God has spoken the word of mercy in this written Revelation, He has not spoken it anywhere; and we have seen, that unless He has spoken such a merciful word somewhere, no human transgressor can be certain of anything but stark unmitigated justice and retribution. Do you tell us that God is too good to punish men, and that therefore it must be that He is merciful? We tell you, in reply, that God is good when He punishes sin, and your own conscience, like that of Plutarch, re-echoes the reply. Sin is a wicked thing, and when the Holy One visits it with retribution, He is manifesting the purest moral excellence and the most immaculate perfection of character that we can conceive of. But if by goodness you mean mercy, then we say that this is the very point in dispute, and you must not beg the point but must prove it. And now, if you deny the authority and credibility of the Scriptures of the Old and New Testaments, we ask you upon what ground you venture to affirm that God will pardon man's sin. You cannot demonstrate it upon any *a priori* and necessary principles. You cannot show that the Deity is obligated to remit the penalty due to transgression. You can prove the necessity of the exercise of justice, but you cannot prove the necessity of the exercise of mercy. It is purely optional with God, whether to pardon or not. If, therefore, you cannot establish the fact of the Divine clemency by *a priori* reasoning,—if you cannot make out a necessity for the exercise of mercy,—you must betake yourself to the only other method of proof that remains to you, the method of testimony. If you have the declaration and promise of God, that He will forgive iniquity, transgression, and sin, you may be certain of the fact,—as certain as you would be, could you prove the absolute necessity of the exercise of mercy. For God's promise cannot be broken. God's testimony is sure. But, by the supposition, you deny that this declaration has been made, and this promise has been uttered, in the written Revelation of the Christian Church. Where then do you send me for the information, and the testimony? Have you a private revelation of your own? Has the Deity spoken to you in particular, and told you that He will forgive your sin, and my sin, and that of all the generations? Unless this declaration has been made either to you or to some other one, we have seen that you cannot establish the certainty that God will forgive sin. It is a purely optional matter with Him, and whether He will or no depends entirely upon His decision, determination, and declaration. If He says that He will pardon sin, it will certainly be done. But until He says it, you and every other man must be remanded to the inexorable decisions of conscience which thunder out: "The soul that sinneth it shall die." Whoever, therefore, denies that God in the Scrip-

tures of the Old and New Testaments has broken through the veil that hides eternity from time, and has testified to the human race that He will forgive sin, and has solemnly promised to do so, takes away from the human race the only ground of certainty which they possess, that there is pity in the heavens, and that it will be shown to sinful creatures like themselves. But this is to shut them up again, to the doubt and hopelessness of the pagan world,—a world without Revelation.

2. In the second place, it follows from this subject, that mankind must take the declaration and promise of God, respecting the exercise of mercy, precisely as He has given it. They must follow the record implicitly, without any criticisms or alterations. Not only does the exercise of mercy depend entirely upon the will and pleasure of God, but, the mode, the conditions, and the length of time during which the offer shall be made, are all dependent upon the same sovereignty. Let us look at these particulars one by one.

In the first place, the method by which the Divine clemency shall be manifested, and the conditions upon which the offer of forgiveness shall be made, are matters that rest solely with God. If it is entirely optional with Him whether to pardon at all, much more does it depend entirely upon Him to determine the way and means. It is here that we stop the mouth of him who objects to the doctrine of forgiveness through a vicarious atonement. We will by no means concede, that the exhibition of mercy through the vicarious satisfaction of justice is an optional matter, and that God might have dispensed with such satisfaction, had He so willed. We believe that the forgiveness of sin is possible even to the Deity, only through a substituted sacrifice that completely satisfies the demands of law and justice,—that without the shedding of expiating blood there is no remission of sin possible or conceivable, under a government of law. But, without asking the objector to come up to this high ground, we are willing, for the sake of the argument, to go down upon his low one; and we say, that even if the metaphysical necessity of an atonement could not be maintained, and that it is purely optional with God whether to employ this method or not, it would still be the duty and wisdom of man to take the record just as it reads, and to accept the method that has actually been adopted. If the Sovereign has a perfect right to say whether He will or will not pardon the criminal, has He not the same right to say how He will do it? If the transgressor, upon principles of justice, could be sentenced to endless misery, and yet the Sovereign Judge concludes to offer him forgiveness and eternal life, shall the criminal, the culprit who could not stand an instant in the judgment, presume to quarrel with the method, and dictate the terms by which his own pardon shall be secured? Even supposing, then, that there were no intrinsic necessity for the offering of an infinite sacrifice to satisfy infinite justice, the Great God might still take the lofty ground of sovereignty, and say to the criminal: "My will shall stand for my reason; I decide to offer you amnesty and eternal joy, in this mode, and upon these terms. The reasons for my method are known to myself. Take mercy in this method, or take justice. Receive the forgiveness of sin in this mode, or else receive the eternal and just punishment of sin. Can I not do what I will with mine own? Is thine eye evil because I am good?" God is under no necessity to offer the forgiveness of sin to any criminal upon any terms; still less is He hedged up to a method of forgiveness prescribed by the criminal himself.

Again, the same reasoning will apply to the time during which the offer of mercy shall be extended. If it is purely optional with God, whether He will pardon my sin at all, it is also purely optional with Him to fix the limits within which He will exercise the act of pardon. Should He tell me, that if I would confess and forsake my sins to-day, He would blot them out forever, but that the gracious offer should be withdrawn tomorrow, what conceivable ground of complaint could I discover? He is under no necessity of extending the pardon at this moment, and neither is He at the next, or any future one. Mercy is grace, and not debt. Now it has pleased God, to limit the period during which the work of Redemption shall go on. There is a point of time, for every sinful man, at which "there remaineth no more sacrifice for sin" (Heb. x. 26). The period of Redemption is confined to earth and time; and unless the sinner exercises repentance towards God and faith in the Lord Jesus Christ, before his spirit returns to God who gave it, there is no redemption for him through eternal ages. This fact we know by the declaration and testimony of God; in the same manner that we know that God will exercise mercy at all, and upon any conditions whatever. We have seen that we cannot establish the fact that the Deity will forgive sin, by any *a priori* reasoning, but know it only because He has spoken a word to this effect, and given the world His promise to be gracious and merciful, In like manner, we do not establish the fact that there will be no second offer of forgiveness, in the future world, by any process of reasoning from the nature of the case, or the necessity of things. We are willing to concede to the objector, that for aught that we can see the Holy Ghost is as able to take of the things of Christ, and show them to a guilty soul, in the next world, as He is in this. So far as almighty power is concerned, the Divine Spirit could convince men of sin, and righteousness, and judgment, and incline them to repentance and faith, in eternity as well as in time. And it is equally true, that the Divine Spirit could have prevented the origin of sin itself, and the fall of Adam, with the untold woes that proceed therefrom. But it is not a question of power. It is a question of intention, of determination, and of testimony upon the part of God. And He has distinctly declared in the written Revelation, that it is His intention to limit the converting and saving influences of His Spirit to time and earth. He tells the whole world unequivocally, that His spirit shall not always strive with man, and that the day of judgment which occurs at the end of this Dispensation of grace, is not a day of pardon but of doom. Christ's description of the scenes that will close up this Redemptive Economy,—the throne, the opened books, the sheep on the right hand and the goats on the left hand, the words of the Judge: "Come ye blessed, depart ye cursed,"—proves beyond controversy that "now is the accepted time, and now is the day of salvation." The utterance of our Redeeming God, by His servant David, is: "To-day if ye will hear His voice harden not your hearts." St. Paul, in the Epistle to the Hebrews, informs the world, that as God sware that those Israelites who did not believe and obey His servant Moses, during their wanderings in the desert, should not enter the earthly Canaan, so those, in any age and generation of men, who do not believe and obey His Son Jesus Christ, during their earthly pilgrimage, shall, by the same Divine oath, be shut out of the eternal rest that remaineth for the people of God (Hebrews iii. 7-19). Unbelieving men, in eternity, will be deprived of the benefits of Christ's redemption, by the oath, the solemn decision, the judicial determination of God. For, this exercise of mercy, of which we are speaking, is not a matter of course, and of necessity, and which therefore continues forever and forever. It is optional. God is entirely at liberty to pardon, or not to pardon. And He is entirely at liberty to say when, and how, and how long the offer of pardon shall be extended. He had the power to carry the whole body of the people of Israel over Jordan, into the promised land, but He sware that those who proved refractory, and disobedient, during a certain definite period of time, should never enter Canaan. And, by His apostle, He informs all the generations of men, that the same principle will govern Him in respect to the entrance into the heavenly Canaan. The limiting of the offer of salvation to this life is not founded upon any necessity in the Divine Nature, but, like the offer of salvation itself, depends upon the sovereign pleasure and determination of God. That pleasure, and that determination, have been distinctly made known in the Scriptures. We know as clearly as we know anything revealed in the Bible, that God has decided to pardon here in time, and not to pardon in eternity. He has drawn a line between the present period, during which He makes salvation possible to man, and the future period, when He will not make it possible. And He had a right to draw that line, because mercy from first to last is the optional, and not the obligated agency of the Supreme Being.

Therefore, fear lest, a promise being left us of entering into His rest, any of you should seem to come short of it. For unto you is the gospel preached, as well as unto those Israelites; but the word, did not profit them, not being mixed with faith in them that heard it. Neither will it profit you, unless it is mixed with faith. God limiteth a certain day, saying in David, "To-day, after so long a time,"—after these many years of hearing and neglecting the offer of forgiveness,—"to-day, if ye will hear His voice, harden not your hearts." Labor, therefore, now, to enter into that rest, lest any man fall, after the same example of unbelief, with those Israelites whom the oath of God shut out of both the earthly and the heavenly Canaan.

[**Note 1:** *Compare, also, the very full announcement of mercy as a*
Divine attribute that was to be exercised, in Exodus xxxiv. 6, 7.
This is the more noteworthy, as it occurs in connection with the giving of the law.]
[**Note 2:** *Their creed lives in the satire of YOUNG (Universal Passion. Satire VI.),—as full of*
sense, truth, and pungency now, as it was one hundred years ago.
"From atheists far, they steadfastly believe
God is, and is Almighty—to forgive.
His other excellence they'll not dispute;
But mercy, sure, is His chief attribute.
Shall pleasures of a short duration chain
A lady's soul in everlasting pain?
Will the great Author us poor worms destroy,
For now and then a sip of transient joy?
No, He's forever in a smiling mood;
He's like themselves; or how could He be good?
And they blaspheme, who blacker schemes suppose.
Devoutly, thus, Jehovah they depose,

The Pure! the Just! and set up in His stead,
A deity that's perfectly well-bred."]

[**Note 3**: Plutarch supposes a form of punishment in the future world that is disciplinary. If it accomplishes its purpose, the soul goes into Elysium,—a doctrine like that of purgatory in the Papal scheme. But in case the person proves incorrigible, his suffering is endless. He represents an individual as having been restored to life, and giving an account of what he had seen. Among other things, he "informed his friend, how that Adrastia, the daughter of Jupiter and Necessity, was seated in the highest place of all, to punish all manner of crimes and enormities, and that in the whole number of the wicked and ungodly there never was any one, whether great or little, high or low, rich or poor, that could ever by force or cunning escape the severe lashes of her rigor. But as there are three sorts of punishment, so there are three several Furies, or female ministers of justice, and to every one of these belongs a peculiar office and degree of punishment. The first of these was called [Greek: Poinae] or Pain; whose executions are swift and speedy upon those that are presently to receive bodily punishment in this life, and which she manages after a more gentle manner, omitting the correction of slight offences, which need but little expiation. But if the cure of impiety require a greater labor, the Deity delivers those, after death, to [Greek: Dikae] or Vengeance. But when Vengeance has given them over as altogether incurable, then the third and most severe of all Adrastia's ministers, [Greek: 'Erinys] or Fury, takes them in hand, and after she has chased and coursed them from one place to another, flying yet not knowing where to fly for shelter and relief, plagued and tormented with a thousand miseries, she plunges them headlong into an invisible abyss, the hideousness of which no tongue can express." PLUTARCH: Morals, Vol. IV. p. 210. Ed. 1694. PLATO (Gorgias 525. c.d. Ed. Bip. IV. 169) represents Socrates as teaching that those who "have committed the most extreme wickedness, and have become incurable through such crimes, are made an example to others, and suffer forever ([Greek: paschontas ton aei chronon]) the greatest, most agonizing, and most dreadful punishment." And Socrates adds that "Homer (Odyssey xi. 575) also bears witness to this; for he represents kings and potentates, Tantalus, Sysiphus, and Tityus, as being tormented forever in Hades" ([Greek: en adon ton aei chronon timoronmenos]).-In the Aztec or Mexican theology, "the wicked, comprehending the greater part of mankind, were to expiate their sin in a place of everlasting darkness." PRESCOTT: Conquest of Mexico, Vol. I. p. 62.]

[**Note 4**: It may be objected, at this point, that mercy also is a necessary attribute in God, like justice itself,—that it necessarily belongs to the nature of a perfect Being, and therefore might be inferred a priori by the pagan, like other attributes. This is true; but the objection overlooks the distinction between the existence of an attribute and its exercise. Omnipotence necessarily belongs to the idea of the Supreme Being, but it does not follow that it must necessarily be exerted in act. Because God is able to create the universe of matter and mind, it does not follow that he must create it. The doctrine of the necessity of creation, though held in a few instances by theists who seem not to have discerned its logical consequences, is virtually pantheistic. Had God been pleased to dwell forever in the self-sufficiency of His Trinity, and never called the Finite into existence from nothing, He might have done so, and He would still have been omnipotent and "blessed forever." In like manner, the attribute of mercy might exist in God, and yet not be exerted. Had He been pleased to treat the human race as He did the fallen angels, He was perfectly at liberty to do so, and the number and quality of his immanent attributes would have been the same that they are now. But justice is an attribute which not only exists of necessity, but must be exercised of necessity; because not to exercise it would be injustice.-For a fuller exposition of the nature of justice, see SHEDD: Discourses and Essays, pp. 291-300.]

XIX - Christianity Requires the Temper of Childhood

MARK x. 15.— *"Verily I say unto you, whosoever shall not receive the kingdom of God as a little child, he shall not enter therein."*

These words of our Lord are very positive and emphatic, and will, therefore, receive a serious attention from every one who is anxious concerning his future destiny beyond the grave. For, they mention an indispensable requisite in order to an entrance into eternal life. "Whosoever shall not receive the kingdom of God as a little child, he shall not enter therein."

The occasion of their utterance is interesting, and brings to view a beautiful feature in the perfect character of Jesus Christ. The Redeemer was deeply interested in every age and condition of man. All classes shared in His benevolent affection, and all may equally partake of the rich blessings that flow from it. But childhood and youth seem to have had a special attraction for Him. The Evangelist is careful to inform us, that He took little children in His arms, and that beholding an amiable young man He loved him,—a gush of feeling went out towards him. It was because Christ was a perfect man, as well as the infinite God, that such a feeling dwelt in His breast. For, there has never been an uncommonly fair and excellent human character, in which tenderness and affinity for childhood has not been a quality, and a quality, too, that was no small part of the fairness and excellence. The best definition that has yet been given of genius itself is, that it is the carrying of the feelings of childhood onward into the thoughts and aspirations of manhood. He who is not attracted by the ingenuousness, and trustfulness, and simplicity, of the first period of human life, is certainly wanting in the finest and most delicate elements of nature, and character. Those who have been coarse and brutish, those who have been selfish and ambitious, those who have been the pests and scourges of the world, have had no sympathy with youth. Though once young themselves, they have been those in whom the gentle and generous emotions of the morning of life have died out. That man may become hardhearted, skeptical and sensual, a hater of his kind, a hater of all that is holy and good, he must divest himself entirely of the fresh and ingenuous feeling of early boyhood, and receive in its place that malign and soured feeling which is the growth, and sign, of a selfish and disingenuous life. It is related of Voltaire,— a man in whom evil dwelt in its purest and most defecated essence,—that he had no sympathy with the child, and that the children uniformly shrank from that sinister eye in which the eagle and the reptile were so strangely blended.

Our Saviour, as a perfect man, then, possessed this trait, and it often showed itself in His intercourse with men. As an omniscient Being, He indeed looked with profound interest, upon the dawning life of the human spirit as it manifests itself in childhood. For He knew as no finite being can, the marvellous powers that sleep in the soul of the young child; the great affections which are to be the foundation of eternal bliss, or eternal pain, that exist in embryo within; the mysterious ideas that lie in germ far down in its lowest depths,—He knew, as no finite creature is able, what is in the child, as well as in the man, and therefore was interested in its being and its well-being. But besides this, by virtue of His perfect humanity, He was attracted by those peculiar traits which are seen in the earlier years of human life. He loved the artlessness and gentleness, the sense of dependence, the implicit trust, the absence of ostentation and ambition, the unconscious modesty, in one word, the child-likeness of the child.

Knowing this characteristic of the Redeemer, certain parents brought their young children to Him, as the Evangelist informs us, "that He should touch them;" either believing that there was a healthful virtue, connected with the touch of Him who healed the sick and gave life to the dead, that would be of benefit to them; or, it may be, with more elevated conceptions of Christ's person, and more spiritual desires respecting the welfare of their offspring, believing that the blessing (which was symbolized by the touch and laying on of hands) of so exalted a Being would be of greater worth than mere health of body. The disciples, thinking that mere children were not worthy of the regards of their Master, rebuked the anxious and affectionate parents. "But,"—continues the narrative,—"when Jesus saw it he was much displeased, and said unto them, Suffer the little children to come unto me, and forbid them not, for of such is the kingdom of God;" and then immediately explained what He meant by this last assertion, which is so often misunderstood and misapplied, by adding, in the words of the text, "Verily I say unto you, whosoever shall not receive the kingdom of God as a little child" that is with a child-like spirit, "he shall not enter therein." For our Lord does not here lay down a doctrinal position, and affirm the moral innocence of childhood. He does not mark off and discriminate the children as sinless, from their parents as sinful, as if the two classes did not belong to the same race of beings, and were not involved in the same apostasy and condemnation. He merely sets childhood and manhood over-against each other as two distinct stages of human life, each possessing peculiar traits and tempers, and affirms that it is the meek spirit of childhood, and not the proud spirit of manhood, that welcomes and appropriates the Christian salvation. He is only contrasting the general attitude of a child, with the general attitude of a man. He merely affirms that the trustful and believing temper of childhood, as compared with the self-reliant and skeptical temper of manhood, is the temper by which both the child and the man are to receive the blessings of the gospel which both of them equally need.

The kingdom of God is represented in the New Testament, sometimes as subjective, and sometimes as objective; sometimes as within the soul of man, and sometimes as up in the skies. Our text combines both representations; for, it speaks of a man's "receiving" the kingdom of God, and of a man's "entering" the kingdom of God; of the coming of heaven into a soul, and of the going of a soul into heaven. In other passages, one or the other representation appears alone. "The kingdom of God,"—says our Lord to the Pharisees,—"cometh not with observation. Neither shall they say, Lo here, or lo there: for behold the kingdom of God is within you." The apostle Paul, upon arriving at Rome, invited the resident Jews to discuss the subject of Christianity with him. "And when they had appointed him a day, there came many to him into his lodging, to whom he expounded and testified the kingdom of God,"—to whom he explained the nature of the Christian religion,—"persuading them concerning Jesus, both out of the law of Moses, and out of the prophets, from, morning till evening." The same apostle teaches the Romans, that "the kingdom of God is not meat and drink; but righteousness, and peace, and joy in the Holy Ghost;" and tells the Corinthians, that "the kingdom of God is not in word, but in power." In all these instances, the subjective signification prevails, and the kingdom of God is simply a system of truth, or a state of the heart. And all are familiar with the sentiment, that heaven is a state, as well as a place. All understand that one half of heaven is in the human heart itself; and, that if this half be wanting, the other half is useless,—as the half of a thing generally is. Isaac Walton remarks of the devout Sibbs:

"Of this blest man, let this just praise be given, Heaven was in him, before he was in heaven."

It is only because that in the eternal world the imperfect righteousness of the renewed man is perfected, and the peace of the anxious soul becomes total, and the joy that is so rare and faint in the Christian experience here upon earth becomes the very element of life and action,—it is only because eternity completes the excellence of the Christian (but does not begin it), that heaven, as a place of perfect holiness and happiness, is said to be in the future life, and we are commanded to seek a better country even a heavenly. But, because this is so, let no one lose sight of the other side of the great truth, and forget that man must "receive" the kingdom as well as "enter" it. Without the right state of heart, without the mental correspondent to heaven, that beautiful and happy region on high will, like any and every other place, be a hell, instead of a paradise.[1] A distinguished writer represents one of his characters as leaving the Old World, and seeking happiness in the New, supposing that change of place and outward circumstances could cure a restless mind. He found no rest by the change; and in view of his disappointment says: "I will return, and in my ancestral home, amid my paternal fields, among my own people, I will say, Here, or nowhere, is America."[2] In like manner, must the Christian seek happiness in present peace and joy in the Holy Ghost, and must here in this life strive after the righteousness that brings tranquillity. Though he may look forward with aspiration to the new heavens and the new earth wherein dwelleth a perfected righteousness, yet he must remember that his holiness and happiness there is merely an expansion of his holiness and happiness here. He must seek to "receive" the kingdom of God, as well as to "enter" it; and when tempted to relax his efforts, and to let down his watch, because the future life will not oppose so many obstacles to spirituality as this, and will bring a more perfect enjoyment with it, he should say to himself: "Be holy now, be happy here. Here, or nowhere, is heaven."

Such being the nature of the kingdom of God, we are now brought up to the discussion of the subject of the text, and are prepared to consider: In what respects, the kingdom of God requires the temper of a child as distinguished from the temper of a man, in order to receive it, and in order to enter it.

The kingdom of God, considered as a kingdom that is within the soul, is tantamount to religion. To receive this kingdom, then, is equivalent to receiving religion into the heart, so that the character shall be formed by it, and the future destiny be decided by it. What, then, is the religion that is to be received? We answer that it is the religion that is needed. But, the religion that is needed by a sinful man is very different from the religion that is adapted to a holy angel. He who has never sinned is already in direct and blessed relations with God, and needs only to drink in the overflowing and everflowing stream of purity and pleasure. Such a spirit requires a religion of only two doctrines: First, that there is a God; and, secondly, that He ought to be loved supremely and obeyed perfectly. This is the entire theology of the angels, and it is enough for them. They know nothing of sin in their personal experience, and consequently they require in their religion, none of those doctrines, and none of those provisions, which are adapted to the needs of sinners.

But, man is in an altogether different condition from this. He too knows that there is a God, and that He ought to be loved supremely, and obeyed perfectly. Thus far, he goes along with the angel, and with every other rational being made under the law and government of God. But, at this point, his path diverges from that of the pure and obedient inhabitant of heaven, and leads in an opposite direction. For he does not, like the angels, act up to his knowledge. He is not conformed to these two doctrines. He does not love God supremely, and he does not obey Him perfectly. This fact puts him into a very different position, in reference to these two doctrines, from that occupied by the obedient and unfallen spirit. These two doctrines, in relation to him as one who has contravened them, have become a power of condemnation; and whenever he thinks of them he feels guilty. It is no longer sufficient to tell him. that religion consists in loving God, and enjoying His presence,—consists in holiness and happiness. "This is very true,"—he says,—"but I am neither holy nor happy." It is no longer enough to remind him that all is well with any creature who loves God with all his heart, and keeps His commandments without a single slip or failure. "This is very true,"—he says again,—"but I do not love in this style, neither have I obeyed in this manner." It is too late to preach mere natural religion, the religion of the angels, to one who has failed to stand fully and firmly upon the principles of natural religion. It is too late to tell a creature who has lost his virtue, that if he is only virtuous he is safe enough.

The religion, then, that a sinner needs, cannot be limited to the two doctrines of the holiness of God, and the creature's obligation to love and serve Him,— cannot be pared down to the precept: Fear God and practise virtue. It must be greatly enlarged, and augmented, by the introduction of that other class of truths which relate to the Divine mercy towards those who have not feared God, and the Divine method of salvation for those who are sinful. In other words, the religion for a transgressor is revealed religion, or the religion of Atonement and Redemption.

What, now, is there in this species of religion that necessitates the meek and docile temper of a child, as distinguished from the proud and self-reliant spirit of a man, in order to its reception into the heart?

I. In the first place, the New Testament religion offers the forgiveness of sins, and provides for it. No one can ponder this fact an instant, without perceiving that the pride and self-reliance of manhood are excluded, and that the meekness and implicit trust of childhood are demanded. Pardon and justification before God must, from the nature of the case, be a gift, and a gift cannot be obtained unless it is accepted as such. To demand or claim mercy, is self-contradictory. For, a claim implies a personal ground for it; and this implies self-reliance, and this is "manhood" in distinction from "childhood." In coming, therefore, as the religion of the Cross does, before man with a gratuity, with an offer to pardon his sins, it supposes that he take a correspondent attitude. Were he sinless, the religion suited to him would be the mere utterance of law, and he might stand up before it with the serene brow of an obedient subject of the Divine government; though even then, not with a proud and boastful temper. It would be out of place for him, to plead guilty when he was innocent; or to cast himself upon mercy, when he could appeal to justice. If the creature's acceptance be of works, then it is no more of grace, otherwise work is no more work. But if it be by grace, then it is no more of works (Rom. xi. 6). If the very first feature of the Christian religion is the exhibition of clemency, then the proper and necessary attitude of one who receives it is that of humility.

But, leaving this argument drawn from the characteristics, of Christianity as a religion of Redemption, let us pass into the soul of man, and see what we are taught there, respecting the temper which he must possess in order to receive this new, revealed kingdom of God. The soul of man is guilty. Now, there is something in the very nature of guilt that excludes the proud, self-conscious, self-reliant spirit of manhood, and necessitates the lowly, and dependent spirit of childhood. When conscience is full of remorse, and the holy eye of law is searching us, and fears of eternal banishment and punishment are rakeing the spirit, there is no remedy but simple confession, and childlike reliance upon absolute mercy. The sinner must be a softened child and not a hard man, he must beg a boon and not put in a claim, if he would receive this kingdom of God, this New Testament religion, into his soul. The slightest inclination to self-righteousness, the least degree of resistance to the just pressure of law, is a vitiating element in repentance. The muscles of the stout man must give way, the knees must bend, the hands must be uplifted deprecatingly, the eyes must gaze with a straining gaze upon the expiating Cross,—in other words, the least and last remains of a stout and self-asserting spirit must vanish, and the whole being must be pliant, bruised, broken, helpless in its state and condition, in order to a pure sense of guilt, a godly sorrow for sin, and a cordial appropriation of the atonement. The attempt to mix the two tempers, to mingle the child with the man, to confess sin and assert self-righteousness, must be an entire failure, and totally prevent the reception of the religion of Redemption. In relation to the Redeemer, the sinful soul should be a vacuum, a hollow void, destitute of everything holy and good, conscious that it is, and aching to be filled with the fulness of His peace and purity.

And with reference to God, the Being whose function it is to pardon, we see the same necessity for this child-like spirit in the transgressor. How can God administer forgiveness, unless there is a correlated temper to receive it? His particular declarative act in blotting out sin depends upon the existence of penitence for sin. Where there is absolute hardness of heart, there can be no pardon, from the very nature of the case, and the very terms of the statement. Can God say to the hardened Judas: Son be of good cheer, thy sin is forgiven thee? Can He speak to the traitor as He speaks to the Magdalen? The difficulty is not upon the side of God. The Divine pity never lags behind any genuine human sorrow. No man was ever more eager to be forgiven than his Redeemer is to forgive him. No contrition for sin, upon the part of man, ever yet outran the readiness and delight of

God to recognize it, and meet it with a free pardon. For, that very contrition itself is always the product of Divine grace, and proves that God is in advance of the soul. The father in the parable saw the son while he was a great way off, before the son saw him, and ran and fell on his neck and kissed him. But while this is so, and is an encouragement to the penitent, it must ever be remembered that unless there is some genuine sorrow in the human soul, there can be no manifestation of the Divine forgiveness within it. Man cannot beat the air, and God cannot forgive impenitency.

II. In the second place, the New Testament religion proposes to create within man a clean heart, and to renew within him a right spirit. Christianity not only pardons but sanctifies the human soul. And in accomplishing this latter work, it requires the same humble and docile temper that was demanded in the former instance.

Holiness, even in an unfallen angel, is not an absolutely self-originated thing. If it were, the angel would be worthy of adoration and worship. He who is inwardly and totally excellent, and can also say: I am what I am by my own ultimate authorship, can claim for himself the glory that is due to righteousness. Any self-originated and self-subsistent virtue is entitled to the hallelujahs. But, no created spirit, though he be the highest of the archangels, can make such an assertion, or put in such a claim. The merit of the unfallen angel, therefore, is a relative one; because his holiness is of a created and derived species. It is not increate and self-subsistent. This being so, it is plain that the proper attitude of all creatures in respect to moral excellence is a recipient and dependent one. But this is a meek and lowly attitude; and this is, in one sense, a child-like attitude. Our Lord knew no sin; and yet He himself tells us that He was meek and lowly of heart, and we well know that He was. He does not say that He was penitent. He does not propose himself as our exemplar in that respect. But, in respect to the primal, normal attitude which a finite being must ever take in reference to the infinite and adorable God, and the absolute underived Holiness; in reference to the true temper which a holy man or a holy angel must possess; our Lord Jesus Christ, in His human capacity, sets an example to be followed by the spirits of just men made perfect, and by all the holy inhabitants of heaven. In other words, He teaches the whole universe that holiness in a creature, even though it be complete, does not permit its possessor to be self-reliant, does not allow the proud spirit of manhood, does not remove the obligation to be child-like, meek, and lowly of heart.

But if this is true of holiness among those who have never fallen, how much more true is it of those who have, and who need to be lifted up out of the abyss. If an angel, in reference to God, must be meek and lowly of heart; if the holy Redeemer must in His human capacity be meek and lowly of heart; if the child-like temper, in reference to the infinite and everlasting Father and the absolutely Good, is the proper one in such exalted instances as these; how much more is it in the instance of the vile and apostate children of Adam! Besides the original and primitive reason growing out of creaturely relationships, there is the superadded one growing out of the fact, that now the whole head is sick and the whole heart is faint, and from the sole of the foot even unto the head there is no soundness in human nature.

Hence, our Lord began His Sermon on the Mount in these words: "Blessed are the poor in spirit; for theirs is the kingdom of heaven. Blessed are they that mourn; for they shall be comforted. Blessed are the meek; for they shall inherit the earth. Blessed are they which do hunger and thirst after righteousness; for they shall be filled."[3] The very opening of this discourse, which He intended should go down through the ages as a manifesto declaring the real nature of His kingdom, and the spirit which His followers must possess, asserts the necessity of a needy, recipient, asking mind, upon the part of a sinner. All this phraseology implies destitution; and a destitution that cannot be self-supplied. He who hungers and thirsts after righteousness is conscious of an inward void, in respect to righteousness, that must be filled from abroad. He who is meek is sensible that he is dependent for his moral excellence. He who is poor in spirit is, not pusillanimous as Thomas Paine charged upon Christianity but, as John of Damascus said of himself, a man of spiritual cravings, vir desideriorum.

Now, all this delineation of the general attitude requisite in order to the reception of the Christian religion is summed up again, in the declaration of our text: "Whosoever shall not receive the kingdom of God as a little child, he shall not enter therein." Is a man, then, sensible that his understanding is darkened by sin, and that he is destitute of clear and just apprehensions of divine things? Does his consciousness of inward poverty assume this form? If he would be delivered from his mental blindness, and be made rich in spiritual knowledge, he must adopt a teachable and recipient attitude. He must not assume that his own mind is the great fountain of wisdom, and seek to clear up his doubts and darkness by the rationalistic method of self-illumination. On the contrary, he must go beyond his mind and open a book, even the Book of Revelation, and search for the wisdom it contains and proffers. And yet more than this. As this volume is the product of the Eternal Spirit himself, and this Spirit conspires with the doctrines which He has revealed, and exerts a positive illuminating influence, he must seek communion therewith. From first to last, therefore, the darkened human spirit must take a waiting posture, in order to enlightenment. That part of "the clean heart and the right spirit" which consists in the knowledge of divine things can be obtained only through a child-like bearing and temper. This is what our Lord means, when He pronounces a blessing upon the poor in spirit, the hungry and the thirsting soul. Men, in their pride and self-reliance, in their sense of manhood, may seek to enter the kingdom of heaven by a different method; they may attempt to speculate their way through all the mystery that overhangs human life, and the doubts that confuse and baffle the human understanding; but when they find that the unaided intellect only "spots a thicker gloom" instead of pouring a serener ray, wearied and worn they return, as it were, to the sweet days of childhood, and in the gentleness, and tenderness, and docility of an altered mood, learn, as Bacon did in respect to the kingdom of nature, that the kingdom of heaven is open only to the little child.

Again, is a man conscious of the corruption of his heart? Has he discovered his alienation from the life and love of God, and is he now aware that a total change must pass upon him, or that alienation must be everlasting? Has he found out that his inclinations, and feelings, and tastes, and sympathies are so worldly, so averse from spiritual objects, as to be beyond his sovereignty? Does he feel vividly that the attempt to expel this carnal mind, and to induce in the place thereof the heavenly spontaneous glow of piety towards God and man, is precisely like the attempt of the Ethiopian to change his skin, and the leopard his spots?

If this experience has been forced upon him, shall he meet it with the port and bearing of a strong man? Shall he take the attitude of the old Roman stoic, and attempt to meet the exigencies of his moral condition, by the steady strain and hard tug of his own force? He cannot long do this, under the clear searching ethics of the Sermon on the Mount, without an inexpressible weariness and a profound despair. Were he within the sphere of paganism, it might, perhaps, be otherwise. A Marcus Aurelius could maintain this legal and self-righteous position to the end of life, because his ideal of virtue was a very low one. Had that high-minded pagan felt the influences of Christian ethics, had the Sermon on the Mount searched his soul, telling him that the least emotion of pride, anger, or lust, was a breach of that everlasting law which stood grand and venerable before his philosophic eye, and that his virtue was all gone, and his soul was exposed to the inflictions of justice, if even a single thought of his heart was unconformed to the perfect rule of right,—if, instead of the mere twilight of natural religion, there had flared into his mind the fierce and consuming splendor of the noonday sun of revealed truth, and New Testament ethics, it would have been impossible for that serious-minded emperor to say, as in his utter self-delusion he did, to the Deity: "Give me my dues,"—instead of breathing the prayer: "Forgive me my debts." Christianity elevates the standard and raises the ideal of moral excellence, and thereby disturbs the self-complacent feeling of the stoic, and the moralist. If the law and rule of right is merely an outward one, it is possible for a man sincerely to suppose that he has kept the law, and his sincerity will be his ruin. For, in this case, he can maintain a self-reliant and a self-satisfied spirit, the spirit of manhood, to the very end of his earthly career, and go with his righteousness which is as filthy rags, into the presence of Him in whose sight the heavens are not clean. But, if the law and rule of right is seen to be an inward and spiritual statute, piercing to the dividing asunder of the soul and spirit, and becoming a discerner of the thoughts and intents of the heart, it is not possible for a candid man to delude himself into the belief that he has perfectly obeyed it; and in this instance, that self-dissatisfied spirit, that consciousness of internal schism and bondage, that war between the flesh and the spirit so vividly portrayed in the seventh chapter of Romans, begins, and instead of the utterance of the moralist: "I have kept the everlasting law, give me my dues," there bursts forth the self-despairing cry of the penitent and the child: "O wretched man that I am.! who shall deliver me? Father I have sinned against heaven and before thee."

When, therefore, the truth and Spirit of God, working in and with the natural conscience, have brought a man to that point where he sees that all his own righteousness is as filthy rags, and that the pure and stainless righteousness of Jehovah must become the possession and the characteristic of his soul, he is prepared to believe the declaration of our text: "Whosoever shall not receive the kingdom of God as a little child, he shall not enter therein." The new heart, and the right spirit,—the change, not in the mere external behavior but, in the very disposition and inclination of the soul,—excludes every jot and tittle of self-assertion, every particle of proud and stoical manhood.

Such a text as this which we have been considering is well adapted to put us upon the true method of attaining everlasting life. These few and simple words actually dropped, eighteen hundred years ago, from the lips of that august Being who is now seated upon the throne of heaven, and who knows this very instant the effect which they are producing in the heart of every one who either reads or hears them. Let us remember that these few and simple words do verily contain the key to everlasting life and glory. In knowing what they mean, we know, infallibly, the way to heaven. "I tell you, that many prophets and kings have desired to see those things which we see, and have not seen them: and to hear those things which we hear, and have not heard them." How many a thoughtful pagan, in the centuries that have passed and gone, would in all probability have turned a most attentive ear, had he heard, as we do, from the lips of an unerring Teacher, that a child-like reception of a certain particular truth,—and that not recondite and metaphysical, but simple as childhood itself, and to be received by a little child's act,—would infallibly conduct to the elysium that haunted and tantalized him.

That which hinders us is our pride, our "manhood." The act of faith is a child's act; and a child's act, though intrinsically the easiest of any, is relatively the most difficult of all. It implies the surrender of our self-will, our self-love, our proud manhood; and never was a truer remark made than that of Ullmann, that "in no one thing is the strength of a man's will so manifested, as in his having no will of his own."[4] "Christianity,"—says Jeremy Taylor,—"is the easiest and the hardest thing in the world. It is like a secret in arithmetic; infinitely hard till it be found out by a right operation, and then it is so plain we wonder we did not understand it earlier." How hard, how impossible without that Divine grace which makes all such central and revolutionary acts easy and genial to the soul,—how hard it is to cease from our own works, and really become docile and recipient children, believing on the Lord Jesus Christ, and trusting in Him, simply and solely, for salvation.

*[**Note 1:** "Concerning the object of felicity in heaven, we are agreed that it can be no other than the blessed God himself, the all-comprehending good, fully adequate to the highest and most enlarged reasonable desires. But the contemperation of our faculties to the holy, blissful object, is so necessary to our satisfying fruition, that without this we are no more capable thereof, than a brute of the festivities of a quaint oration, or a stone of the relishes of the most pleasant meats and drinks." HOWE: Heaven a State of Perfection.]*
*[**Note 2:** GOETHE: Wilhelm Meister, Book VII., ch. iii.]*
*[**Note 3:** Compare Isaiah lxi. 1.]*
*[**Note 4:** ULLMANN: Sinlessness of Jesus, Pt. I., Ch. iii., § 2.]*

XX - Faith the Sole Saving Act

JOHN vi. 28, 29.—"Then said they unto him, What shall we do, that we might work the works of God? Jesus answered and said unto them, This is the work of God, that ye believe on him whom he hath sent."

In asking their question, the Jews intended to inquire of Christ what particular things they must do, before all others, in order to please God. The "works of

God," as they denominate them, were not any and every duty, but those more special and important acts, by which the creature might secure the Divine approval and favor. Our Lord understood their question in this sense, and in His reply tells them, that the great and only work for them to do was to exercise faith in Him. They had employed the plural number in their question; but in His answer He employs the singular. They had asked, What shall we do that we might work the works of God,—as if there were several of them. His reply is, "This is the work of God, that ye believe on Him whom He hath sent." He narrows down the terms of salvation to a single one; and makes the destiny of the soul to depend upon the performance of a particular individual act. In this, as in many other incidental ways, our Lord teaches His own divinity. If He were a mere creature; if He were only an inspired teacher like David or Paul; how would He dare, when asked to give in a single word the condition and means of human salvation, to say that they consist in resting the soul upon Him? Would David have dared to say: "This is the work of God,—this is the saving act,—that ye believe in me?" Would Paul have presumed to say to the anxious inquirer: "Your soul is safe, if you trust in me?" But Christ makes this declaration, without any qualification. Yet He was meek and lowly of heart, and never assumed an honor or a prerogative that did not belong to Him. It is only upon the supposition that He was "very God of very God," the Divine Redeemer of the children of men, that we can justify such an answer to such a question.

The belief is spontaneous and natural to man, that something must be done in order to salvation. No man expects to reach heaven by inaction. Even the indifferent and supine soul expects to rouse itself up at some future time, and work out its salvation. The most thoughtless and inactive man, in religious respects, will acknowledge that thoughtlessness and inactivity if continued will end in perdition. But he intends at a future day to think, and act, and be saved. So natural is it, to every man, to believe in salvation by works; so ready is every one to concede that heaven is reached, and hell is escaped, only by an earnest effort of some kind; so natural is it to every man to ask with these Jews, "What shall we do, that we may work the works of God?"

But mankind generally, like the Jews in the days of our Lord, are under a delusion respecting the nature of the work which must be performed in order to salvation. And in order to understand this delusion, we must first examine the common notion upon the subject.

When a man begins to think of God, and of his own relations to Him, he finds that he owes Him service and obedience. He has a work to perform, as a subject of the Divine government; and this work is to obey the Divine law. He finds himself obligated to love God with all his heart, and his neighbor as himself, and to discharge all the duties that spring out of his relations to God and man. He perceives that this is the "work" given him to do by creation, and that if he does it he will attain the true end of his existence, and be happy in time and eternity. When therefore he begins to think of a religious life, his first spontaneous impulse is to begin the performance of this work which he has hitherto neglected, and to reinstate himself in the Divine favor by the ordinary method of keeping the law of God. He perceives that this is the mode in which the angels preserve themselves holy and happy; that this is the original mode appointed by God, when He established the covenant of works; and he does not see why it is not the method for him. The law expressly affirms that the man that doeth these things shall live by them; he proposes to take the law just as it reads, and just as it stands,—to do the deeds of the law, to perform the works which it enjoins, and to live by the service. This we say, is the common notion, natural to man, of the species of work which must be performed in order to eternal life. This was the idea which filled the mind of the Jews when they put the question of the text, and received for answer from Christ, "This is the work of God, that ye believe on him whom he hath sent." Our Lord does not draw out the whole truth, in detail. He gives only the positive part of the answer, leaving His hearers to infer the negative part of it. For the whole doctrine of Christ, fully stated, would run thus: "No work of the kind of which you are thinking can save you; no obedience of the law, ceremonial or moral, can reinstate you in right relations to God. I do not summon you to the performance of any such service as that which you have in mind, in order to your justification and acceptance before the Divine tribunal. This is the work of God,—this is the sole and single act which you are to perform,—namely, that you believe on Him whom He hath sent as a propitiation for sin. I do not summon you to works of the law, but to faith in Me the Redeemer. Your first duty is not to attempt to acquire a righteousness in the old method, by doing something of yourselves, but to receive a righteousness in the new method, by trusting in what another has done for you."

I. What is the ground and reason of such an answer as this? Why is man invited to the method of faith in another, instead of the method of faith in himself? Why is not his first spontaneous thought the true one? Why should he not obtain eternal life by resolutely proceeding to do his duty, and keeping the law of God? Why can he not be saved by the law of works? Why is he so summarily shut up to the law of faith?

We answer: Because it is too late for him to adopt the method of salvation by works. The law is indeed explicit in its assertion, that the man that doeth these things shall live by them; but then it supposes that the man begin at the beginning. A subject of government cannot disobey a civil statute for five or ten years, and then put himself in right relations to it again, by obeying it for the remainder of his life. Can a man who has been a thief or an adulterer for twenty years, and then practises honesty and purity for the following thirty years, stand up before the seventh and eighth commandments and be acquitted by them? It is too late for any being who has violated a law even in a single instance, to attempt to be justified by that law. For, the law demands and supposes that obedience begin at the very beginning of existence, and continue down uninterruptedly to the end of it. No man can come in at the middle of a process of obedience, any more than he can come in at the last end of it, if he proposes to be accepted upon the ground of obedience. "I testify," says St. Paul, "to every man that is circumcised, that he is a debtor to do the whole law" (Gal. v. 3). The whole, or none, is the just and inexorable rule which law lays down in the matter of justification. If any subject of the Divine government can show a clean record, from the beginning to the end of his existence, the statute says to him, "Well done," and gives him the reward which he has earned. And it gives it to him not as a matter of grace, but of debt. The law never makes a present of wages. It never pays out wages, until they are earned,—-fairly and fully earned. But when a perfect obedience from first to last is rendered to its claims, the compensation follows as matter of debt. The law, in this instance, is itself brought under obligation. It owes a reward to the perfectly obedient subject of law, and it considers itself his debtor until it is paid. "Now to him that worketh, is the reward not reckoned of grace, but of debt. If it be of works, then it is no more grace: otherwise work is no more work" (Rom. iv. 4; xi. 6).

But, on the other hand, law is equally exact and inflexible, in case the work has not been performed. It will not give eternal life to a soul that has sinned ten years, and then perfectly obeyed ten years,—supposing that there is any such soul. The obedience, as we have remarked, must run parallel with the entire existence, in order to be a ground, of justification. Infancy, childhood, youth, manhood, old age, and then the whole immortality that succeeds, must all be unintermittently sinless and holy, in order to make eternal life a matter of debt. Justice is as exact and punctilious upon this side, as it is upon the other. We have seen, that when a perfect obedience has been rendered, justice will not palm off the wages that are due as if they were some gracious gift; and on the other hand, when a perfect obedience has not been rendered, it will not be cajoled into the bestowment of wages as if they had been earned. There is no principle that is so intelligent, so upright, and so exact, as justice; and no creature can expect either to warp it, or to circumvent it.

In the light of these remarks, it is evident that it is too late for a sinner to avail himself of the method of salvation by works. For, that method requires that sinless obedience begin at the beginning of his existence, and never be interrupted. But no man thus begins, and no man thus continues. "The wicked are estranged from the womb; they go astray as soon as they be born, speaking lies" (Ps. lviii. 3). Man comes into the world a sinful and alienated creature. He is by nature a child of wrath (Eph. ii. 3). Instead of beginning life with holiness, he begins it with sin. His heart at birth is apostate and corrupt; and his conduct from the very first is contrary to law. Such is the teaching of Scripture, such is the statement of the Creeds, and such is the testimony of consciousness, respecting the character which man brings into the world with him. The very dawn of human life is clouded with depravity; is marked by the carnal mind which is at enmity with the law of God, and is not subject to that law, neither indeed can be. How is it possible, then, for man to attain eternal life by a method that supposes, and requires, that the very dawn of his being be holy like that of Christ's, and that every thought, feeling, purpose, and act be conformed to law through the entire existence? Is it not too late for such a creature as man now is to adopt the method of salvation by the works of the law?

But we will not crowd you, with the doctrine of native depravity and the sin in Adam. We have no doubt that it is the scriptural and true doctrine concerning human nature; and have no fears that it will be contradicted by either a profound self-knowledge, or a profound metaphysics. But perhaps you are one who doubts it; and therefore, for the sake of argument, we will let you set the commencement of sin where you please. If you tell us that it begins in the second, or the fourth, or the tenth year of life, it still remains true that it is too late to employ the method of justification by works. If you concede any sin at all, at any point whatsoever, in the history of a human soul, you preclude it from salvation by the deeds of the law, and shut it up to salvation by grace. Go back as far as you can in your memory, and you must acknowledge that you find sin as far as you go; and even if, in the face of Scripture and the symbols of the Church, you should deny that the sin runs back to birth and apostasy in Adam, it still remains true that the first years of your conscious existence were not years of holiness, nor the first acts which you remember, acts of obedience. Even upon your own theory, you begin with sin, and therefore you cannot be justified by the law.

This, then, is a conclusive reason and ground for the declaration of our Lord, that the one great work which every fallen man has to perform, and must perform, in order to salvation, is faith in another's work, and confidence in another's righteousness. If man is to be saved by his own righteousness, that righteousness must begin at the very beginning of his existence, and go on without interruption. If he is to be saved by his own good works, there never must be a single instant in his life when he is not working such works. But beyond all controversy such is not the fact. It is, therefore, impossible for him to be justified by trusting in himself; and the only possible mode that now remains, is to trust in another.

II. And this brings us to the second part of our subject. "This is the work of God, that ye believe on him whom He hath sent." It will be observed that faith is here denominated a "work." And it is so indeed. It is a mental act; and an act of the most comprehensive and energetic species. Faith is an active principle that carries the whole man with it, and in it,—head and heart, will and affections, body soul and spirit. There is no act so all-embracing in its reach, and so total in its momentum, as the act of faith in the Lord Jesus Christ. In this sense, it is a "work." It is no supine and torpid thing; but the most vital and vigorous activity that can be conceived of. When a sinner, moved by the Holy Ghost the very source of spiritual life and energy, casts himself in utter helplessness, and with all his weight, upon his Redeemer for salvation, never is he more active, and never does he do a greater work.

And yet, faith is not a work in the common signification of the word. In the Pauline Epistles, it is generally opposed to works, in such a way as to exclude them. For example: "Where is boasting then? It is excluded. By what law? of works? Nay, but by the law of faith. Therefore we conclude that a man is justified by faith, without the deeds of the law. Knowing that a man is not justified by the works of the law but by the faith of Jesus Christ, even we have believed in Jesus Christ, that we might be justified, by the faith of Christ and not by the works of the law. Received ye the Spirit, by the works of the law, or by the hearing of faith?"[1] In these and other passages, faith and works are directly contrary to each other; so that in this connection, faith is not a "work." Let us examine this point, a little in detail, for it will throw light upon the subject under discussion.

In the opening of the discourse, we alluded to the fact that when a man's attention is directed to the subject of his soul's salvation, his first spontaneous thought is, that he must of himself render something to God, as an offset for his sins; that he must perform his duty by his own power and effort, and thereby acquire a personal merit before his Maker and Judge. The thought of appropriating another person's work, of making use of what another being has done in his stead, does not occur to him; or if it does, it is repulsive to him. His thought is, that it is his own soul that is to be saved, and it is his own work that must save it. Hence, he begins to perform religious duties in the ordinary use of his own faculties, and in his own strength, for the purpose, and with the expectation, of settling the account which he knows is unsettled, between himself and his Judge. As yet, there is no faith in another Being. He is not trusting and resting in another person; but he is trusting and resting in himself. He is not making use of the work or services which another has wrought in his behalf, but he is employing his own powers and faculties, in performing these his own works, which he owes, and which, if paid in this style, he thinks will save his soul. This is the spontaneous, and it is the correct, idea of a "work,"—of what St. Paul so often calls a "work of the law." And it is the exact contrary of faith.

For, faith never does anything in this independent and self-reliant manner. It does not perform a service in its own strength, and then hold it out to God as something for Him to receive, and for which He must pay back wages in the form of remitting sin and bestowing happiness. Faith is wholly occupied with another's work, and another's merit. The believing soul deserts all its own doings, and betakes itself to what a third person has wrought for it, and in its stead. When, for illustration, a sinner discovers that he owes a satisfaction to Eternal Justice for the sins that are past, if he adopts the method of works, he will offer up his endeavors to obey the law, as an offset, and a reason why he should be forgiven. He will say in his heart, if he does not in his prayer: "I am striving to atone for the past, by doing my duty in the future; my resolutions, my prayers and alms-giving, all this hard struggle to be better and to do better, ought certainly to avail for my pardon." Or, if he has been educated in a superstitious Church, he will offer up his penances, and mortifications, and pilgrimages, as a satisfaction to justice, and a reason why he should be forgiven and made blessed forever in heaven. That is a very instructive anecdote which St. Simon relates respecting the last hours of the profligate Louis XIV. "One day,"—he says,—"the king recovering from loss of consciousness asked his confessor, Pere Tellier, to give him absolution for all his sins. Pere Tellier asked him if he suffered much. 'No,' replied the king, 'that's what troubles me. I should like to suffer more, for the expiation of my sins.'" Here was a poor mortal who had spent his days in carnality and transgression of the pure law of God. He is conscious of guilt, and feels the need of its atonement. And now, upon the very edge of eternity and brink of doom, he proposes to make his own atonement, to be his own redeemer and save his own soul, by offering up to the eternal nemesis that was racking his conscience a few hours of finite suffering, instead of betaking himself to the infinite passion and agony of Calvary. This is a work; and, alas, a "dead work," as St. Paul so often denominates it. This is the method of justification by works. But when a man adopts the method of justification by faith, his course is exactly opposite to all this. Upon discovering that he owes a satisfaction to Eternal Justice for the sins that are past, instead of holding up his prayers, or alms-giving, or penances, or moral efforts, or any work of his own, he holds up the sacrificial work of Christ. In his prayer to God, he interposes the agony and death of the Great Substitute between his guilty soul, and the arrows of justice.[2] He knows that the very best of his own works, that even the most perfect obedience that a creature could render, would be pierced through and through by the glittering shafts of

174

violated law. And therefore he takes the "shield of faith." He places the oblation of the God-man,—not his own work and not his own suffering, but another's work and another's suffering,—between himself and the judicial vengeance of the Most High. And in so doing, he works no work of his own, and no dead work; but he works the "work of God;" he believes on Him whom God hath set forth to be a propitiation for his sins, and not for his only but for the sins of the whole world.

This then is the great doctrine which our Lord taught the Jews, when they asked Him what particular thing or things they must do in order to eternal life. The apostle John, who recorded the answer of Christ in this instance, repeats the doctrine again in his first Epistle: "Whatsoever we ask, we receive of Him, because we keep His commandment, and do those things that are pleasing in His sight. And this is His commandment, that we should believe on the name of His Son Jesus Christ" (1 John iii, 22, 23). The whole duty of sinful man is here summed up, and concentrated, in the duty to trust in another person than himself, and in another work than his own. The apostle, like his Lord before him, employs the singular number: "This is His commandment,"—as if there were no other commandment upon record. And this corresponds with the answer which Paul and Silas gave to the despairing jailor: "Believe on the Lord Jesus Christ,"—do this one single thing,—"and thou shalt be saved." And all of these teachings accord with that solemn declaration of our Lord: "He that believeth on the Son hath everlasting life; and he that believeth not the Son shall not see life; but the wrath of God abideth on him." In the matter of salvation, where there is faith in Christ, there is everything; and where there is not faith in Christ, there is nothing.

1. And it is with this thought that we would close this discourse, and enforce the doctrine of the text. Do whatever else you may in the matter of religion, you have done nothing until you have believed on the Lord Jesus Christ, whom God hath, sent into the world to be the propitiation for sin. There are two reasons for this. In the first place, it is the appointment and declaration of God, that man, if saved at all, must be saved by faith in the Person and Work of the Mediator. "Neither is there salvation in any other: for there is none other name under heaven given among men, whereby we must be saved" (Acts iv. 12). It of course rests entirely with the Most High God, to determine the mode and manner in which He will enter into negotiations with His creatures, and especially with His rebellious creatures. He must make the terms, and the creature must come to them. Even, therefore, if we could not see the reasonableness and adaptation of the method, we should be obligated to accept it. The creature, and particularly the guilty creature, cannot dictate to his Sovereign and Judge respecting the terms and conditions by which he is to be received into favor, and secure eternal life. Men overlook this fact, when they presume as they do, to sit in judgment upon the method of redemption by the blood of atonement and to quarrel with it.

In the first Punic war, Hannibal laid siege to Saguntum, a rich and strongly-fortified city on the eastern coast of Spain. It was defended with a desperate obstinacy by its inhabitants. But the discipline, the energy, and the persistence of the Carthaginian army, were too much for them; and just as the city was about to fall, Alorcus, a Spanish chieftain, and a mutual friend of both of the contending parties, undertook to mediate between them. He proposed to the Saguntines that they should surrender, allowing the Carthaginian general to make his own terms. And the argument he used was this: "Your city is captured, in any event. Further resistance will only bring down upon you the rage of an incensed soldiery, and the horrors of a sack. Therefore, surrender immediately, and take whatever Hannibal shall please to give. You cannot lose anything by the procedure, and you may gain something, even though it be little."[3] Now, although there is no resemblance between the government of the good and merciful God and the cruel purposes and conduct of a heathen warrior, and we shrink from bringing the two into any kind of juxtaposition, still, the advice of the wise Alorcus to the Saguntines is good advice for every sinful man, in reference to his relations to Eternal Justice. We are all of us at the mercy of God. Should He make no terms at all; had He never given His Son to die for our sins, and never sent His Spirit to exert a subduing influence upon our hard hearts, but had let guilt and justice take their inexorable course with us; not a word could be uttered against the procedure by heaven, earth, or hell. No creature, anywhere can complain of justice. That is an attribute that cannot even be attacked. But the All-Holy is also the All-Merciful. He has made certain terms, and has offered certain conditions of pardon, without asking leave of His creatures and without taking them into council, and were these terms as strict as Draco, instead of being as tender and pitiful as the tears and blood of Jesus, it would become us criminals to make no criticisms even in that extreme case, but accept them precisely as they were offered by the Sovereign and the Arbiter. We exhort you, therefore, to take these terms of salvation simply as they are given, asking no questions, and being thankful that there are any terms at all between the offended majesty of Heaven and the guilty criminals of earth. Believe on Him whom God hath sent, because it is the appointment and declaration of God, that if guilty man is to be saved at all, he must be saved by faith in the Person and Work of the Mediator. The very disposition to quarrel with this method implies arrogance in dealing with the Most High. The least inclination to alter the conditions shows that the creature is attempting to criticise the Creator, and, what is yet more, that the criminal has no true perception of his crime, no sense of his exposed and helpless situation, and presumes to dictate the terms of his own pardon!

2. We might therefore leave the matter here, and there would be a sufficient reason for exercising the act of faith in Christ. But there is a second and additional reason which we will also briefly urge upon you. Not only is it the Divine appointment, that man shall be saved, if saved at all, by the substituted work of another; but there are needs, there are crying wants, in the human conscience, that can be supplied by no other method. There is a perfect adaptation between the Redemption that is in Christ Jesus, and the guilt of sinners. As we have seen, we could reasonably urge you to Believe in Him whom God hath sent, simply because God has sent Him, and because He has told you that He will save you through no other name and in no other way, and will save you in this name and in this way. But we now urge you to the act of faith in this substituted work of Christ, because it has an atoning virtue, and can pacify a perturbed and angry conscience; can wash out the stains of guilt that are grained into it; can extract the sting of sin which ulcerates and burns there. It is the idea of expiation and satisfaction that we now single out, and press upon your notice. Sin must be expiated,—expiated either by the blood of the criminal, or by the blood of his Substitute. You must either die for your own sin, or some one who is able and willing must die for you. This is founded and fixed in the nature of God, and the nature of man, and the nature of sin. There is an eternal and necessary connection between crime and penalty. The wages of sin is death. But, all this inexorable necessity has been completely provided for, by the sacrificial work of the Son of God. In the gospel, God satisfies His own justice for the sinner, and now offers you the full benefit of the satisfaction, if you will humbly and penitently accept it. "What compassion can equal the words of God the Father addressed to the sinner condemned to eternal punishment, and having no means of redeeming himself: 'Take my Only-Begotten Son, and make Him an offering for thyself;' or the words of the Son: 'Take Me, and ransom thy soul?' For this is what both say, when they invite and draw man to faith in the gospel."[4] In urging you, therefore, to trust in Christ's vicarious sufferings for sin, instead of going down to hell and suffering for sin in your own person; in entreating you to escape the stroke of justice upon yourself, by believing in Him who was smitten in your stead, who "was wounded for your transgressions and bruised for your iniquities;" in beseeching you to let the Eternal Son of God be your Substitute in this awful judicial transaction; we are summoning you to no arbitrary and irrational act. The peace of God which it will introduce into your conscience, and the love of God which it will shed abroad through your soul, will be the most convincing of all proofs that the act of faith in the great Atonement does no violence to the ideas and principles of the human constitution. No act that contravenes those intuitions and convictions which are part and particle of man's moral nature could possibly produce peace and joy. It would be revolutionary and anarchical. The soul could not rest an instant. And yet it is the uniform testimony of all believers in the Lord Jesus Christ, that the act of simple confiding faith in His blood and righteousness is the most peaceful, the most joyful act they ever performed,—nay, that it was the first blessed experience they ever felt in this world of sin, this world of remorse, this world of fears and forebodings concerning judgment and doom.

Is the question, then, of the Jews, pressing upon your mind? Do you ask, What one particular single thing shall I do, that I may be safe for time and eternity? Hear the answer of the Son of God Himself: "This is the work of God, that ye believe on Him whom He hath sent."

*[**Note 1:** Romans iii. 27, 28; Galatians ii. 16, iii. 2.]*
*[**Note 2:** The religious teacher is often asked to define the act of faith, and explain the way and manner in which the soul is to exercise it. "How shall I believe?" is the question with which the anxious mind often replies to the gospel injunction to believe. Without pretending that it is a complete answer, or claiming that it is possible, in the strict meaning of the word, to explain so simple and so profound an act as faith, we think, nevertheless, that it assists the inquiring mind to say, that whoever asks in prayer for any one of the benefits of Christ's redemption, in so far exercises faith in this redemption. Whoever, for example, lifts up the supplication, "O Lamb of God who takest away the sins of the world, grant me thy peace," in this prayer puts faith in the atonement, He trusts in the atonement, by pleading the atonement,—by mentioning it, in his supplication, as the reason why he may be forgiven. In like manner, he who asks for the renewing and sanctifying influences of the Holy Ghost exercises faith, in these influences. This is the mode in which he expresses his confidence in the power*

of God to accomplish a work in his heart that is beyond his own power. Whatever, therefore, be the particular benefit in Christ's redemption that one would trust in, and thereby make personally his own, that he may live by it and be blest by it,—be it the atoning blood, or be it the indwelling Spirit,—let him ask for that benefit. If he would trust in the thing, let him ask for the thing.

Since writing the above, we have met with a corroboration of this view, by a writer of the highest authority upon such points. "Faith is that inward sense and act, of which prayer is the expression; as is evident, because in the same manner as the freedom of grace, according to the gospel covenant, is often set forth by this, that he that believes, receives; so it also oftentimes is by this, that he that asks, or prays, or calls upon God, receives. 'Ask and it shall be given you; seek and ye shall find; knock and it shall be opened unto you. For every one that asketh, receiveth; and he that seeketh, findeth; and to him that knocketh, it shall be opened. And all things whatsoever ye shall ask in prayer, believing, ye shall receive (Matt. vii. 7, 8; Mark xi. 24). If ye abide in me and my words abide in you, ye shall ask what ye will, and it shall be done unto you' (John xv. 7). Prayer is often plainly spoken of as the expression of faith. As it very certainly is in Romans x. 11-14: 'For the Scripture saith, Whosoever believeth on him shall not be ashamed. For there is no difference between the Jew and the Greek: for the same Lord over all is rich unto all that call upon him; for whosoever shall call upon the name of the Lord shall be saved. 'How then shall they call on him in whom they have not believed.' Christian prayer is called the prayer of faith (James v. 15). 'I will that men everywhere lift up holy hands, without wrath and doubting (1 Tim. ii. 8). Draw near in full assurance of faith' (Heb. x. 22). The same expressions that are used, in Scripture, for faith, may well be used for prayer also; such as coming to God or Christ, and looking to Him. 'In whom we have boldness and access with confidence, by the faith of him' (Eph. iii. 12)." EDWARDS: Observations concerning Faith.]
[**Note 3**: Livius: Historia, Lib. xxi. 12.]
[**Note 4**: ANSELM: Cur Deus Homo? II. 20.]

www.ingramcontent.com/pod-product-compliance
Lightning Source LLC
Chambersburg PA
CBHW051821170626
46807CB00003B/968